If you have a home computer with Internet access you may:
- request an item to be placed on hold.
- renew an item that is not overdue or on hold.
- view titles and due dates checked out on your card.
- view and/or pay your outstanding fines online (over $5).

To view your patron record from your home computer click on Patchogue-Medford Library's homepage: www.pmlib.org

The Tell-Tale Art

Poe in Modern Popular Culture

CHRISTINE A. JACKSON

McFarland & Company, Inc., Publishers

Jefferson, North Carolina, and London

ALSO OF INTEREST: *Marcia Muller and the Female Private Eye: Essays on the Novels That Defined a Subgenre*. Edited by Alexander N. Howe and Christine A. Jackson (McFarland, 2008). *Myth and Ritual in Women's Detective Fiction*. Christine A. Jackson (McFarland, 2002).

LIBRARY OF CONGRESS CATALOGUING-IN-PUBLICATION DATA

Jackson, Christine A., 1951–
 The tell-tale art : Poe in modern popular culture /
Christine A. Jackson.
  p.   cm.
 Includes bibliographical references and index.

 ISBN 978-0-7864-6318-3
 softcover : 50# alkaline paper ∞

 1. Poe, Edgar Allan, 1809–1849 — Criticism and
interpretation. 2. Poe, Edgar Allan, 1809–1849 — Influence.
3. Popular culture and literature. I. Title.

 PS2638.J27 2012   818'.309 — dc23   2011039643

BRITISH LIBRARY CATALOGUING DATA ARE AVAILABLE

On the cover: Reproduction of the "Ultima Thule" daguerreotype of Edgar Allan Poe, 1848 (Library of Congress); background © 2012 Shutterstock

Manufactured in the United States of America

McFarland & Company, Inc., Publishers
 Box 611, Jefferson, North Carolina 28640
 www.mcfarlandpub.com

Contents

Acknowledgments

With deep gratitude, I recognize my family for our many hours shared in the lively art of tale-telling. Over the decades, we have swapped uncountable stories, from the haunted to the hilarious. I am also fortunate in receiving jolts of energy from a network of live-wire friends and colleagues interested in ideas and supportive of my projects. James Doan, Ph.D., chair of the Faculty Lecture Series at Nova Southeastern University, earns acknowledgment, as he first suggested that my hour-long Poe lecture for the Series could grow into an actual book. Most importantly, with his unswerving support, love, and belief in me, my husband Harold has been a moving force in my storyline.

Preface

The late-night scene in a chilly library evokes a *déjà vû* familiar to all insomniacs. Before a dying fire, the grieving hero searches the bookshelves for a distraction, anything, to halt the downward spiral into depression. He starts to nod off when a noise outside startles him. Nerves jangling, he rushes to confront the rude, unwanted guest pressing for entry. He opens the door to find — no one.

> Deep into that darkness peering, long I stood there wondering, fearing,
> Doubting, dreaming dreams no mortals ever dared to dream before ["The Raven" ll.25–26, 1845].

These innovative narratives that Poe dared to dream and write about are so central to the human psyche that mortals have been reading, viewing, and living these same dreams and nightmares ever since. What does the persistence of Poe's fiction narratives say about American literature and culture?

The purpose of this book is to examine Poe's fearful dreams with a critical eye. The discussion poses and attempts to answer key questions about the effective features of these narratives, and the ways they have influenced popular entertainment. Our culture maintains a long-standing fascination with stories about greed and guilt, about codes needing to be deciphered, about murder plots born of madness. Clearly, motifs from Poe's carefully constructed fiction continue to matter.

In "The Masque of the Red Death," Poe lays out an intricate floor plan for Prince Prospero's "imperial suite."

The unusual design of the masked ball's location comes from the Prince's eccentric decorating tastes, his "love of the *bizarre*" (269; Vintage ed., 1979; all subsequent passages from Poe are from this edition, cited in-text). The irregular shape to each of the seven rooms limits a viewer's perspective. "There was a sharp turn at every twenty or thirty yards, and at each turn a novel effect." Each successive room is a different color, a progression through a spectrum of garish hues. The last chamber is black, viewed through a red-tinted window. An observer only vaguely grasps a room's signature color, due to the unusual way the seven chambers are lit:

> There was no light of any kind emanating from lamp or candle within the suite of chambers. But in the corridors that followed the suite, there stood, opposite to each window, a heavy tripod, bearing a brazier of fire, that projected its rays through the tinted glass and so glaringly illuminated the room. And thus were produced a multitude of gaudy and fantastic appearances [270].

Prince Prospero's imperial suite is soon to be a crime scene. The prince and his guests fall to a series of bloody murders by a highly mysterious assailant. However, like Plato's cave, the complicated architecture of these successive rooms presents a metaphor of limited comprehension. The rooms define liminal spaces between illusion and reality. As such, the architectural design serves as an apt emblem of the multi-part method informing this critical study. The *Tell-Tale Art*'s approach is eclectic, breaking down Poe's fiction into motifs and patterns of images. Different critical theories provide the lenses for viewing in this hard-to-see environment. For this range of material, the chapters use methods from psychoanalysis, structuralism, narratology, philosophy, myth and media criticism, and reader/viewer response theory.

As for focus, the book zooms in on seven chambers in Poe's house of fiction. Each is furnished with elaborate concepts that find their way into today's books, films, television programs and even video games. Stories of detection featuring C. Auguste Dupin and the unnamed narrator sidekick present a double-sided perspective on death and reports on death that novelists and scriptwriters have used in American entertainment for decades. Tales dotted with codes and ciphers set a precedent for code-tracker films like *National Treasure* and forensic dramas such as *CSI*. Poe's extreme psychological landscapes illustrate ways that films blend a character's trauma with a nightmarish setting to achieve a "unity of effect." Tales featuring diffuse personalities advance Poe's pioneering methods of character development. These stories explore to the outer edge of the psyche and lead the way for dramas about moral dilemmas dividing and distending the self.

Poe's place as the creator of horror has long been acknowledged. However, emotional undercurrents of his blood-soaked narratives, such as "The Masque of the Red Death," have yet to be linked to today's television programs set in hospitals or morgues. Tracking the debt of current extreme reality television to Poe's *Pym* leads to an instructive narrative comparison highlighting similar structural patterns. Poe's only novel pits the human will against the environment in a taut blend of action-adventure. Another subgenre of reality television, a program set in a kitchen, affords an opportunity to assess Poe's qualities of extreme guilt and sadomasochism in the context of today's competitive narratives of creativity that take no prisoners. Lastly, Poe's "interdisciplinary" approaches to story through image, sound, and motion continue to mark our entertainment on screens large and small. From the mall Cineplex to the framed stories on laptops and cell phones, Poe announces his taleteller's art. The truth in Poe's art is like an elusive, fleeing figure, a self-reflecting infinite regression. Compared to these stories' thick gloom of effects, theories about narrative structure or dreams seem as inadequate as the indirect braziers of fire for lighting the interior of Prospero's palace. The genius of Poe's tale-telling art is that it strikes us with a genuine view of experience that resists comprehensive analysis.

Discussion of each subgenre begins with a Poe short story as the prototype of a narrative subgenre. Then the argument follows the influence of that story type as it seeps into books, films, television programs, and video games of smaller screens. Lit with braziers of fire that are inevitably inadequate, this study's critical method is descriptive, analytical, and comparative. It defines elements of these repeated narrative structures, comparing them across a span of subgenres in popular culture.

The discussion of each subgenre proceeds mostly chronologically. Since a long shelf life in the marketplace typically measures a work's commercial success and reflects enthusiastic audience response, longevity is a central criterion for my selection of narratives and characters for close study. The examples in this book involve stories shaping films with sequels and television shows with multiple seasons. Each character chosen for the discussion appears over a long time and in many works. He or she generally casts a long shadow.

In myriad guises, Poe's designs for tale-telling continue to fascinate American audiences. What are the characteristics of these narrative patterns and what makes them a strong match for the tastes and expectations of American consumers in today's entertainment marketplace?

The book starts by explaining terminology about story telling from well-established theories of narrative. The study makes judicious use of this lexicon to clarify and distinguish ideas, not to obfuscate with jargon or technicalities. Each subsequent chapter then uses one or two examples from Poe's fiction to illustrate a narrative template.

Poe's tales pose and sometimes answer questions. Who committed the murders in the Rue Morgue illustrates Poe's contribution to the template of the detective story. However, his fiction sets many other narrative models addressing other mysteries. These involve profound issues of human existence: knowledge of one's own identity, the powers and limitations of language, workings of the body and its deterioration over time, human interaction with the natural environment, and the role of narrative in a culture. Each chapter deals with a particular story pattern addressing these mysteries. Our discussion then traces Poe's model narratives as they appear across today's cultural landscape, in the pages of best-sellers and on the screens of movie theaters, televisions, laptops, and even iPhones. This book does not claim to chart the entire field of Poe's influence, which would be a daunting task for an entire series, let alone one study. However, from this close analysis emerge ideas that we hope warrant additional exploration.

Poe's biographers dig hard, as if clues to the work are hidden among details of his life. To be sure, actual events provide perspective on Poe's art, but the source of his power comes from the complex swirl of imagination occurring between tale and teller. This study follows a similar path blazed by the collection of essays called *Poe's Children: Connections Between Tales of Terror and Detection* (Magistrale and Poger, 1999).

In this incisive literary and cultural history, two New England academics trace Poe's legacy in works by Arthur Conan Doyle and Robert Louis Stevenson through time to more recent books and contemporary films. Magistrale and Poger note that "Edgar Allan Poe never produced any biological offspring during his lifetime, but clearly his literary children are everywhere" (9). Since 1999, more of Poe's literary offspring have flooded bookstores, films, television, and the internet. Providing an update, this present study could be summed up as *Poe's Grandchildren, the Next Generation*.

This study appeals to a wide readership. It uses scholarly sources as well as examples familiar to a lay audience. Mystery readers and writers as well as academics teaching mystery fiction in a context of popular culture may find ideas about form and function to add to their collections. This book examines a wide selection of today's detective and thriller novels, films, an array of television programs from diverse genres, and video games. From my perspective, these pieces of pop culture carry evidence that Poe has twisted the screws for jaw-tightening impact on today's readers and viewers.

It's difficult to conceive how today's popular entertainment might be different without Poe's narrative design. An absence of detectives is impossible to imagine. Mystery fiction is the quintessential American literary form. Using Poe's methods of storytelling and suspense, today's best mystery fiction infuses characters with psychological depth. Works by Linda Fairstein, Laura Lippman, Dennis Lehane and other novelists pose incisive questions about America's justice system and explore issues of identity. They keep us reading long into the night, whether we flip paper pages or trace a finger across the screen of an e-book reader. Recognizing these tightly wound narrative patterns helps us to better understand messages from writers and filmmakers, today's dream followers.

Undoubtedly, a writer like Poe would have come along eventually, given the nineteenth-century cultural setting of Civil War horrors and tense economic reversal. A Poe-less heritage for writers and film producers might have opened the door wider for Melville's ironically comic spirit.

The many dramas exploring conflicts in business, the military, or sports stem most likely from Melville's constructed "band of brothers" context and his simultaneous embrace and critique of the democratic ideal. There may not have been room for marginalized eccentrics like Poe's C. Auguste Dupin or William Legrand. Without Poe's genius of pairing Dupin with an observant narrator, our emblematic characters might have been cut from the same rough cloth as Ahab or Bartleby. They might have developed into Ishmael-like loners, adrift on seas of epistemological speculation. Fortunately for us, however, Poe's writing did catch on with a public eager to track down clues, and he is an immense presence in our popular culture. The detailed development and ongoing popularity of his narratives in contemporary guises attest to the inventive sturdiness of Poe's designs for telling a story. They testify to his visionary genius.

Introduction: A Sound Structure

What qualities of Poe's work give it longevity? Because the writer's pervasive influence says a great deal about our contemporary consumer culture, it pays to define the long-lasting qualities of his fiction.

As a poet, Poe is first and last concerned with sound. In his lifetime, the short story had not yet coalesced into a separate prose form. Poe considered that sounds of words serving as the basis for poetry should bleed into the prose form and vice versa. He conceived of a literary text with its own soundscape, not merely through the harmonies of words, but with an aural dimension essentially "playing" in the background. For instance, as part of his legacy, he wanted "Eureka," a late prose work that reads like a philosophical tract, to be regarded as a poem after he was gone: "It is as a Poem only that I wish this work to be judged after I am dead" (Black, ed., *The Works of Edgar Allan Poe*, 1927 edition, 820).

Other writers searched ways to power fiction with accurate-sounding speech through dialogue, even though the convention of modern dialogue had not yet fully developed. Writing at the same time as Poe, Hawthorne was extremely interested in creating an aural dimension to a text. In his journals, he remarks on storytelling sessions he heard on the docks in Salem. He enjoyed these legends from veterans of seafaring men, with whom he worked at the Custom House, and felt frustration that he could not capture on the page the same swagger and color of stories by these rascals (Mellow 271–273). Hawthorne's technique was to recreate spoken legends, but without the specificity or directness of the stories themselves. Hawthorne uses the concept of a report or rumor as an allegory, instead of actually rendering how a spoken story sounds.

In early-nineteenth-century America, fiction had just begun to incorporate colloquial style. Post-Revolution novelist Tabitha Tenney strikes her own blow for freedom in fiction through inventive uses of vernacular dialogue. In *Female Quixoticism: The Romantic Opinions and Extravagant Adventures of*

Dorcasina Sheldon (1798), Dorcasina's gardener Scipio lets loose with a wild barrage as he protects the garden from a thief: "You dog, take dat next time come teal our melon. I teach you better manners!" Sarah Orne Jewett's "A White Heron" (1886) relies on local color speech for a minor character. The protagonist, a young girl named Sylvy, leaves her crowded household to stay with her grandmother in the country. The old woman tends to drop letters and incorporate local idioms in her speech: "I guess she won't be troubled no great with 'em up to the old place!" Later, she tells the bird-hunting stranger about the hunting prowess of her son, Sylvy's father: "I never wanted for pa'tridges or gray squer'ls while he was to home." The convention of recreating spoken speech on the page reaches a full development with Twain. His stylistic achievement with dialogue blends character and voice against a backdrop of spoken tales and rumors that create an entire region.

Like Hawthorne, Poe stumbles over the fledgling nineteenth-century convention of dialogue. In "The Gold Bug," he uses an awkward colloquial style to represent the speech of Jupiter, Legrand's servant. "The Premature Burial" is somewhat better at capturing vernacular speech, although Poe's technique is still rough around the edges.

The narrator of this tale is prone to falling into profound sleeping spells described as being "superinduced" (264). He becomes obsessed with the fear of being buried alive while in one of these deep sleeps. He customizes the family vault with a bell and a lever for easy opening from inside. During one time of slow waking, he comes to, finding himself enshrouded in darkness, smelling of earth. He screams for help: "A long, wild, and continuous shriek, or yell, of agony, resounded through the realms of the subterranean Night." A chorus of rough voices greets him:

> "Hillo! Hillo, there!" said a gruff voice in reply.
> "What the devil's the matter now!" said a second.
> "Get out o' that!" said a third.
> "What do you mean by yowling in that ere kind of style, like a catty-mount?" said a fourth ["The Premature Burial" 267].

The narrator and his friends had taken emergency shelter aboard a sloop. The nightmare figures, diggers of his too-soon grave, are in actuality members of the vessel's crew. This passage marks one of the few times that Poe makes more than a passing effort to recreate idiosyncratic speech.

Instead, Poe spends his energy developing a rich symphony of sounds serving essentially as background noises, a "soundtrack" accompanying the action. Readers do not hear distinctive sounds of people talking, but the background speaks for them. Bells chime, hearts thud, furniture scrapes, and women shriek. Poe does not need mimicked sounds of voices in discursive speech when he can achieve this sound dimension by other means. There is a reason Emerson once referred to Poe as "the jingle man."

Without doubt, Poe had an ear for music. His wife Virginia played the piano and sang. Poe wrote to his friend George Eveleth that it was during one of her vocal recitals that she began to have a throat hemorrhage (Silverman 334). Poe also uses melody as a metaphor to represent the height of poetic expression.

In "Israfel," he makes a specific reference to the inspiration of the angel Israfel as coming from his lute of a heart. The angel's song is so beautiful that even the "giddy stars" making their music of the spheres stop to listen and "attend the spell of his voice." At the end of the poem, the narrator expresses a wish to change places with this divine, omnipotent muse:

> If I could dwell
> Where Israfel
> Hath dwelt, and he where I,
> He might not sing so wildly well
> A mortal melody,
> While a bolder note than this might swell
> From my lyre within the sky [971–972].

The poet expresses frustration over not being a better "singer." He longs to feel more than earth-bound truth with his lute-like heart. To reach this empyrean sphere where Israfel sings, Poe raises an intense "mortal melody," through a blend of image and sound.

Once soundtracks in cinema developed, technology to infuse sound into a story finally caught up with the fullness of Poe's imagination. The author's technique of using sound effects, from harmonious to discordant, in a well-orchestrated aural backdrop makes his works ready-made for film adaptation, as well as for new electronic media with its high-definition visual and aural dimensions.

The sense of the ineffable as the goal of a chase or inquiry seems to find a corollary in the dark mysteries of music. Music counts on time for its existence, and Poe's fiction evokes suspense by engaging time, stretching moments or speeding up action. Story elements of uncertainty, fear, and disturbances to the nervous system find their corollary in auditory qualities suggesting dissonance, rapidity, and unexpected rhythms. A held note may evoke suspense. It is not merely the "notes" of Poe's work, the disparate elements of character or plot, that evoke this fear, but the mood in the interstices of narrative. Poe develops a dramatic backdrop of vocal expressions to simulate and intensify a unified emotional effect. Shrieks, groans, and hisses reverberate across the page, disturbing the silence of the reader.

Poe often incorporates music in his writing, not only in subject, but through sounds. It may be that the relative lack of organized music in nineteenth-century America contributed to this aural direction of Poe's artistry. The United States lagged far behind Europe's long and established musical traditions. Dozens of stringed instruments simulated supernatural events and ineffable realms. In Europe, music gave the Gothic sensibility full expression. Two striking examples contemporaneous with Poe are Schubert's "The Erlking" and "Symphonie Fantastique" (1830) by Hector Berlioz.

"The Erlking" narrative had existed as a written text in Goethe's *Der Erlkönig* (1782) before Schubert used it in his *lied*, or art song, of the same title. In Schubert's version, the boy is seated behind his father on horseback. The boy continues to exclaim to his father about a sinister, troll-like figure, the erlking, hiding in the forest luring the child toward death. The boy's hysterical pleas gather more energy, until finally, the father's steed clatters into the courtyard. The man's son is still seated behind him on the horse, slumped in death. Poe had read Goethe, but whether he knew this exact work is not clear. Much of Poe's work, such as "The Pit and the Pendulum" or "The Black Cat," captures this same sense of mounting terror and sudden loss.

Berlioz's *Symphonie Fantastique* traces the opium-induced visions of a hero who ends up being executed for killing his beloved, whom he had suspected as being unfaithful. Then, as the work's final movement starts, the hero comes to life in hell, with his wife taunting him during the "Witches' Sabbath." The elements of this work are reminiscent of Poe as events spiral out of the protagonist's control, and he slips into madness. Essentially Poe re-shapes the sound of European Gothic into an American context. He infuses literary form with the intense feelings carried by music. He creates a hybrid art form.

With musical adaptations of poetry, the composer Claude Debussy also ventured into blending melody and literary text. Arthur Wenk notes the influences that the French symbolist poets had on Debussy and his successful compositions. Wenk's study traces Debussy's debt to poetry. The composer developed a musical idiom that smoothly fit the emotional lassitude of poems by Baudelaire, Mallarmé, Verlaine and others. Debussy's well-known "Prelude to an Afternoon of a Faun" (*Prélude à l'après-midi d'un faune*, 1894) succeeds in capturing the nuanced dreaminess of Mallarmé's style.

Because of Debussy's affinity with these poets, in 1908 he undertook a project to write music for a ballet based on Poe's "The Fall of the House of Usher" ("*La Chute de la Maison Usher*"). The enterprise intrigued him. "Edgar Allan Poe had the most original imagination in the world; he struck an entirely new note. I shall have to find its equivalent in music," he told one of his agents (Vallas 224). He signed a contract for the Poe project while he was still working on his opera *Pelléas et Mélisande* (1902). For two years, between 1908 and 1910, Debussy was obsessed with Poe, whose words he considered as dramatizing the "influence of stones on the minds of neurasthenic people." He wrote to friends that "the exterior world hardly exists for me.... [I] hardly ever leave the House of Usher" (Vallas 223).

Debussy stayed on the project for several more years, exchanging letters about it with his publisher, obsessing over it. Ultimately, he finished only the libretto and a few sketches for the piano. Ultimately, due to postponements and Debussy's feelings of being overwhelmed by the material, he never completed the orchestration. The project never became a reality.

In a study of Debussy's influences from the *Symboliste* poets, Wenk concludes that Debussy perhaps could not create music without a program. For the composer, inspiration from the spiderweb connections between music and poetry in the end stayed in the realm of the subconscious. "After having examined levels of meaning in Debussy's relation to poetry ... [Wenk concludes] such associations belong to the province of dream, for Debussy the wellspring of artistic inspiration" (Wenk 276). As tuned into nuance as Debussy was, he could not hear Poe's dreams. Some ethereal quality of Poe's literature defied expression in musical form.

In recreating the mind's travels along dream landscapes, Poe was a visionary. It would take a combination of sound and image to reproduce Poe's vision in the performing arts, that is, through film.

Through a direct emotional connection with readers, Poe's style comes closer to the intense feeling and audibility of music than fiction by his contemporaries. Cooper's *Last of the Mohicans* (1826) is a case in point. While the narrative arc of the story has an epic grandeur and originality in the character of Natty Bumppo, Cooper's plot proceeds in spurts. Sentences move as if in iron boots, not moccasins. Later, in a scathing commentary, Mark Twain famously details Cooper's numerous "literary offences." "Cooper's art has some defects. In one place in 'Deerslayer,' and in the restricted space of two-thirds of a page, Cooper has scored 114 offences against literary art out of a possible 115. It breaks the record."

Works by Poe and Cooper have similar storytelling values in that both Dupin and Natty Bumppo as take the initiative in righting injustices. Still, the contrast between the two authors stylistically is striking. Probably because Cooper did not write poetry, his prose lacks a pace and rhythm that a reader would recognize as "musical."

One *can* gather information about a book from its title. Irving's title of "Strange Stories by a Nervous Gentleman" (1824) lacks the imagistic power of "A Descent into the Maelström" or "The Tell-Tale Heart." The static label falls short on the suspense of Poe's title of "The Thousand and Second Tale of Scheherazade" or the dramatically wrong time element of "The Premature Burial."

While Poe's entire narrative makes a solid impression of horror or psychological confusion, his stories are highly wrought, artificial constructions. He ruffles the surface of his storylines through stories within stories. Just as a musical theme creates an ominous or sweeping emotion for a music listener, embedded text in language is a sign to the reader of a storyline's dramatic shifts. Writing on narratology, Mieke Bal provides a way for readers to follows these narrative insets.

Bal notes the often clashing testimonies of witnesses in a courtroom setting: "for people conversant with the practice of law, the notion that narrative is a construction, rather than a reconstruction, must seem pretty obvious, if not 'natural'" (220). Bal's definitions on parts of narrative go a long way toward furthering an approach to the "constructed" quality of Poe's tales.

Mise en abîme is "an embedded text presenting a story that resembles the primary fabula" (57–58). This construction equates to an infinite regress. In heraldry, the medallion in the middle of a shield gives a smaller graphic that serves as an emblem of the outer border of the shield. In language the insert occurs in a less than "ideal" form, what Bal labels as "mirror-text" (58).

Where the mirror text occurs in the primary text determines its function for a reader. Placed at the beginning of the narrative, the emblem foreshadows action, but this tie is oblique, making an impact only through "abstraction" (58). The reader figures out the relationship between embedded text and fundamental narrative only at the story's end, once the entire narrative has played out. "Thus suspense is maintained, but the prefiguring effect of the mirror-text is lost" (Bal 58). To gain the full effect of this prefiguring, the reader must return to the story's beginning, assessing how the introduction has shaped the ending. Poe's story "William Wilson" benefits from such an approach. The narrator relates a tragic downturn in fortunes that seems to occur at some point after the narrative ends and before the tale-teller begins speaking at the beginning.

Another pattern reverses an embedded story's dramatic impact. "The question that the reader raises is not 'How does it end?' but 'Will the character discover in time?'" (58). Both reader and character remain in the dark over a suspenseful event. The ending to *The Narrative of A. Gordon Pym* seems constructed from this placement of an embedded story. The embedded fragmented journal entries catalogue Pym's journey into an immense, ambiguous whiteness, creating an ongoing conundrum for critics and readers.

Mirror text at the end of a story changes from a predictive to a "retrospective" effect (58). This after-the-fact placement enhances meaning and dramatic suspense. The mirror text lifts or drops the narration to another thematic level, with universal meaning. An author's slow-motion control over the story may work as a "magnifying glass" (Bal 107). Actions that we know to take only a short time stretch out on the page, as occurs in the narrator's ruined murder plot during "The Tell-Tale Heart." For contrast, frequency and repetition builds a rapid pace. Bal places into this category "different events or alternative presentations of events" (112). A barrage of spinning detail creates disorientation during "A Descent into the Maelström," for instance.

Another element of Poe's fiction linking his style to music is an infusion of metaphors. Paul Ricoeur's definition of metaphor emphasizes a spatio-temporal quality similar to the space between musical tones. Ricoeur sees metaphor as a process of "bringing together terms that at first seem 'distant,' then suddenly 'close.' The relationship between two thoughts varies this distance to create, again, a quality of music through 'concordance and discordance'" (Ricoeur 3–4). Poe's multi-linear story lines recreate a musical quality akin to melody, and through the controlled distance between items being compared, figurative comparisons evoke a quality of harmony and discord.

The thrust of Ricoeur's *The Rule of Metaphor* is that a metaphor takes us away from the communicative quality of language and brings us to another reality "inaccessible to direct description" (xi). Narrative and stylistic theories from Bal and Ricoeur help us access distant regions in Poe's imagination that emerge as a force in contemporary novels.

Variations in Form

What are some uses of Poe's narrative in recent fiction and with what effects? Martha Grimes' *The Black Cat* (2010) proudly announces a Poe connection.

The Richard Jury novels by Grimes are all set in London and are titled with the names of London pubs. Although author Grimes lives in Washington, D.C., her character Richard Jury is the superintendent and a high-ranking detective with London's Metropolitan Police. A woman has been found dead on the grounds outside a pub called the Black Cat. The book is dedicated to "My old cat, Blackie, November 1989–April 23, 2007," so Grimes has written the book as a tribute, a release from grief.

In Poe's story "The Black Cat" (1843), the narrator slips into a crippling alcoholism and takes his self-hatred out on his wife's pet cat. First, he grabs the creature, and it bites him. In retribution, he cuts out its eye. The wound heals but the cat's presence is a constant reminder to the narrator of his weakness. Eventually, the narrator gives in to his impulse to be rid of the thing, and he hangs it from a tree in the yard. After the hanging, his house burns down, all except for one wall on which is an outline of a giant cat.

He discovers another cat, similar to the first, perched on a wine cask in a bar. He brings it home, thinking to undo his previous horrific act. The cat's appearance starts to change. The small white patch on its fur takes on the shape of the gallows. The image predicts the narrator's fate, as the cat's very presence annoys him to the point of murder. "Evil thoughts became my sole intimates" (228).

He raises an axe against the creature, but his wife halts him. "Goaded by this interference into a rage more than demoniacal, I withdrew my arm from her grasp and buried the axe in her brain. She fell dead upon the spot without a groan" (228). Ultimately, the mewling cat survives as evidence that incriminates him.

Grimes' novel *The Black Cat* sets up a similar situation in that a cat has witnessed a murder and carries the key to the murderer's identity. The solution to this case is less a supernatural awareness or even the cat's actual ability to tip off Jury about the murder. There are many animals in this book, three cats and three dogs. The closing scene involves Jury and his sidekick, the former aristocrat Melrose Plant, throwing a stick for his new dog. However, the actual function of the cat in this murder case is as a projection of human emotions, which indicts Richard Jury as a feeling human being.

Jury experiences a welter of feelings, since the woman he loves, Lu Aguilar, lies in a hospital bed, probably never able to walk again, as the result of a car accident. When Jury contemplates going to visit, he speaks to himself, "Don't go there," but he goes anyway. He has set up a series of mental barriers to protect himself from feeling.

In Lu's hospital room, Jury sees how much weight she has lost. She is frail, and he thinks about how she's lost her edge. He senses the "sheer bone" of her. He also thinks about the impossibility of him finding a way of being with her, by "marrying her or taking care of her somehow." Lu would be too proud to take him up on it, he thinks, since she would see it as stemming from pity and she shuns all that.

> Jury felt his walk down the white corridor must be almost as painful as hers, lying in that bed.
> *You're off the hook.*
> He did not want to explore that rush of feeling, distinctly like relief. He had been on the hook all right. He realized now that the hook had been sexual.... .
> The long white corridor seemed endless, the bank of elevators, the bright red "Exit" sign never getting any closer.
> The way out never did [25].

Poe's technique of using the supernatural in an expressionistic way to evoke repressed emotion comes through in Grimes' rendition of *The Black Cat*. As in Poe's tale, the cat speaks when a person cannot.

Poe and True Crime

The outlines of the current spate of "true crime" television reality programs situate the viewer in the same circumstance as the reader of Poe's tales. This subgenre of crime programs present in video form the same outline of "true crime" as Poe's innovation in the Dupin story "The Mystery of Marie Rogêt" (1842), which was based on an actual crime, the killing of Mary Rogers in New York, that Poe had known about.

In "The Mystery of Marie Rogêt," Poe sets a model of graphic crime at a distance, as Dupin and his help-mate learn of the crime much later from newspaper accounts. Dupin goes through the evidence, alibis, and testimony. The narrator collects newspaper accounts, so Dupin can combine all the versions into a coherent whole, an *ur* story, piecing together what had happened, through a comparison. Three-quarters of the way through the tale, Dupin emphasizes the likely truth about the case, along with the revelation of the murderer.

A young woman, engaged to be married, had disappeared for a time then returned. A few weeks afterward, a young woman's body was found floating in the Seine and determined to be the missing girl. Accounts include statements from eyewitnesses noting the last time they had seen the girl or premonitions that something might happen to her.

Dupin's helper summarizes specifics of the victim's condition when found. Poe does not shy away from graphic phrases such as "the face was suffused with dark blood, some of which issued from the mouth" and "the flesh of the neck was much swollen" (174). While the story makes liberal use of forensic details about the decaying body to unsettle or appeal to the reader's morbid interest, the focus is proportionately less on gore and more on how Dupin pieces together what probably happened. He uses police reports and stories featuring the crime in the tabloid newspapers of Paris.

These news accounts earn Dupin's scorn. In assessing each article's credibility, Dupin cites errors of reporting or counters the newspapers' assertions based on medical truths that everyone supposedly knows. The narrator prompts Dupin in his discussion:

"And what are we to think," I asked, "of the article in *Le Soleil*?"

"That it is a vast pity its inditer was not born a parrot — in which case he would have been the most illustrous parrot of his race. He has merely repeated the individual items of the already published opinion; collecting them with laudable industry, from this paper or that" [190].

Another of Dupin's key techniques is to place himself in the mind of the killer. "Let us see. An individual has committed the murder. He is alone with the ghost of the departed. He is appalled by what lies motionless in front of him" (200). As a result of his critique on the shoddy reporting and "mind meld" with the murderer, Dupin draws a conclusion about what might have actually happened to Marie Rogêt. Witness statements place the girl earlier in the company of a man with somewhat "swarthy" complexion. From sailor's knots binding the body and the timing of the victim's previous absence coinciding with schedules of sailors' deployments, Dupin alleges that the girl had planned an elopement with a man in the navy. He is most likely the murderer, not the girl's fiancé or other men in her life. The reader sees the facts laid out and achieves a distance from the horror of the crime.

Today's "true crime" television programs follow a similar format. These mystery docudramas certainly fail to pass muster as legal evidence, but the witness statements and reports, like Poe's story, are larded with gossip and innuendo. The onscreen narrator attempts to sort calmly through the varying accounts to create a distance for the viewer between sensational crime and its emotional aftermath.

The cases chosen for these so-called "true crime" dramas cannot be a garden variety wrongdoing. The shows rarely involve a crime motivated by poverty or desperation or random violence. Instead, the crime victims are typically upper middle class. Through the audience's eyes, crime is like a ferocious zoo animal kept behind bars, removed from the viewer by being behind a TV screen. These cases seem to have an interest because they represent some aspect of insolubility, whether it's that the murderer is never found or they reveal a strange, unbelievable quirk of human behavior. Television viewers need the combined voyeuristic connection with the crime and the objective distance of its step-by-step solution.

The idea of having a journalist or journalist-seeming guide take us through the case is another appeal of these programs. The investigator might be young and competent, or older, with a long-term media presence for credibility. The journalist host seemingly has access to all the police files, sometimes speaking directly with the police. At times, as the case makes its way through the courts, the camera goes into the courtroom for that moment of the verdict. The camera zooms in on the defendant for a moment of high drama as the verdict is read. This scene resonates as a duplicate of footage from the 1995 O.J. Simpson trial.

Journalistic details make the cases seem clinical, as does the narration itself. But at the heart of the narrative formula are portraits of people we recognize. These persons have some traits we identify with, but not too much, as with the objectified stereotype of a swarthy sailor in Dupin's solution to Marie Rogêt case. Dowler and Fleming observe the importance of the victim's being a blend of recognizable qualities and features that mark him or her as "other." They note the prevalence in crime reporting of the adage "if it bleeds, it leads," but discount the saying's accuracy: "It really depends on who is bleeding" (841).

Events in Poe's narrative structure overlap each other to create places for an embedded conundrum in today's true-crime dramas. In this sense, the elements of story represent seven steps across a narrative tightrope. Suspense over the killer's identity and what actually happened drives the story.

1. **Body Drops**—Death announces itself. This first segment introduces us to the context of the crime, the geographical locale, the victim, and others surrounding the victim.
2. **Summons**—Investigators are called onto the scene. They comb the area where the body was found, collecting evidence.
3. **Line Up**—Family and friends react to the death. The story recovers from grief and maintains its suspense as investigators assemble another line-up of witnesses and alibis.
4. **Rewind**—Camera shots can rewind the crime's enactment very exactly. Viewers experience the stabbing or gunshot in minute detail. Frequently, when the narrative returns after a commercial break, the camera takes another run through the horrible night to bring new viewers up to speed. Alibis and times are crucial during this phase.
5. **Ah-Ha! Moment (The Reveal)**—A courtroom drama or explicit evidence found by the police points the finger at the killer. Friends and family react with shock, if the killer is known to them, or relief that their long ordeal is nearly over.
6. **Encounter with Evil**—The camera may enter the convicted killer's cell to record his hollow pleas of innocence with investigators. Or the camera may sit as a welcome guest at a kitchen table of the suspect whom the jury found innocent.
7. **Restoration**—Life continues. The camera records moments of family solidarity, a meal or a graduation to emphasize that the rift in the community has closed, but only partially.

Dateline NBC, 48 Hours and *Hard Case* exemplifies the true-crime drama following Poe's template. In the case of a murdered French citizen, Hugues la Plaza, covered by *48 Hours* for its episode "A Case for Murder" in 2009, viewers see immediately that the victim is physically attractive, and he knows many women. He was at a bar called Underground San Francisco in the hours before his death, and his murder remains unsolved, surrounded by an investigation filled with ambiguities. La Plaza fits the bill as the featured personality of the reality crime drama. As a transplant to the States, la Plaza has the requisite status of being "other" that allows viewers to separate themselves from the trauma of the crime. Still, he leaves a devoted girlfriend behind, who presses authorities to continue the investigation and ensures that la Plaza will be not forgotten.

In the *48 Hours* episode entitled "The Lady in the Harbor" (2009), the victim's daughter is suspected of murdering her mother. Still, the girl maintains her innocence straight down the line. The narrative about each case represents an attempt to control the ineffable in human behavior.

Another case emphasizes the insidious role played by small town gossip. A man in Savannah, Tennessee, is dead from an overdose of a drug used to treat diabetes. The odd part is that the man, Freddie, was not a diabetic. Where did he gain access to this drug? Who could have administered it?

Freddie's wife Sharron is a nurse. Did she poison her own husband? She is brought to trial. Since Savannah is a town made up of closely knit social circles, the nurse suffers from the questioning eyes of community members about causes of her husband's death. The jury deliberates for ninety minutes. Sharron is found not guilty of killing her husband, Freddie, but she feels that her life is ruined.

True-crime television programs emphasize Poe's same formula of attempted solutions in an hour-long format. The shows also issue a warning of the show's graphic content and how it might be disturbing for some viewers. The warning is thereby guaranteed to keep viewers riveted through the commercials with the implication of horrors to come.

Because of the public's need to keep horrors of crime at a distance, the constructed narratives of Poe serve a key role in our culture. They represent a sort of narrative "firewall" to protect us from violence and anomalous crime. By viewing these narratives, we keep the world's random violence in check.

A Wired Writer for Our Time

What lies behind the upsurge in Poe's popularity over recent decades? There are no pat answers, although two phenomena are strong contenders and both involve wiring.

In *The Scarecrow* (2010), Michael Connelly's protagonist Jack McEvoy is a Los Angeles–based police reporter. McEvoy has been downsized from his job on the crime beat. Despite his newspaper's waning influence, or maybe because of it, he is eager to hang on to the purity of reporting truth. After receiving a pink slip, McEvoy assesses his situation:

> Like the paper and ink newspaper itself, my time was over. It was about the Internet now. It was about hourly uploads to online editions and blogs. It was about television tie-ins and Twitter updates. It was about filing stories *on your*

phone instead of using it to call rewrite. The morning paper might as well be called the *Daily Afterthought*. Everything in it was posted on the web the night before [Connelly 12].

With his usual insight, Connelly captures the despair of a writer floundering in the sea-changes of 21st-century communication.

Poe knew these changes well. As a writer he struggled to make a living and a difference in an unstable literary market. He developed his narratives partially in response to a time of clashing changes in audience taste and expectations. The telegraph and the railroad compressed the world and sped up communications. The life-and-death rhetoric of the decades leading up to the Civil War kept public discourse at a white-hot temperature. Antebellum writers faced an uncertain future. Newspapers and magazines folded. Conflicts over copyrights interfered with writers making a living. The publishing market struggled to establish a distinctive American literary voice and form. Poe intensified the short-form prose "sketch" into a short story dramatizing insoluble dilemmas; contemporary writers cross novel genres or try alternative marketing to compete in a world of electronic publishing and the instant internet.

Another state of being "wired" relates to why readers might gravitate toward Poe's nervous excitability. Stress-inducing artificial situations stream into our homes via television, films, and DVDs. This de-stabilizing situation keeps us on edge and ready.

Ready for what? Does a book or TV drama show us what to do should we be involved in a crime? Somewhere, a serial killer has shattered the lives of real families. Actual people have endured the traumas of sitting through a murder trial. Obviously crime touches more people than it should, but the percentage of the general populace affected by violent crime is surprisingly low.

The Federal Bureau of Investigation notes about all categories of violent crime: "Preliminary figures indicate that, as a whole, law enforcement agencies throughout the Nation reported a decrease of 5.5 percent in the number of violent crimes brought to their attention for 2009 when compared with figures reported for 2008." Although we would not suspect this fact, due to the nightly line-up of crime-associated television shows, homicide is also on the decline. Per capita murder rates in the United States peaked at 10.2 in 1980, rose again to 9.5 in 1993, and since then has steadily decreased over the past ten years to a low of 5.4 in 2008 ("Crime in the United States"). The chances of being a crime victim are relatively rare. The sensational appeal of danger has little to do with actual crime.

Despite the unmitigated awfulness of actual violence, people continue to crave the thrill of walking a precipice. These entertainments provoke visceral reactions to potentially horrible, fictive experiences. Poe pitches his narratives toward the reader's appetite for experiences of the night. While his fiction has a vivid, psychic immediacy, it is far from realistic. Instead, it highlights the same lack of rationality, confusion of time and place, and metaphoric duality that we associate with dreams.

Murder as entertainment is popular, then, not because an on-page narrative strikes a chord from our waking lives. Rather, a murder we read about in a novel or see onscreen may simulate the fears we try to escape in our sleep. A television drama about murder presents the resolution we struggle toward in our nightmares.

Life as a Dream or a Dream as Life?

A thorough study of the dream process is too complex for full presentation here. However, the latest theories on why we dream refute Freud's hypothesis about "hidden impulse" messages and posit a physiological genesis for the activity. During sleep, dreams fire our brains to keep cognitive functions honed. This body of oneirological research illustrates that the narrative structures of dreaming have been with us a long time. They lie in our developing brains from infancy on. Obviously the shapes of dreams precede and inform verbal structures. A scary late-night film does not cause nightmares; rather, we like these dramas because watching stressful narratives is good for us. Detective fiction, films, and TV shows exert a primal force. While awake, we are drawn to these stories because they remind us of the storm of chemical/electrical activity essential to healthy brain function. In addition, the narratives we experience while awake offer the kind of content resolution and completion that we cannot reach during our nocturnal chases.

This combination of theories also sheds light on Poe's storytellers. The author's almost claustrophobic brand of first-person perspective serves at once to highlight and restrain character. The tension resulting from this distinctive method creates a flexible balance that fits smoothly into 21st-century America's media. Today's readers and viewers crave complete immersion into the action. They gravitate toward "step-aside moments" of commentary, a technique common on *faux* reality shows. This blend of subjectivity and objective observation opens a textual space for narrative interactivity appealing to American audiences. As if sitting in the driver's seat of first-person role-player video games, the reader/viewer may then solve the crime, tolerate the most incredible justification for outrageous behavior, or witness up-close destruction of a psyche. This technique grants an illusion of user control over direction of the text. Poe's perspective finds broad application to American entertainment

CHAPTER 1

The Sidelong Glance

Poe's first tale of detection featured the French genius C. Auguste Dupin. He was not the narrator of events. The "seated" perspective, home base for the reader, is the narrator who clearly admires Dupin, serves as a helper and as a retriever of documents, has more money than Dupin (and probably pays), and is unobservant, a less finely honed power of observation than Dupin, but not necessarily a dim bulb.

Poe's pair of protagonists unifies method and material. As Charles May notes, "The most significant contribution Poe's detective stories make to the development of the short story consists of their basing a story's central theme and structure on the very process by which the reader perceives that unifying structure and pattern" (May 82). Poe himself recognized the innovative quality to his stories. In an 1846 letter to his friend Philip Pendeleton Cooke, he wrote, "These tales of ratiocination owe more to their popularity to being something in a new key. I do not mean to say that they are not ingenious — but people think them more ingenious than they are — on account of their method and *air* of method. In 'Murders of the Rue Morgue,' for instance, where is the ingenuity of unraveling a web which you yourself (the author) have woven for the express purpose of unravelling?" (May 85).

The narrator of "The Murders in Rue Morgue" (1848) is unnamed. He discusses the role of cognition, which itself cannot be analyzed; we can only see its effects. "As the strong man exults in his physical ability, delighting in such exercises as call his muscles into action, so glories the analyst in that moral activity which *disentangles*" [italics original] (144).

Bonding over literature situates their relationship from the outset in the world of symbol. The two meet in a library, sharing a similar interest in the same volume. The narrator has a powerful pull toward Dupin. Phrases like "brought into closer communion," "deeply interested," "astonished," and "I felt my soul enkindled" show that he is drawn to Dupin's wild yet unique imagination (143). Readers also may focus attention on Dupin, bypassing the boring narrator.

With the focus on Dupin's brilliant methods, the more plodding narrator seems to get short shrift. However, a grounded examination requires that we examine the two together to note the complementary and competitive nature of their relationship. The dual relationship is what makes its way into our popular culture. It's the narrator who first considers Dupin's moods, the narrator who thinks about Dupin's "bi-part soul" and conjures up the concept of a "double Dupin — the creative and the resolvent" (144). Dupin is not the only solver of personalities. The tale teller performs a major function in laying out the story of this eccentric character.

"We existed within ourselves alone." They are isolated, in a kind of honeymoon. Dupin loves the night, the dark, and many other gloomy things. The narrator explains Dupin's predisposition toward things nocturnal as a "freak of fancy." But the boring narrator also has his wild side. Dupin pulls in the narrator: "into this *bizarrerie,* as unto all his others, I quietly fell" (144).

One day, Dupin and his companion read a newspaper account of a horrible crime. The graphic details of the crime contrast with the twilight aestheticism of their domestic life. Neighbors hear shrieks in the upstairs flat of a mother and daughter. The neighbors race upstairs, only to encounter a locked entrance. They break down the door. Once inside, they discover the dead body of the daughter, jammed feet first up the chimney. They find the mother outside, body mutilated. Her throat has been cut. When the neighbors try to pick the mother up, her head flops off.

When the newspaper account is clearly not enough, Dupin and the narrator visit the crime scene. Since Dupin has assisted the police on crimes in the past, the two are allowed to cross the yellow tape. They discover the room strewn with hanks of coarse hair and puddles of blood. The following passage shows us Dupin's decisive investigative method. It also illustrates the relationship between Dupin and the narrator. Note that the "I" of the story is hardly Dupin's intellectual equal, but a sounding board for Dupin's investigation.

> "Dupin!" I said, completely unnerved; "this hair is most unusual — this is no human hair."
>
> "I have not asserted that it is," said he; "but, before we decide this point, I wish you to glance at the little sketch I have here traced upon this paper. It is a facsimile drawing of what has been described in one portion of the testimony as 'dark bruises, and deep indentations of finger nails,' upon the throat of Mademoiselle L'Espanaye" [161–162].

Except for the actual visit onto the horrific scene, Dupin and the narrator solve the murders from a distance through the page. Dupin is poor and he spends his inheritance on books. "By courtesy of his creditors, there still remained in his possession a small remnant of his patrimony; and, upon the income arising from this, he managed, by means of a rigorous economy, to procure the necessities of life, without troubling himself about its superfluities. Books, indeed, were his sole luxuries" (143). So both he and his friend are well versed in experiences received second-hand. The story unfolds through a series of newspaper articles, during which we as readers learn along with Dupin and the narrator about the accounts of various witnesses.

Dupin follows events without much comment until the police make an arrest: "It was only after the announcement that Le Bon had been imprisoned, that he asked me my opinion respecting the murders. I could merely agree with all Paris in considering them an insoluble mystery" (152). The narrator has no contribution beyond what "all Paris" might hold as an opinion.

This story makes explicit the manipulation of a text. Only by absorbing the printed word does Dupin learn about the crime in the first place. Dupin reads about the crime and absorbs verbal information before rearranging the data. The resulting word construction reveals the previously hidden narrative of the crime.

Dupin notes that the best way to see is to look at the situation sideways. "To look at a star by glances — to view it in a side-long way, by turning toward it the exterior portions of the *retina* (more susceptible of feeble impressions of light than the interior), is to behold the star distinctly —" (153). With the dual protagonists of Dupin and the narrator, Poe structures a tale by putting the sidelong glance into practice. Through the sideways processing of information between this duo, mysterious events and hidden phenomena gain definition.

The detective fits the ordinary detail into a larger pattern in the same way that the writer selects bits of everyday life, every hair and fiber, and fits them into the larger fabric of human experience. Charles May notes the significance of Poe's technique of having Dupin relay this information to his narrator, the proto-Dr. Watson: "The transformation of ordinary detail, previously mere verisimilitude, into contextually meaningful motifs is a key factor in the creation of not only the detective story but the short story as a genre" (May 83). In many ways, Poe has built into the detective narrative less of the detective and more of the writer, working among the clues of sensation to find words. The narrator helps in piecing words together to tell the story.

The narrator of the Dupin mysteries often receives short shrift, being seen through the filter of Conan Doyle's construction of Watson, the helpmeet. Still, the reader is positioned among this duo to receive the information from the narrator in an uneven distribution. The reader is, as Charles May notes, "in a crucial hermeneutic situation between the narrator and the protagonist" (May 83). The reader does not have access to Dupin's mind, but may know more than the anonymous holder of the story's point of view. Reading is a key part of their relationship. They meet in a library. The two men are on the trail of the same rare book. They hit it off and soon are sharing an apartment, essentially living like vampires.

> At the first dawn of the morning we closed all the mossy shutters of our old building; lighted a couple of tapers which, strongly perfumed, threw out only the ghastliest and feeblest of rays.... We then busied our souls in dreams — reading, writing, or conversing.... [At] the Advent of true Darkness, [t]hen we sallied forth into the streets until a late hour, seeking, amid the wild lights and shadows of the populous city, that infinity of mental excitement [141].

While Dupin is very precise in tracing cause and effect from close observations, the passage makes it clear that he does not proceed solely from a rational perspective. Dupin's crime-solving method relies on a potent blend of empirical reasoning and a poet's imagination.

Because Conan Doyle's Sherlock Holmes picks up the "logical" method as a means of investigation, early critics of Poe viewed Dupin through a ratiocinative lens. In "The Deluded Detectives," Gerald Kennedy discusses how early critics placed too much emphasis on the empiricism of Dupin. Kennedy finds that however much Poe railed against the vagueness of Coleridge or the transcendentalists, he was immersed in the Romanticism of his time, reacting against the Age of Reason. In "The Purloined Letter" (1845), Dupin sharpens his vision, that is, his inner intuitive faculties, by plunging into darkness. The case requires the most delicate handling. It revolves around a compromising letter written by a female "royal personage." A minor government functionary has taken the letter and is now using it to blackmail the lady. The police know who took the letter, and they turn the man's apartment upside down looking for it. They unscrew furniture legs, poke into upholstery, and dig into the carpets. Still, the incriminating letter continues to elude them. Dupin focuses his full mind, both the rational and the intuitive sides, on the problem: "'If it is any point requiring reflection,' observed Dupin, as he forbore to enkindle the wick, 'we shall examine it to better purpose in the dark'" (208).

Dupin visits the villain, a Minister D—. As a result of Dupin's "I see better in the dark" approach, he finds the special letter. It sits tucked in a letter holder among everyday correspondence, hidden in plain sight. Beforehand, he has paid local street urchins to create a diversion. During a momentary lapse in Minister D's attention, Dupin steals the letter back and lords his success over the Prefect of Police:

> "But," said the Prefect, a little discomposed, "*I* am *perfectly* willing to take advice and to pay for it. I would *really* give fifty thousand francs to anyone who would aid me in the matter."
> "In that case," replied Dupin, opening a drawer and producing a check-book, "you may as well fill me up a check for the amount mentioned. When you have signed it, I will hand you the letter" [214].

Once again, Dupin has efficiently solved the case, outwitting both the Prefect and the letter-snatching villain. In solving the crime, he himself enacts the original crime. A man with the last initial of "D" repeats the larceny. Again, words and "letters" play an essential part in the nature of the solution.

Poe's creation of C. Auguste Dupin predates Sherlock Holmes by thirty years. In the Dupin stories, several durable conventions of the detective character are in place. He is an eccentric genius, a night traveler with a sidekick. His method is to investigate with every resource at his disposal, emotion or intuition as well as logic. He is not above working with street informants, the street children who stir up a distraction. He also maintains a friendly rivalry with police.

Poe's two investigators make their way onto current films by way of the recent *Sherlock Holmes* (2009), directed by Guy Ritchie and starring Robert Downey Jr. and Jude Law. While it might be argued that this work is about Conan Doyle's creation, many elements of Poe's original concept emerge in this movie. A sequel is soon to follow. Ritchie anticipates a long franchise, as with Conan Doyle's original creation.

The work presents itself as an amalgam of Poe's mysticism, contemporary crime scene investigation (CSI) strategies and "steam punk," a Victorian-era blend of steel and romance.

From the outset, the film's self-conscious adaptation and referential nature bleeds through the screen. Holmes himself is in a self-referential mode, thinking through the blows he needs to throw on the man standing guard over Lord Blackwood's sacrificial murder of a young woman. In his mind, Holmes runs through his pugilistic moves as if the items are on a checklist. He detects the guard's vulnerabilities, adds them up and offers a prognosis for the solution on how long it will take his unfortunate opponent to recover. A CSI-like slow-motion filming is used as Holmes plans out the punches and karate strategy he'll use to whip his opponent in the ring. The slow-mo runs through the body for gory details — cracked ribs, broken kneecap, broken jaw, flesh ripples back from the energy of the thrown punch. The camera also zooms in on the body parts and pig carcasses in the laboratory of Reardon, the mad scientist. This materiality of the world contrasts with the film's "cerebral" side in a replication of Dupin's "Bi-Part Soul."

The film inserts by-the-way incidents of Holmes' scientific whimsy. When Watson catches Holmes shooting in his apartment, Holmes claims to be on the trail of inventing a new firearm suppressor. But Watson knows that Holmes is bored and he needs a new case. He is idly pursuing experiments, using sounds from his violin bow to make the flies all fly counterclockwise. He has also experimented with a new anesthesia on Gladstone, their English bulldog.

The film equates Holmes' manipulation of dogs to his exploitation of Watson. When the two arrive on the crime scene, Blackwood the villain sneers, "If it isn't Sherlock Holmes, and your loyal dog," which refers to Watson.

Watson expresses outrage over Gladstone's lying motionless on the floor. Watson's fiancée Mary is also concerned when she first visits their flat on 221B Baker Street. She notes that Gladstone (i.e., Watson) is seemingly unconscious. Once Gladstone comes to, Watson joins Holmes in the case and Mary nods her acceptance. Throughout the film, scenes with Gladstone echo those of Holmes' manipulation of Watson. Even at the end, when Watson packs in preparation of leaving the flat and asserting his independence, Holmes says, "Quick, close the door," both so Gladstone will not escape and so Watson will remain trapped in the flat. Being a helper to Holmes is dangerous.

The film casts a knowing wink at a possible homoerotic relationship between Holmes (Robert Downey Jr.) and Watson (Jude Law). There is much domestic blather about their house, their dog, and Holmes sharing Watson's clothes. The two squabble like a long-time married couple. Watson plans to buy an engagement ring. A fortune-teller they encounter on the way to the jewelers reads Watson's palm and sets up a guilt-inducing situation: "There are two brothers, not of blood, but of bond." The soothsayer has, of course, been paid off by Holmes.

The film's clear-eyed awareness about stereotypes of two men living together updates the relationship between Holmes and Watson for a modern audience. The shift in tone that Ritchie has created asserts the basic solidity of Poe's original construction. Readers and viewers know that the bond between Holmes and Watson, as the tie between Dupin and the narrator of their adventures, is really their work together on the case.

Watson gets as drawn into a case as Holmes. Watson might be fed up with the immature aspects of Holmes' personality, but he still cannot resist the draw of solving the next mystery. The film may move to today's context in a few ways, but mostly stays within Poe's original model.

When Watson's fiancée Mary encounters Holmes at Watson's bedside after the explosion, she tells Holmes, "You love him as much as I do." After all, Watson had saved Holmes' life, Damon and Pythias-style, from the explosion, warning him off the charges set by Blackwood.

For a modern action film, Ritchie's version retains a number of self-referential dimensions to the Holmes-Watson adventures. First is the idea of processes of thought for moving the storyline. Count Blackwood's crime involves the dark arts, seemingly beyond empirical reality. The film attempts to delve into the mysteries of consciousness, primarily through Holmes's prodigious reasoning. Blackwood may owe his supernatural side to trickery, but ultimately, Holmes and Watson use reasoning to figure out Blackwood's moves.

Like the narrator of the Dupin mysteries, who gathers the news clippings for Dupin to process in "The Mystery of Marie Rogêt," Watson is the word man. He is the one to "pronounce" Count Blackwood dead, to render the pulse of life into words. He is the one keeping the notes of their "adventures," so he can later tell about his exploits with the legendary Holmes. He is the "reader" of code. He reveals the secret message on the nearly burned paper they find in Reardan's laboratory. When he pours the dropper of liquid onto the document, an image of the Four Orders crest gradually emerges in a parallel of old-fashioned photographic development. Watson's excited conclusion of course comes after Holmes is already leaping ahead to answer the next question.

Watson continues to attempt the draw the line on how much he assists Holmes, but his resistance is feeble. When he is packing his books to move out of their flat, he continues to be drawn in by Holmes' next case. Holmes interrupts the packing process and drapes a body across a table. Watson cannot resist looking closely at the corpse and participates in gathering observations to determine that the man had worked at a slaughterhouse — coal dust in the vicinity of the place. When Holmes hurries off in a rush, urging Watson to come along, the words man finds the words to resist. Then Watson sees that Holmes has left his revolver on the table, Watson recognizes that "he did it on purpose." Also, Watson in the end is ultimately the keeper of the notes, "scribbles, really" of their "adventures." He is the means by which these diverse encounters will make it to the page for a larger readership. Although Count Blackwood says that *he* is only the channel for the dark arts to emerge on the world of the living, Watson the tale teller is ultimately the only channel to carry the alchemy of story to readers.

The name of the villain, Blackwood, may allude to *Blackwood Magazine*, where Poe freelanced from 1837 to 1838. Cryptography and the ultimate mystery involved in language comes into the film through the hodge-podge of markings, measurements, symbols, words, and math formulas scribbled first on the wall of Blackwood's cell and later the room imprisoning Holmes.

A raven, Poe's signature emblem, makes its appearance throughout the film after key scenes. The bird lands outside Count Blackwood's cell at his death, then in the cemetery after Blackwood has ostensibly risen from the dead. It appears as a kind of familiar to Blackwood after the murder of Sir Thomas, and it caws raucously at the film's conclusion from the top girder of the bridge under construction over the Thames. Despite the film's updates, it uses a myriad of Poe references.

Blackwood also alludes to another realm, one beyond reach. He stands on the verge of an unknowable universe. He is only the channel, he tells Holmes, when Holmes visits him in his cell. Count Blackwood's character is very vampiric, supposedly coming back from the dead. His plan is to take over the living world in a mass conspiracy. The final scene is of two halves of an unfinished bridge. Count Blackwood hangs in the middle, dead, like the symbol of that insoluble puzzle of what happens after death. Irene Adler says, "The storm is coming," and then Holmes and Adler allude to Moriarty, the chalk-marked professor. Clearly the professor is poised to play a central role in the sequel.

The relationship between Holmes and Watson (Dupin and the narrator) is of a different quality than a doppelgänger. Whereas the doppelgänger reflects a moral dimension of right and wrong, or convention versus lack of inhibition, this two-teaming is more pliable. It emphasizes two sides of problem solving, conception versus pragmatism, ideas versus implementation. It raises involved questions of epistemology.

"If the writer does his work properly, if he is successful in building up a sense of the mysterious, of some dark secret or intricately knotted problem, then he has to face the fact that there simply exists no hidden truth or guilty knowledge whose revelation will not seem anticlimactic compared to an antecedent sense of mystery and the infinite speculative possibilities it permits" (Irwin 28). The allure is in the mystery.

The Investigation

These "pairs from Poe" have blossomed into many forms and variations in both fiction and film. The unequal partnership of Dupin and the narrator has evolved through the Holmes/Watson dynamic into a mix and match of crime-solving duos. John Cawelti says that the Poe's construct of Dupin and the narrator gained more acceptance through Holmes and Watson:

> Poe's version ... does not really develop the middle-class family circle as the basic ... milieu of crime. Perhaps because of this, the detective story did not become immediately popular after Poe invented it. Rather, it had to wait until the later nineteenth century and the enormous success of Sherlock Holmes, for it is in Doyle's work that the relation between crime and the family circle is fully elaborated [Cawelti 99].

During the early decades of television, this double-sided perspective was comprised of male detectives with women as helpmates. In Erle Stanley Gardiner's *Perry Mason* series, Perry worked with the private investigator Paul Drake, and Perry worked with his secretary Della Street, but the balance of power in solving the case was never evenly distributed among the three. They occasionally went out for dinner to celebrate the end of a case, but Perry would be the one in charge. In "The Case of the Curious Bride" (1958), Perry dispatches Paul onto a field trip in the classic Thunderbird. Paul gets instructions to watch a house and locate a witness at a local bar.

Back at the office, Perry needs insight into a skittish woman client's identity. Della sits across from Perry's desk where the client had just been sitting. Ever the super-efficient secretary, Della literally pulls the woman's purse out from under her to give Perry the key information he needs. Still, Perry is inevitably the focal point of the instructions. He is "Mason," builder of the foundation. Paul Drake is inevitably in the field, with his name "drake" connoting a solitary wanderer bird out in nature. "Street" situates Della in an urban identity apart from the lawyer's profession. Her name also may carry a sexualized connotation of "street walker." While the televised version of the mysteries rarely emphasized the sensual version of Della, her status as secondary to the men is clear.

As the stature of the investigator as a lone agent grew on television, the status of women did become more sexualized (Stark 230–232). In *The Rockford Files*, Jim Rockford was the only investigator. He had a bumbling helper, a man named Angel, and occasionally his father, Rocky, who assisted on the occasion. Still, Rockford was alone, living in a trailer, on the margins of respectable society. His telephone message machine played at the start of many programs. At times, these messages kicked off the case. More frequently, they emphasized Rockford's recent love life. In a sense, Jim Rockford's absence of the middle-class family life did not matter. He drove a muscle car and was beaten up nearly every episode. The show emphasized the hyper-masculine domination of the PI series on television.

By the late 1990s, original thinkers working with Poe's sidelong convention continued to reshape the formula with varied relationships between the two crime solvers. Male detectives share crime-solving with women and at times even turn over the major investigation duties to women. The variations expand the sphere of influence for the crime-solving pair. With the detective and his sidekick being of different ethnicities, the writer gives voice to original identities and develops unusual challenges for the lead character. To keep excessive violence away from the head detective but to allow violence on the page or onscreen, the protagonist takes on a sociopathic buddy. This allows the sidekick to bust heads, while the hero detective uses his or her head to piece clues together. Alternating points of view provide an ongoing shift in perspective and control. The variation can refresh a multi-volume detective series, presenting readers with new fields of vision for investigators.

The sociopath helper has been a recent placeholder in the "pairs from Poe" convention. The hero deploys a strong-armed thug to do the dirty work in a hyper-masculinized, semi-articulate manner. This buddy, often a violent hitman, allows the hero to dispatch firepower without compromising his own morality. Once released to commit mayhem, these characters go off and do bad things. Spenser's Hawk, created by Robert Parker, is extremely well spoken, listens to Ornette Coleman, and has a rarefied taste. With Hawk's creation, Parker goes against an ethnic stereotype, avoiding any associations of Hawk with a gangster image. Still, Hawk goes where Spenser fears to tread. He and Hawk are blood brothers with a strong bond of silence.

Spenser and Hawk contrast with the two-teaming detectives of Dupin and the narrator. They do not speak about what they do. These two are not word guys. One is the brain, the other is the muscle. The musclemen are not narrators of action. Their actions are offstage, only implied. The reader has to infer what has happened to the corrupt politician or likely killer who got away with it. But there might be a scene when the tough guy storms onto the scene like an avenging angel at a crucial moment.

Frequently the brute characters are of a different ethnicity from the main character and have an odd quirk. C. J. Box's Nate Romanowski is from Russia and has a falcon. *The Master Falconer* features Nate. Joe Pickett has had to take care of Nate's pet. *Nowhere to Run* is another volume featuring Nate. Robert Crais's Elvis Cole has his bully boy in Joe Pike, an ex–Marine. *The Watchman* (2007) and *The First Rule* (2010) focus on Pike.

In an interview for *January* magazine, Dennis Lehane discusses his high-testosterone creation, Bubba Rogowski. The interviewer asks if Bubba is based on a real person. "No. I knew some guys growing up who might have had a couple of screws loose. But he just sorta showed up in the first book."

Lehane's *Moonlight Mile* (2010) is the latest installment in the Patrick/ Angie series. Essentially, the book is a sequel to *Gone, Baby, Gone* (1999), which was made into a film ten years later. In *Moonlight Mile*, Patrick can mull over if he was right to return a kidnapped girl to an abusive family life. In previous books, Bubba Rogowski is the oversized strong man whom nobody wants to mess with. But in this outing, he turns into Uncle Bubba, a babysitter and protector of the child. He gives her a teddy bear.

S. J. Rozan places her own stamp on Poe's convention of the double-headed investigation. In the ongoing Lydia Chin/Bill Smith series by S. J. Rozan, the two lead characters are not only of different genders but different cultures. For each new book in the series, the sidekick and the protagonist switch seats as the controlling perspective. In *On the Line* (2010), Bill Smith has to rescue Lydia, who has been kidnapped. So she is out of sight. *Shanghai Moon* has Lydia as a focal point and Bill takes a secondary role.

Absent Friends (2002) is a stand-alone novel about the attack on New York City on September 11, 2001. According to notes on Rozan's author website: "Working on that got me intrigued with the multi-voice novel. That's a format that I thought wouldn't work for Lydia and Bill, because they each narrate in the first person." In *Shanghai Moon* (2008), Rozan uses diverse materials, documents, interviews, and diaries to create other voices from the past. She also maintains an active online presence through her blog, which frequently discusses the writing process. She gives the reader a backstage glimpse of her books as she writes them. She takes the reader into the kitchen to experience the food preparation before the food is served. Rozan is articulate about the writing process. In a sense, the reader becomes one of the parties receiving her sidelong glance.

Rozan may have pried open the crime-solving duo team into a trio through her website. On the website for *Shanghai Moon*, Rozan revealed that she was writing a new book with Bill Smith as the narrator. Lydia Chin has been kidnapped, and the kidnapper continues to call Bill and taunt him with clues he must solve to find Lydia before the kidnapper kills her. Rozan mentioned that the book was nearly finished, but she did not yet know the title. The fact alarmed her because a title will usually come to her as she completes the book. Later, she held a contest and the winning entry was *On the Line*. Given the book's situation of crucial telephone calls, the phrase presents a condensed meaning of being on the telephone and on the spot.

Rozan's technique of alternating perspectives keeps the series fresh, allowing the author the opportunity to approach each case from distinctive perspectives. There's no single formula dictating that one investigator should be brilliant and the other should play obtuse. Rozan's approach allows a more inventive storytelling structure that unfolds more opportunities to reveal the psychology of Lydia and Bill.

S. J. Rozan sees the writing process as a dual stream of the author's consciousness. She explained in an interview that she introduced two characters in *On the Line* so they could help Bill, and they stuck around, refusing to leave, seemingly developing wills of their own. When the interviewer asked if a writer's characters actually do that, Rozan responded:

> Of course not. The rational part of a writer, in charge most of the time, knows they don't because they don't exist except inside our heads. But the irrational part is often in charge during the actual writing of a book. Then it seems to the rational part like the characters are doing whatever they want and were just running alongside writing it down.

In 2010, S. J. talked about her current writing project, with Lydia next in line as narrator, called *Ghost Hero*. As of this writing, the novel is not yet published. Obviously, this technique of alternating the Dupin/narrator fragments of her consciousness works for her and gives variety to the novel's development.

Marcia Muller uses a similar technique to keep her series fresh, but with different protagonists and an entirely different set of characters. In a sense, Muller has to create different worlds to have these unusual perspectives. Muller has said that she may abandon her long-time protagonist Sharon McCone, taking a break to write a stand-alone or have an alternative main character with a different occupation from crime solving. She has swerved into three different series with some crossover characters. She continues with one character until Sharon McCone taps her on the shoulder and lets her know that it's time to return to McCone.

Marcia Muller and S. J. Rozan are two creators of women's detective fiction not afraid to talk about the uncanny sense a writer may experience that characters somehow take over and seem to haunt the creative process. Poe grasped this concept of the unknowable in "The Murders in the Rue Morgue": "The mental features discoursed of as the analytical are, in themselves, but little susceptible of analysis."

Poe has influenced generations of works featuring crime-solving partners. The convention carries many variants. In the film *Sherlock Holmes*, the dialogue of Dupin and the narrator (i.e., Holmes and Watson) evolves into a postmodernist writer/text connection. In this case, Watson becomes very obviously the words man. He is the direct legatee to Poe's storytelling narrator. This Watson takes a more active role in constructing the case.

At times, the partnership can become a triad of main characters. The underlying narrative structure shifts into Freudian territory with the tension distributed among three parts of the writer's subconscious. The pairing moves from one character being the chief inquirer and the other serving as a sounding board, to the audience, which makes up the triad. The narrative construct is therefore a triangle of writer/text/reader or ego/id/superego. The writer is the controlling consciousness. The story with its imaginative stirrings and releases holds the energy of the id, while the reader serves as superego, chief selector and regulator of information.

The crime-solving pair developed by Poe shows up regularly on today's television offerings. One inventive example among many occurs on the long-running television program *Monk*. It features Adrian Monk, an obsessive-compulsive detective. This crime show had a seven-year run on the USA network, garnering many nominations and three Emmy wins for its star, Tony Shaloub. Debuting in the summer of 2002, this program hit its stride in the post 9–11 atmosphere of paranoia, with the possibility of toxic substances showing up in the most everyday places. While new episodes are no longer filmed, the show appears regularly through syndication.

On this show, the secondary is Monk's woman caretaker, first Sharona Fleming (Bitty Schram) and then Natalie Teeger (Traylor Howard). The show is set in San Francisco. With images familiar from Hitchcock's *Vertigo*, the city's steep hills and convoluted streets reinforce the overwhelming emotional disequilibrium that upends Adrian's daily life.

Monk is a damaged man. As a homicide detective with the San Francisco PD, he had excelled at his job. Although he already had shown obsessive-compulsive behavior, his extreme fastidiousness made him a success in closing cases. However, his career took an abrupt turn when his wife Trudy was blown up by a car bomb, and Monk suspected the bomb was intended for him. Throughout the series, Monk focuses on the case at hand, but each day, he feels overwhelming guilt and the pressure to channel his investigative energies on locating the person responsible for Trudy's death.

Monk's companion prompts him on the case. She asks questions and sometimes inadvertently pieces together evidence that leads him to a revelatory moment that cracks the case. The difference here, in addition to the secondary being a woman, is that Monk explicitly needs a caretaker to function. The roles of tale and teller are imbalanced.

Monk receives a psychological discharge from the police force. He has undergone a psychic split from the trauma over his wife's death. The result is that he now struggles to live despite numerous phobias and obsessions. In "Mr. Monk and the Three Pies" (2003), viewers learn more about Adrian's family background to understand that even before Trudy's death, the detective already suffered from OCD due to his father's abandonment of the family.

The most notable of Monk's phobias is his obsession with cleanliness. As one might assume, this phobia makes difficult, if not impossible, his continuing his job, fingerprinting suspects, chasing quarries down dark alleys, walking the mean streets. Humor comes in when the job's major requirement is the detective's obsession for gathering clues. Adrian's abilities in crime-solving may make him inept for everyday living, but he excels at putting together a case against a suspect. He has instant recall of all objects in a room so he knows what may have been disturbed or removed from a crime scene. Like Dupin, he has preternatural powers of observation. Another comic situation occurs when the killers are in a car chasing Adrian, who is on foot. He dashes along the sidewalk and has to count the parking meters, stopping at each one, while the car menaces. The program emphasizes that Adrian's mind is so filled with clutter that the addition of one more piece of data that calls for him to change behavior is more than he can handle.

There is poignance about why Adrian is as he is. Some of the episodes take us back to before Trudy died, and suggest how Adrian might have prevented her death. In nearly every episode, Adrian's thoughts plague him on how he could solve her murder.

In "Mr. Monk and the Red Herring" (2004), Adrian has to hire a replacement for Sharona. This episode lays out all his foibles. Interviews with the ostensible job candidates go badly as no one in a right mind would care to deal with Monk, since he is not in his right mind. Monk manages to sabotage each of the interviews. But by way of a woman who needs assistance after a home invasion, Monk finds his eventual caretaker.

Natalie Teeger has a pre-teen daughter, Julie. Monk shows his worth in helping Julie and deciding to overlook his obsessions with cleanliness. When trying to decide between retrieving a precious moon rock or saving Julie's pet fish, he opts to pick up the slimy fish.

Due to the daughter's participation in a school science fair, Monk, Natalie, and Julie attend exhibits at the San Francisco Science Museum. The setting in a museum emphasizes the press of the past that Monk has to understand to relieve his psychological imbalance. In one scene, Adrian and Natalie gaze through a Plexiglas coffin at a partially mummified skeleton. The skeleton is frosted with ice. Adrian says, "This man did not freeze to death. He was murdered. Look at this wound on his neck." Natalie says, "That case was 30,000 years ago." Monk's shrug and facial expression emphasize that the time of a past trauma is irrelevant. The trauma persists.

At the museum, a man dressed as a giant white corpuscle approaches Natalie asking if she wants to know the kinds of diseases and germs that he protects against. Natalie wins points with Adrian by her emphatic refusal. Another exhibit in the museum dramatizes one of Monk's phobias. Monk and Natalie join a line of schoolchildren ready to enter an exhibit called "The Miracle of Birth." The first phase leads through an orangey/pink tunnel to represent the birth canal, with a path leading to the womb. Monk's face is terror-stricken, and he can barely force himself to pass the entryway, turning his body one way then another to avoid the unsanitary sides of the tunnel. "It'll be okay," Natalie says. "Take my hand." Adrian refuses to touch her, of course, but with great effort manages to squeeze himself inside the recess.

Once he is inside, Natalie explains how reproduction is natural and the life of a new person is a joyous event, but all her attempts to calm him fail. "This way to the Fallopian tubes," the museum guide says blithely. "I can't go up there," Monk says, visibly quaking. "I didn't even know this woman." Halfway through the canal, in the throes of a major anxiety attack, Monk spies the lit door of an emergency exit and makes a frantic dash, saying, "I think this is going to be a Caesarean."

While many aspects of Adrian's germ-phobia come across for comic effect, this episode presents in condensed form the difficulties that Monk encounters in trying to break out of his grief. The narrative shows the persistence of trauma, and how far away the concept of a new existence for Monk would be. His phobias short-circuit any possibility of his own re-emergence as a person who is healed.

Monk is an expert at solving locked-room crimes. In one episode, the suspect is a man weighing four hundred pounds whose alibi was that he could not leave his bed. Monk proved the man's guilt beyond any doubt. He understands these problems of inertia all too well. While *Monk* may at times verge on parody, the comic elements cannot overcome the basic poignance of Adrian Monk's struggle to overcome his phobias. With each case, he fights against the overwhelming psychological forces keeping him in his own locked room.

The Closer is a detective program that started in 2005. Standing in for Dupin and the unnamed narrator is the crime-solving pair, Deputy Chief Brenda Lee Johnson (Kyra Sedgwick) and her now husband, FBI Special Agent Fritz Howard (Jon Tenney). On several levels, Sedgwick's character represents a new take on the woman detective. She is the first woman head of Special Crimes, an elite unit in the Los Angeles PD. The team is called in for particularly difficult homicide cases.

Like Jane Tennison, played by Helen Mirren on the successful BBC series *Prime Suspect*, Brenda spends much of the first season enlisting the loyalty of the hard-nosed officers assigned to her. The crew is made up of officers from various ethnicities, which is entirely credible in Los Angeles. Lieutenant Tao is the techno-geek; Detective Sanchez is the street-wise gang guy. Robbery-Homicide Commander Russell Taylor (Robert Gossett) has been a huge thorn in Chief Johnson's side from the beginning, and the two have had numerous power struggles. After a few seasons, she has won even him over.

Since Chief Johnson is from Atlanta and clueless on the busy Los Angeles highways, she at first needed a driver who could deliver her to the crimes scenes on time. Sergeant Gabriel is an African American who serves as her driver, and she wins him over by the end of the first episode. Many of the older men make fun of her ultra-femininity. She carries a big purse, wears floppy hats, and has a yen for chocolate that she tries to hide. She yells "Yoo-hoo" to say hello, or ends up thanking people excessively. However, these veterans on the force gradually fall in line, as Brenda wins them over through her tough questioning that closes cases.

Another unusual way the program develops issues of gender and authority is to show that Brenda has already had a romantic attachment with her boss, Will Pope (J. K. Simmons). His role as her former lover casts him against a romantic lead type, since he is bald yet virile authoritative figure.

In the most recent season, Pope is the victim of political shenanigans. Brenda is competing with Will for a top post, and as a woman, she possibly has the edge over him in landing the job in a politically charged climate. Pope is a favorite for getting the job, but she has been told that it is hers if she wants it. It turns out that she does not. She tells Fritz that she wouldn't take it even if offered, because Pope is still a close friend. But Fritz, who is married to Brenda, reminds her that Will would not retain his loyalty to her if the situation were reversed.

Johnson is also innovative in playing against the *Law and Order* type of investigator. Whereas District Attorney Jack McCoy runs up against a wall of the suspect's silence, Brenda makes the person confess in their own words through inventive twists.

As shown in "The Purloined Letter," Dupin is never humble about his insights that solve a case. By contrast, Brenda's strategy is to make the suspect underestimate her capabilities. However, like Dupin, Brenda believes in making progress against a suspect through distractions.

Typically, to catch the guilty party, Brenda's team uses much sleight of hand and role playing. At times, she will work with the person she suspects is guilty to give the guilty party the idea that he or she is helping the police to nail the wrong suspect. As another crime-solving strategy, Brenda's squad often goes undercover. Detective Sanchez and another young woman on the squad change into a young Hispanic couple with a new baby strolling outside a house. To nab a ring suspected of a murder involving the sale of illegal drugs, her team members pretend to be owners of a suspicious head shop on one of L.A. shabbier streets. They give themselves street cred by wearing earrings and tee-shirts.

Brenda uses canny methods to obtain evidence in surreptitious ways. In a 2010 episode entitled "Living Proof, Part 1," a suspect refuses to give the police access to his son so they can take a DNA sample. Brenda places herself close to the boy. When she sees him chewing gum, she arranges for him to receive a medical exam in another part of the building. Brenda quickly says, "No gum in the exam room." She holds up a napkin, and he spits it out. The saliva on the gum provides the much-needed DNA sample to prove the son's relationship to suspect.

She wields another smart technique to nail criminals in "Strike Three" (2009). To wring out the confessions, she puts the two suspects together in the back seat of the squad car. Before she slams the door, she says to one of them, "Don't forget what we talked about." Going on the philosophy that there's no honor among thieves, Brenda raises the suspects' suspicions and then has her team search the house and grounds, with the perps watching. The squad car is wired for sound. She uses their comments to steer the search and direct her team to the hidden drugs, the evidence they need to convict these two for killing two policemen and a young man.

For the past two seasons, Brenda has tangled with Captain Sharon Raydor (Mary McDonnell). They try to find new ways to trip each other up. Raydor often blocks Brenda's investigations. As an example, Raydor makes the death notification to the mother of the victim, forestalling Brenda's under-the-radar questioning of the victim's mother. Raydor shakes her head in skepticism when Brenda issues efficient orders to her team. When Brenda conducts surveillance on a suspected location, Raydor shows up prematurely to confiscate evidence. The competition between the two drives the personal storyline, the alternate narrative apart from the case.

In the early seasons, Brenda's dithering about making a commitment to Fritz provides a sharp counter to her go-ahead attitude in solving a case. Initially, she did not want to introduce him to her parents, did not want him to move in, and she certainly did not want to be married. Having to face her parents throws her right back into pre-teenhood. She acts like a little girl in front of them. When they tell her they plan to move from Atlanta to LA, she maintains a frozen smile of delight on her face, a chipper voice of acceptance, then takes a phone call. "Deputy Chief Johnson, help me. Uh, I mean how can I help you?"

Brenda Lee and Fritz are life partners, but they also collaborate on cases. For Brenda, the best part of having an FBI agent in the family is that he has access to information she couldn't otherwise get. However, at times they are competitive. For instance, in "Next of Kin, Part 1" (2007), Chief Johnson must question a key witness. The witness has fled to Georgia. Brenda sees this as an opportunity for her and Fritz to visit her parents for the holidays.

She finds the witness in jail. She asks the local sheriff if she can question the man. The sheriff refuses, pulling rank on her. "Sweetheart, where's your warrant? You show me a badge and a warrant and you can get in there." Of course, she has neither.

Luckily Fritz has his FBI shield, and he flaunts this at the sheriff, who is amazingly impressed. The Sheriff admires Fritz and shares that recently he had attended a seminar up at Quantico. Fritz gains access to the witness when Brenda had failed. She fumes about the sheriff's blatant sexism, and Fritz says, "You want somebody to question him or do you want to strike a blow for women everywhere?" Then as Fritz questions the witness, making modest gains, an officer arrives outside the cell door to announce that the questioning has ended. The witness has been bailed out.

The witness's benefactor, of course, is Brenda, who then has access to her key to the case. Ultimately, however, Fritz has the last word in this power struggle based on economic control. He complains, "Brenda, we don't have the money. You keep acting as if we do."

This problem sets up another obstacle for the next phase in the plot. Brenda ups the ante. When the issue of traveling back to Los Angeles comes up, Brenda wants to fly back. At this time, however, her parents learn that her reason for visiting them wasn't for them. Brenda feels tremendously guilty. She solves this problem by going cross-country in the parents' RV. This way she manages to spend more time with her parents, as well as have time to question the suspect. She can also escort the witness to LA.

Debuting in 2005, the same year as *The Closer*, *Bones* is now in Season 6. Bones is the nickname of forensic anthropologist Temperance Brennan (Emily Deschanel). Her other half is FBI Special Agent Seeley Booth (David Boreanaz). The show is set in a large crime-solving institute in Washington, D.C. This institutional setting gives the organization many elaborate resources, including the technology to recreate the form of a living body from human remains. The machine is a holograph that looks like a shimmery fish tank. In the middle of the rectangle, the machine projects a three-dimensional image of what a skeleton's face might look like, with flesh added.

Temperance Brennan is based on the character created in the novels by Linda Reichs. Reichs is like Linda Fairstein, author of *Entombed*, in that she has legal criminal experience. Reichs' career before she turned to writing was forensic anthropology. Brennan's character on the show is a dry academic, focused on science. Her colleagues often tease her for not knowing idioms or pop culture references. At one point, in giving information to her forensics team, she says, "And here's the kick." Booth gently corrects her with "kicker."

Bones' compatriot Booth fits his metaphoric name in that he cares for Bones, but resists any clear expression of his feelings. She presents scientific techniques; he carries out crime investigation techniques. The tension of their romance, the human connection, gives the program at times a comic cushion to ease the tension of the grisly ways of death they encounter. The name "Booth" gives an accurate sense of the second crime solver's character; he is hermetically sealed emotionally, as if in a small room. In a postmodernist self-reference, the television character of Bones writes a mystery series in what little spare time she has, with a main character named Kathy Reichs. The writer writes the detective writing the writer.

Nothing succeeds like success, and the formula of a crime-fighting duo as women in charge in the squad rooms is set to have a run on television for a while. These women in charge have to be tough in ways that Pepper Anderson of *Police Woman* or Cagney and Lacey never had to be. These programs reflect the increased numbers of women in law enforcement. They also take advantage of women's skills with words. Television program executives continue to mine books for programming material.

Rizzoli and Isles focuses on a crime-solving pair based on the series of books by Tess Gerritsen. Jane Rizzoli is a working-class, tough street cop, woman warrior, and Maura Isles is genteel, a Dupin-like empiricist. Isles is often out of her element on the streets of Boston, like, for instance, when she wears three-inch designer heels to a crime scene. Like Kyra Sedgwick's Chief Johnson, Isles is ultra-feminine, but her rigid character makes the pair more cut and dried than in the relationship between Brenda and Fritz. The development of Rizzoli and Isles as characters proceeds according to convention.

Rizzoli is too gruff, and Isles is a bit of a stick in the mud, using high-flown speech that makes her the butt of her colleagues' jokes. One potential for a different development is that there is an easygoing repartée between these two, as well as a sensual undertone that plays off a subtle homoerotic subtext. In one episode, these characters end up chastely sleeping next to each other, like girls in a slumber party. The show seems to revel in finding ways to illustrate this ongoing physical flirtation as the women josh each other to show they really care. Dupin and his narrating helper never had this kind of easygoing, familiar connection.

February 2011 saw the debut of yet another new program featuring a woman in charge: *The Chicago Code*, starring Jennifer Beals. As of this writing, it is uncertain how audiences will respond to this program's format and late time slot. However, already the program has won admiration from critic Ken Tucker, although Tucker acknowledges that a follow-up series from even an excellent writer typically may not make the grade. This one is from Shawn Ryan, who created *The Shield*. The show has "more humor than you would have guessed," Tucker says.

> I didn't quite buy the premise set up in Monday's debut: that Wysocki's ex-partner, Beals' Teresa Colvin, now the city's police superintendent, enlists the honest but hotheaded guy as a key player in an anti-corruption task force, one of whose aims is to get crooked politicians, such as Delroy Lindo's powerful alderman Ronin Gibbons. It's a semi-undercover role for Wysocki, but the guy seems too much of a loose-cannon, showboating hotdogger (have I piled on enough double-barreled cliché adjectives?) to be of much use in a long-term task-force investigation.

Still, Tucker begrudgingly admits: "I think *Chicago Code* is positioned well for ratings success."

A cop show set in Chicago is a natural. In 2011, the city has drawn considerable attention as the home of President Obama and from the frontier city politics kicked up from the dust of former Illinois Governor Rod Blagojevich. The schemes striating his administration, not to mention that the White House's former Chief of Staff Rahm Emanuel is now running for mayor, makes certain that all eyes are on the city that Daly built. Since the 1950s, the roles of women in detective fiction have been a gauge of women's involvement in all professions, and this current increase in women in charge of the law reflects that increase as well.

Except for the payment Dupin takes from Prefect G — in exchange for locating the purloined letter, Dupin and the narrator make no money from their crime observations. They approach the cases as intellectual puzzles. However, since the 1980s, with the influx of more women detectives working on their own, women have taken on more crime-solving roles as supervisors.

While these women characters manage to find some time for home lives and love interests, they are generally extremely professional.

In an analysis of television detective programs of the 1970s, David Bowman notes the frequency of policemen-protagonists working in an institutional setting. "TV cops are not real cops," which is the same as today (Bowman 46). Bowman makes the point that "cop operas" are a reflection of who we are. These cop shows are less accurate reflections of legal issues and more about the melodrama on the airwaves over 30 years ago. Then, as today, "The heroes of cop opera on TV almost inevitably are public employees" (42). Bowman compiles a lengthy list of shows like *McMillan and Wife*, *Mannix*, *Kojak*, *Streets of San Francisco*, *Barnaby Jones*, *Emergency*, and *Perry Mason* to prove his point. Women on these shows are in a helper capacity. Bowman's study is dated before the detective novels featuring women burst onto the crime-fighting scene. Marcia Muller's first novel, *Edwin of the Iron Shoes*, followed in the late 1970s.

One pattern unnoted in Bowman's study is that these programs featuring women in law enforcement have a literary feature. Many of these television characters either come originally from novels or focus on characters who carry out their jobs using verbal data. Does this connection with words have a tie with Poe's method of searching for meaning through language? Chief Brenda Lee Johnson solves crimes by grilling witnesses, using words to trip them up. Bones may not be up on the latest phrases, but she saves her word-smithing for work and the novels she has precious little time to write. Rizzoli knows the lingo of the Boston streets, and Isles is overly articulate, but her high-flown vocabulary never fails to send Rizzoli into gales of laughter.

Yet another television show provides additional evidence that detective programs are showing a literary bent. Poe's metaphor of the artist hero taking part in action, the self-referential narrator as set up in *Pym* and other stories continues in the HBO program *Bored to Death* (2009). This program also seems structured on the rule of three, with the Dupin-narrator partnership being split into a Freudian triad of ego, superego, and id. In this outing, a writer is not merely a metaphor of the detective but a literal detective, a failed writer who advertises his services of spouse surveillance or locating missing items on Craig's list.

During the program's opening credits, a squiggly drawn book morphs into an image of a man snooping as a detective. The series plays off this concept of the protagonist being not only a detective but a writer and the show's writer on top of that. This construct sets up a self-conscious referential quality to the program. It is meta-narrative. The action is set in New York, not in Manhattan, but Brooklyn. The locations are not disco clubs or seedy bars of the lower East Side, but neighborhood pubs where people know each other. Jonathan is an abysmal failure as both a writer and a detective. Pursuits in which he must track down an errant husband or petty thief usually end with him being chased.

The main character, Jonathan Ames (Jason Schwartzman), leads the trio as Superego. He intervenes between Ego, George Christopher (Ted Danson), and Id, Ray Hueston (Zach Galifianakis). George is Jonathan's boss at the magazine where he works and is completely self-absorbed. Ray has written a comic book hero with a twelve-foot-long phallus. His girlfriend has lost a dog named Little Ray.

In a *New Yorker* review, television commentator Nancy Franklin greets this show with enthusiasm: "Danson and Galifianakis steal the show, partly by design. Schwartzman's character is tentative, provisional, making himself up as he goes along; he's like a piece of writing as it's being written — by definition, a work in progress."

This show reverses the usual concept of the hero as frustrated artist bored with his everyday life. Jonathan's life is infinitely more interesting to him than his writing. Although he pretends to be annoyed when dragged into the latest escapade with Ray and George, the would-be artist seems relieved to have a wild life so to escape his failures as an artist. He actually savors these distracting adventures to avoid facing the blank page. The show flips the usual dichotomy of uneventful life and romantic adventure on the page inside out. This is an anti-romantic, postmodernist view of art.

Poe's original crime-solving duality was a sturdy original narrative construct. Over the decades, the double investigator has changed to fit the writers using it. The convention has mirrored social changes. As women and minorities have gained power in the workplace, the investigators reflect a similar shift in the balance of power. The original quality Poe had built into Dupin and his narrator that involved a literary processing of the world, crime-solving through language, continues in films and television. Despite high-tech equipment, the audience's interest in characters and storyline comes about from the main character's abilities to solve the crime through engagement with language.

CHAPTER 2

Codes, Cryptograms, and Crime Scene Investigations

In Poe's "The Gold Bug" (1843), an unnamed narrator relates the story of how he and his friend, an amateur naturalist, with help from his manumitted servant named Jupiter, eventually locate a "treasure of incalculable wealth." "The Gold Bug" won Poe $100 for first prize in a story contest. Still, critics often dismiss "The Gold Bug" as one of his creakiest inventions. William Friedman and Woodrow Hassell take Poe to task for being inconsistent with the story's ciphers and more boastful about his own deductive powers than was warranted. In addition, the story includes an African American stereotype of the treasure hunter's manumitted servant, Jupiter, with an awkward rendition of colloquial style dialogue. ["De bug—I'm berry sartain dat Massa Will bin bit somewhere 'bout de head by dat goole bug" (46).]

More recent criticism has focused on the narrative's misshapen structure. The narrator's elation over the treasure's discovery is dampened by an overlong explanation from Legrand, as the overwrought protagonist belabors his method in deciphering the encoded map to the riches. However, as with most of Poe's fiction, the story ultimately delves into much more than a hunt for buried treasure. Not only has Poe's creation cast a long shadow of influence, from *Treasure Island* action-adventures to the spy novel subgenre, but this story's inclusion of markings to be interpreted and its gradual revelations, Poe attempts to replicate the structure and processes of language.

The story falls into three parts: exposition, excavation, and explanation. An unnamed, first-person narrator takes it upon himself to visit an old friend, William Legrand. The narrator wastes no time telling us, in the second sentence, that Legrand "had once been very wealthy; but a series of misfortunes had reduced him to want" (42). Even so, Legrand has learned to cope with his loss by indulging his interest the outdoors and becoming a naturalist.

The narrator's friend now lives off the coast of Charleston, on Sullivan's

Island, desolate and isolated. The nearby ruins of Fort Moultrie are "miserable frame buildings" (42). The terrain is covered with "bristly palmetto" growing in slimy marsh. Since many spots are "impenetrable," no one ventures there, but those who do are rewarded with a sweetness underneath: "a dense undergrowth of sweet myrtle, burthen[s] the air with its fragrance" (42). As meandering as this landscape description at first appears, the topography is symbolic. This contrast provides a sweet enticement toward the rich possibility of the hidden.

In describing Legrand, Poe sustains this concept of an attractive inner layer. The narrator's friend is nearly identical to the island, isolated, and impenetrable on the outside, but "there was much in the recluse to excite interest and esteem" (42). Throughout, Poe urges the necessity of digging in to find the under layer of meaning.

Legrand tells the narrator about his latest etymological discovery, an unusual gold-colored beetle. Legrand has given the bug to a soldier at Fort Moultrie, so they cannot examine it immediately. Instead, as a man of science as well as an artist, Legrand says, "I can give you some idea of the shape" (44), and he draws a picture of the insect. And so begins the first of many symbol-making discourses that propel the narrative.

Legrand passes the drawing to the narrator as they sit before the fire. The narrator is puzzled. His perception of the drawing is different from Legrand's. The beetle looks almost exactly like "a skull or a death's head" to the narrator. Legrand takes the paper and becomes so agitated that the narrator leaves and returns to Charleston. A month later, Jupiter arrives at the narrator's home with an urgent and suspenseful summons from Legrand. "Since I saw you," he writes, "I have had great cause for anxiety. I have something to tell you, yet scarcely know how to tell it, or whether I should tell it at all" (47). To this missive, Jupiter adds that Legrand is not in his right head, because he had been bitten by the gold bug.

We can characterize the narrative's next phase as "**the excavation**." The narrator finds Legrand in a high state of excitement, similar to the mania shown by Dupin and Roderick Usher. He shakes the narrator's hand nervously, his face is pale, and "his eyes glared with an unnatural lustre" (48). Legrand shows the narrator the actual bug, carries it around at the end of string, and whips it around. He asserts that the insect does not just look golden but it is "a bug of *real gold*" (48). The narrator is more than ever convinced of his friend's loss of mental stability but decides to continue to help.

Legrand, the narrator, and Jupiter travel "through a tract of country wild and desolate where no trace of a human footstep was to be seen" (50), essentially an unmarked territory. Once they reach an ancient tree with many branches, Legrand sends Jupiter up the tree. The servant reports that a skull is nailed to one of the branches. Legrand tells Jupiter to drop the string of the beetle through the left eye socket of the skull. Legrand measures out a distance with a tape measure and goes through a frenzy of digging. The narrator watches the crazed "gold-seeker" from a distance with pity, as the frantic search yields no results. However, they soon realize that Jupiter had erred in dropping the beetle, not knowing right from left. They re-measure and resume digging in the new spot. At this point, the narrator is captivated as well: "I dug eagerly, and now and then caught myself actually looking, with something that very much resembled expectation, for the fancied treasure, the vision of which had demented my unfortunate companion" (55).

Soon, they locate human bones, and clank onto an iron ring, digging up a treasure chest "full to the brim" with "treasure of incalculable value." Gold ornaments, coins, diamonds, rubies, emeralds, all very ancient, and priceless, although the narrator mentions the haul to be worth at least "a million and a half dollars" (57–58).

If this tale were only about a search for gold and riches, their find should close the lid of the treasure chest and end the story. Still, the narrative continues for another twenty pages into a final "**explanation**" phase. Legrand details to the narrator and reader his method in finding the parchment on which he had first drawn the bug and how previously invisible imprints became visible when the parchment was close to the fire.

In addition to the skull becoming visible in the upper left corner, an image of a goat, or a kid, emerged in the lower right. The alphanumeric markings then need deciphering into sentences, which in turn need points of reference to be applied to the island's terrain. At this stage, Legrand finds an ancient local woman with knowledge of local lore. We backtrack through this process and rewind to the incident of the sighting of the skull in the tree.

Legrand also explains reasons for the wrong turns in their digging — that Jupiter had threaded the string of the gold bug through the right eye of the skull, instead of the left. Legrand emphasizes that the perspective allows "no variation." The story ends with the two men noting skeleton bones in the hole. Legrand explains that the original diggers knew the secret burial place. The pirate Captain Kidd had left the skeletons to keep the secret intact.

In a series of seminars that Lacan delivered to psychoanalysts at the Parisian Institute in 1956, later published in *Escrits*, he constructs a comprehensive psychoanalytic approach based on Poe's "The Purloined Letter." Lacan says that we make a mistake thinking of Poe's tale as merely a detective story. Dupin's solution to the lost letter reinforced Lacan's assertion of connections between the language-making faculty and the subconscious. Further, the "missing" letter, like a pirate's *X*, only marks a spot. Lacan notes that "the signifier is a unit in its very uniqueness, being by nature symbol only of an absence" (39). The fact that Freud used the "talking cure" as a way into this subconscious absence emphasizes how language informs the psyche and vice versa. People constructing narratives about their deeply felt traumas helps to structure and resolve or at least address them. Further, Lacan also relies on principles of structural linguistics, as detailed by the French linguist Frederick de Saussure.

Language is both structure and act. De Saussure makes the distinction between signifier (speech sound or speech marking) and signified mental image or meaning that the series of letters conveys (Muller and Richardson 56). The lost symbol can never be fully restored, but through intense scrutiny, its outlines may be discerned. Lacan then lays out his theory of inter-subjectivity between the three characters in "The Purloined Letter." The story's design is somewhat like a pivot, with the letter in the center and Dupin, the minister, and the royal personage, the letter's original owner, rotating around this object to be searched. How the "order of the symbol" affects a person is Lacan's main point.

Poe wrote "The Gold Bug" around six months before "The Purloined Letter." It is clear from the text in the earlier tale that he was trying out some of the narrative structures that later appear in more complex form in the Dupin story.

Poe has many stories focused on the word itself as a narrative twist. In addition to "The Purloined Letter," letters or words as words play a central role in "MS Found in a Bottle" and "The Sphinx." *The Narrative of A. Gordon Pym* includes many segments centered on the necessity of finding the right words. When Pym is stowed away on his friend's boat, he finds an ominous note fragment: "*blood—your life depends upon lying close*" (Chapter III, 770). In addition, chapter 23 includes a series of hieroglyphic markings on the cliffs that Pym and Dirk Peters try to translate to escape from the labyrinth of fissures in the earth as a result of quakes (873). In these cases, understanding language and finding the correct word is linked with pressing urgency, if not actual survival value.

Poe's interest in codes reflected a craze in the early decades of the nineteenth century. Delia Bacon had begun trying to prove that her ancestor was the writer of Shakespeare, and she began reading Shakespeare between the lines looking for clues. People were running fine-tooth combs through texts. Poe was so fascinated with codes and secret writing that, while working at the *Weekly Messenger*, he issued a code "challenge." He was let go from that job before the contest ended, but when he resumed work at *Graham's*, he wrote that he had figured out most of the entries. He published the solutions, emphasizing that the challenge "gave us *no trouble whatsoever* [original italics]" (Silverman 152).

Poe might not have been strictly forthcoming in reporting his record in successfully decoding the entries. His ultimate goal for including the puzzles was not for the puzzle's sake, but to shape these solutions into a narrative and draw interest to his fiction. In July 1841, Poe wrote in *Graham's* that "the reader should bear in mind that the basis of the whole art of solution ... is found in the general principles of the formation of language itself."

In the same way that Lacan asserts "The Purloined Letter" means more than a detective story, we make a mistake to read "The Gold Bug" as a tale about treasure hunting. In a sense, this story's structure is a palindrome, a phrase or sentence reading the same backwards and forwards. A few examples of well-known palindromes are what Eve heard on her first date ("Madam, I'm Adam") or how people characterized Teddy Roosevelt ("A man, a plan, Panama"). This story has a symmetry that makes it read almost the same forwards and backwards.

To start, Legrand has lost wealth and in the end he finds it. Poe also works with a punning on names. In the beginning, Legrand (the Large) is diminished. On the deciphered map, two markings on the treasure map flank the coded message. One is the death's head on the upper left corner and the baby goat or kid diagonally across from the signature. The discovery of the treasure occurs about halfway through, then Legrand works backward explaining his process, going through the steps he had followed during the excavation. The story ends with wry comments on the two skeletons in the pit, the cost of the buried treasure, and people who give their lives to the treasure, which could very well refer to Jupiter and the narrator. If these two are knocked out, the treasure is left solely to Legrand. The palindrome structure seems an apt emblem for the self-reflexive cycle of writing and reading, the shuttling back and forth between signified and signifier implicit in all language.

An additional connection to language processes and structure emerges from Legrand's direct method of finding the treasure. The decoded message tells him to run a line from death's skull dropped through the skull's eyeball socket to the ground. Then, the way to the buried treasure falls underneath. As readers and researchers, we follow this same process. After we read the marks, we search in our heads for the signified meaning, pulling it from the entire semantic ground of our experience.

Carroll Laverty argues persuasively about an expanded meaning for the death's head marking on the beetle. Laverty ties Poe's reference to a "death's head" in this story to a death's head moth in his story "The Sphinx" (89–90). Connected to a Sphinx allusion, then, for Poe, the death's head insect both warns and represents an enigmatic truth that we have yet to fathom.

As writers, we dig around in our heads for that invaluable treasure, *le mot juste*, to reproduce on paper or a laptop screen. Poe has created Legrand's treasure hunting process as a mirror image of the sacred act of both reading and writing.

X marks the spot. The eye lines up so signifier and signified are connected. The point of view must be exactly right. Turning up money from the soil can be thrilling, of course, but even on the level of the treasure hunt, the suspense is more real, more intense and urgent, if we consider that the story is actually about the limitations of language and the hunt for how language means.

Charles May notes, "The bug in the story, if I may be excused for using a mixed metaphor, is actually a red herring, for it has nothing to do with the treasure" (May 86). May somewhat miscalculates. The treasure has nothing to do with money itself; the bug is the key to unlocking the message *about* the treasure — the word.

If we re-conceptualize this story's meaning so the true treasure is language, we can better understand why this subgenre continues to exert such a strong pull in popular culture even today. The narrative template has cast a long shadow of influence, from *Treasure Island* action-adventure films like *Pirates of the Caribbean*, to Conrad's *The Secret Agent*, to Cold War–era spy novels. John LeCarré, Clive Cussler, Ken Follett, and Robert Ludlum set the rhythms for these spy novels, and the main characters' abilities to decipher code and untangle language form a major part of these narratives. Thrillers such as Barry Eisler's John Rain series capitalizes on Rain's facility with language, speaking Japanese to navigate the culture. *The Emperor's Tomb* (2010) and *The Jefferson Key* (2011) are books in the Cotton Malone series by Steve Berry in which Malone's "eidetic" or photographic memory for re-constructing crime scenes or reading cryptic signs carry earth-shattering ramifications. These novels regularly crowd the top of best-seller lists. The spy novel subgenre continues to fuel today's entertainment in bookstores and on screens large and small.

In fiction about espionage, also called "spy-fi," nothing is as it seems: Every secret agent lives a double life by definition. Other narrative elements are equally of a double nature. Drops and exchanges frequently involve diverse messages for both the person delivering the package and the one picking it up. A plant is like a drop, except the one picking up the package may not know about it ahead of time, or may be mistaken about what the plant actually is. Treason, betrayal, and defection also involve duality in the agent's switch of allegiance. Moral ambiguity involves a similar balance of binary choices. The concept of duality blankets everything a double agent does. In most spy-fi narratives, there is a duality of appearance and meaning.

Generic features add much suspense. Typically, the agent works against a ticking clock. The clock ups the ante for the already precipitously high stakes. The object of the search, or the McGuffin, is typically an object price-less beyond measure, such as the Holy Grail, a potion for eternal life, or proof that Christ had a child. A mere stash of gold coins does not measure up. The search for the object might also be a valuable secret by which the possessor can avert the end of a nation. Political thrillers or the end of the world in narratives convey these apocalyptic visions. The causes of the apocalypse might come from space. These could be alien beings, as in *Independence Day* (1996) or *2012* (2009).

Another catalyst could be climate change, an ecological apocalypse. The film *Day After Tomorrow* (2004) marks the instant onset of a glacial age. *The Happening* (2008) tells the story of vegetation issuing toxic gases to strike back against mankind. Television programs depict characters working against the clock for impossibly high stakes, to avert a national disaster, as in the television series *24*, *Jericho*, or *The Event*. Non-fiction Discovery Channel disasters assume a *faux*-documentary tone, yet these dramas featuring asteroids, sunspots, and meteors play off the same kinds of viewer anxieties that commercial films and television shows evoke. Because so many of these narratives involve the correct reading of "signs," the central message is that natural catastrophe and imminent demise for all humankind can be averted if we only communicate.

In spy fiction, the entire narrative moves according to the duality of sign and text. John Cawelti examines this double-ness, which he calls the "clandestine."

In "The Gold Bug," what is hidden must be revealed. The spy story expresses this duality, but it additionally represents the obverse of this concept, that is, what seems obvious and on the up-and-up is actually undercover. A plain building is really spy headquarters. An ordinary housewife is an agent. A squabbling married couple is unaware of their double double-agent status. In *Mr. and Mrs. Smith* (2005), each works for a different spy agency. Cawelti argues that a central draw to spy fiction lies in "the appeal of clandestinity." He also notes the number of activities of a non-secret agent's life that remain hidden. "Crime is another mode of clandestine operation and so are many forms of love" (Cawelti and Rosenburg 12). Lovers may need to keep an affair secret. The secrecy "can give the initial involvement an added impetus" (13). Fantasy and disguise are offshoots from the clandestine. "The spy is invisible in a number of senses: he is the secret observer who, himself unseen, watches through a peephole or, in our modern technological age, through a telescope or some electronic device" (13). Invisibility gives the observer a perceived freedom from moral responsibility.

Another feature of the clandestine code is having access to an exclusive language. Cawelti says, "Clandestinity generates not only a special view of the world based on shared secrets, but a different language as well as a different morality" (16). This coded layer both compels and resists being deciphered.

Agents not only share a special jargon, but frequently, the agent is in a foreign country. This context adds yet another layer of language to the agent's trove of intelligence secrets. As Cawelti underscores, language plays a key role in the agent's struggle to carry out his mission. Cawelti further characterizes the dual nature of the secret agent's life as resembling "the pathology of schizophrenia" (17). An additional rift occurs when the agent's plan diverges from that of the controlling group. Cawelti characterizes the phases of clandestinity that shape the spy-fi narrative:

1. An individual or group conceives of a purpose requiring actions outside the bounds of the law.
2. To pursue these purposes, a secret group is formed; tension arises.
3. The individual is isolated from society as well as other members of the group. [He] has fear of exposure, betrayal, profit [21].

The element of the clandestine is at odds with democracy. Freedom of speech and exercise of the individual will does not fit with the secret world that values above all silence and the pursuit of institutionally proscribed "missions" (29).

In July 2010, the *Washington Post* published "Top Secret America." The study documents the sharp rise in domestic counterterrorism operations since the September 11, 2001, attacks. Based on data gathered by journalists Dana Priest and William M. Arkin, over 800,000 people hold top-security clearances in the United States. This status gives individuals access to significant confidential information, but the agencies monitoring this access are not clearly identified. The information remains difficult to verify. According to the Central Intelligence Agency's website, "Neither the number of employees nor the size of the Agency's budget can, at present, be publicly disclosed." Despite extensive growth in these surveillance operations, relatively few of us work in surveillance or government intelligence. Being a spy is hardly the norm. Still, the mystery surrounding this information advances the notion of a ubiquitous spy class that books, films, and entertainments exploit.

Modes of spying infuse even the most mundane aspects of our daily lives. Cawelti observes that the metaphor of being a spy is extremely common to all who work with language. The spy out in the cold "seems to express the way many people feel about the basic patterns of their lives" (32). When Cawelti was on book tour for *The Spy Story* (1987), he was amazed by the unexpected audience enthusiasm for spy adventures. People from many professions, psychiatrists, professors, feminists, and graduate students, connected with the idea of carrying out missions, living double lives, and keeping secrets. Cawelti says, "Their relationship to society and to their profession or organization made them feel like either a participant in a clandestine world, or a double agent, or both" (32).

The particulars of the spy story have changed in response to shifting trends in political turbulence. Throughout the twentieth century, novels and films have followed the *zeitgeist* of distrust, recreating paranoia from World War I sabotage, diverted bombing raids from World War II codes, Cold War political manipulations, and unpredictable terrorism. Implicit in this long string of discrete narrative units is the duality of language. Inevitably, many spy novels pivot on the agent's retrieval of a secret message or code. Two examples are Adam Hall's *The Mandarin Cypher* and *The Quiller Memorandum*. In these works, a code or written document unlocks the narrative's central mystery. The story is a chain of narrative conventions. Clues and markings serve as signifiers that lead to meaning. The spy searches to fill in the missing message, reading the signifier to figure out what is signified.

X marks the spot. In the film *Raiders of the Lost Ark*, the marker to the Ark of the Covenant is a shaft of light that falls exactly where the treasure can be found. In films based on novels by Dan Brown, such as *The DaVinci Code* (2006) and *Angels and Demons* (2009), art historian Robert Langdon's special weapon is his expertise in reading images as codes. He traces these signifiers to zero in on the hidden signified message. In these novels, Langdon ultimately interprets Christ's legacy as allegedly revealed in "The Last Supper" or follows a coded map around Rome to decipher the Illuminati's plot to destroy the Vatican.

The popularity of Langdon's Poe-inspired detection method has led filmmakers to bring this mystery to home ground with films such as *National Treasure* (2004, dir. Jon Turteltaub) and its sequels. Treasure hunter Benjamin Franklin Gates (Nicholas Cage) leads the investigation. Clues from American history become the signifiers. The menace posed by the secret society of Illuminati is replaced by an equally vague menace of the Freemasons. The Declaration of Independence and Lincoln assassination documents assume secular mythic status. These films take on the near-hysterical tone of many of Poe's narrators. The stories gain power from the assumption that reading the code or secret message is crucial. The clock is ticking. The fate of a nation or even the world is at stake. If the investigator fails, apocalypse looms. Benjamin Franklin Gates has to thwart a conspiracy to steal an object priceless beyond measure, a treasure map on the reverse of the Declaration of Independence, missing pages from the diary of John Wilkes Booth. Ultimately, despite many action sequences involving chases and gunfire, this narrative is based on the investigator's crucial skill of deciphering the secrets of language. The most skilled reader of clues wins the race to where *X* marks the spot. To counter the impotence of human agency in the outside world, communication is the sole defense.

In Poe's "The Gold Bug" and *The Narrative of A. Gordon Pym*, the solution to the narrative hinges on the accurate reading of symbols and signs.

However, a secondary result from this accurate reading is the tale-teller's ability to reconstruct the past or at least a version of history. William Legrand rewinds the clock when he regales the narrator with a lengthy description of what he thinks happened. Pym leaves a journalistic record of his last days sailing into the South Pole, although the outcome of that voyage is never clear.

The urgency of *National Treasure* finds a television presence in the series *Brad Meltzer's Decoded*. The fact that this show airs on the History Channel provides another tip as to why the race toward *X* is so significant. Being able to piece fragmented events together provides a review of the past. While Meltzer's program discusses some of the same topics addressed in the *National Treasure* film franchise, *Decoded* takes on another meaning: the lack of resolution to the past. Despite the best constructed narrative evidence, events from history lie in the same realm as stories and contain the same challenges of an unresolved mystery. *Decoded* purports to be a history lesson for American viewers without much awareness of America's past.

Labeled a "documentary," this program investigates conspiracies, mysteries, and puzzles from America's past. A few episodes from this year have focused on the capture of John Wilkes Booth, the identity of D. B. Cooper, and events surrounding the death of Meriwether Lewis after the Lewis and Clark expedition. The kick-off episode analyzes a mystery hovering over the White House and the Freemasons.

Brad Meltzer is a well-known mystery novelist. His most recent books are *The Book of Lies* (2008), about a man's search for the weapon Cain used to kill Abel, and *The Inner Circle* (2011). This book's lead character works in the National Archives and finds a dictionary that had once belonged to George Washington. The document suggests that Washington had developed his own spy ring, and the group continues to this day. *Decoded* also capitalizes on the opportunity to market Meltzer's novels in the same way that Poe held a deciphering contest to draw attention to himself as a writer. As the program's first show ends, an advertisement announces the weeks-away launch of Meltzer's latest book.

Despite this brazen promotion, this program presents a compelling amalgam of fiction and purported reality. The premise is that novelist Meltzer heads a team of three investigators. Brad says at the beginning of each show, "I spend my life writing stories. The best include signs, symbols, and codes." The focus of each mission is for the team to gather and read signifying clues as they lead to meanings that may be hidden in plain sight.

In the first episode, the three investigators are cruising in an SUV when the car phone trills over the Bluetooth. "What's up, Brad?" they respond. Into this narrative comes the reliable *Charlie's Angels* formula. Brad is Charlie. The angels are Buddy Levy, a professor of literature at Washington State

University; Christine McKinley, whom they call "Mac," an engineer; and lawyer Scott Rolle. Mac's skills come in handy when the team needs figures on the size and weight of the White House cornerstone. Attorney Scott Rolle frequently issues statements about evidence and cautions the other two if they threaten to range too far afield with wild theories or assumptions.

This first episode is entitled "White House." It suggests that the cornerstone for the White House is missing. "Team, find the cornerstone" is Brad's directive. As the team tours the building, the camera follows. The tour takes us through winding corridor and traces a labyrinth through the White House kitchens. We follow the camera's eye along a network of narrow hallways to an underground bomb shelter below the People's House. This tracing of a map-like route is itself a sign, an unreadable hieroglyph.

Before the show breaks for commercial, Brad whets the audience's appetite: "I write cover-ups and this is one of the best." Frequently Brad's transitional comment hangs heavy with the suggestion that more bombshells await. The biggest explosion in this episode is the team's allegation that the cornerstone under the Capitol Building is also missing.

The team members interview people offering possible reasons behind the missing cornerstones. Chris Pinto has written a book outlining a possible conspiracy perpetrated by the Society of the Freemasons. Pinto tells the team about Captain William Morgan in 1826 who risked being killed by publishing the Masonic rituals involving an inner "cabal." The Masons' ultimate agenda is to control the New World order. Pinto asserts that the Masons came to take back what they had originally placed. The cornerstone is a "talisman of power, if you will." Meltzer follows this discussion with "There are some who consider his views extreme. And I'm one of them." Despite Brad's skepticism, he dispatches the team to the Temple of the Freemasons in Washington, D.C. McKinley, the woman engineer, is enthusiastic for this unique opportunity for an inside look. The program does not mention that this museum is open to the public anyway.

Brad Meltzer is soft-spoken and bespeckled, the very image of an author. He wears a sports jacket over a colored tee-shirt and stands before a blackboard. On the board are messages and signs, algebra formulas, varied fonts, and a circle bisected with lines. He breaks into the narrative regularly with comments to cheer the team or scoff at their findings. He never appears with the three on their field trips, which gives the impression that he is a voice of authority from some undisclosed academic location, moving his three members around like pawns on a chessboard.

This approach gives historians, archivists, and writers a chance to be action heroes. Like William Legrand, with his bookish approach to the world, *Brad Meltzer's Decoded* takes on question marks from history. On the surface,

Meltzer's investigation addresses conspiracy theories about world control. However, underlying the search is a mystery about another kind of control, our ability to understand how language shapes or distorts meaning. Historical documents provide certain kinds of information about the past, but they frequently lack the imaginative element. As a writer of fiction, Meltzer knows that this aspect is key to firing up people's ability to envision a story. Programs like Meltzer's pinpoint the dual quality of the word. On the surface, the word is a sign that points to something else. By its very nature it signifies and conceals. As Poe emphasizes, there is always more to relate once the treasure has been located. It makes sense also that Brad Meltzer would host a show about locating a manuscript, secret document, or lost book. As a writer, he spends his day grappling with language.

The team enters the Freemason Temple in Washington, D.C. Like the White House, the building is a labyrinth of passageways. They pass Egyptian statues and miniature sphinxes. The program inserts a mini-seminar for viewers, identifying the number of Masonic symbols and pyramid references in everyday American discourse, including the pyramid on the back of a one-dollar bill. It encloses the eye of an all-seeing God. The team files along a hall, the walls of which are covered with pictures of famous members of the Freemasons, John Glenn, Buzz Aldrin, and Supreme Court Justices. The team takes note.

Following a sign to "The Museum," they find glass-enclosed exhibits, one of which is a piece of a cornerstone. It is etched with markings. The camera then draws an outline over the stone to connect the scratches, in the same way that astronomers might draw a line from star to star to highlight a constellation or archaeologists might construct a form to show the original structure of Stonehenge. The highlights reveal a Masonic symbol. The members of Meltzer's team react with widened eyes.

Buddy Levy, the professor from the team, is busy in the meantime, sorting through pictures of a White House renovation during the Truman era. The workers had dug trenches coming within eight to ten feet of the supposed place of the original cornerstone, but then Buddy learns that Truman supposedly halted the operation. The narrative implies that a conspiracy at the top levels of government worked to keep the stone hidden. The camera cuts to Meltzer: "I was down there. I saw how close they came."

The team members meet with representatives of the official Masons at the museum. The attorney presents a legalistic take: "Their arguments are iron-clad. They came across as very believable, yet I still got the feeling that we weren't hearing it all." What they have not yet heard but soon discover is that the Capitol Building's cornerstone has disappeared as well. The narrative line spirals into yet another tangle of conspiracy in a new location.

The team obtains physical dimensions of the Capitol stone. With MacKinley's laptop at the ready, she figures from the estimated size that the stone must weigh over 18 tons. She sits in awe, staring at the laptop screen.

Northrop Frye has noted that "the mathematical and the verbal universes are doubtless different ways of conceiving the same universe" (355). MacKinley's method approaches this mystery from the numerical angle. The stone was too immense to be moved. The answer to the missing cornerstone is that it never moved at all. Scott the lawyer intones again in lawyerly mode that they should assess all the evidence. Like Dupin's purloined letter, the stone is there, hidden in plain sight.

Through a series of interviews, the team uncovers information about a man named Charlie Scala. Charlie knew the lay of the land under all the Washington, D.C., buildings. They find him in an old picture from the Archives. Looking for the cornerstone, he conducted an unofficial investigation at the behest of a few senators who were Masons. They first encouraged him to look for the cornerstone, but Charlie was taken off the project. The team casts each other meaningful looks. This second sudden cancellation is highly suspicious.

The team worries that this new missing stone might have covered up secret words crucial to the operation of the new nation, an alternative constitution or a plan for developing a different society. "What if they put something in the cornerstone that we could read?"

Ultimately, the team has to rest with the non-resolution to their search. Brad concludes the episode on an anticlimactic note. "When I first started out, I wanted to find it. Something far more important is that if found, it loses its symbolic power. It's still 'missing,' [but it] retains its power as a symbol, [and] keeps us wondering and searching." The conclusion emphasizes a void in the empirical method. When one conclusion is reached, another taunts the searcher and ducks around a corner. Despite the show's pretense at conducting a rational "investigation," it ends up extolling the symbol. Essentially, Meltzer's conclusion is for us to keep the magic. This television program emphasizes several points highlighted in "The Gold Bug." The excitement of knowledge is its pursuit, and the accumulation of knowledge inevitably falls short of the truth.

Another variant on Poe's "codes and clues subgenre" from "The Gold Bug" is the story's influence on police procedurals and crime scene investigation dramas. In the CSI television program and its clones, reading again comes to the fore, only investigators use numeric symbols to access the unknown. Physical measurements represent attempts to control the world outside the mind. Such as method comes to the fore in the film *Murder by Numbers* (dir. Barbet Schroeder, 2002) and the television show *Numb3rs* (CBS 2005–2010).

Murder by Numbers pitches homicide police detective Cassie Mayweather (Sandra Bullock) against two highly intelligent high school misfits. The bored young men make a game out of asserting their "superior" minds to puzzle the police. They murder a woman and plant false evidence, a baboon hair, to incriminate a janitor, who keeps a baboon in a shed. The hair not only forces police to focus on the wrong suspect, but with the hair, the boys set a trap for Cassie. The trap springs when she opens the janitor's shed, and the baboon attacks her. This part of the film makes an explicit nod to Poe, alluding to the orangutan killer in "The Murders in the Rue Morgue."

Whoever holds the tightest control over time and numbers seems to be ahead in the race to enact or evade justice. The teens work out an alibi using the timing device on a water-sprinkler system. Cassie has to "read" the underlying reality of this alibi. The story develops through several twisted expectations and competitive one-upsmanship between the boys and Cassie, even to the final scene. The essential competition between detective and villain that Poe sets up in the Dupin tales drives the plot and characters in *Murder by Numbers*.

The television show *Numb3rs* (2005–2010) also relies on the correct reading of symbols to solve cases. FBI Special Agent Don Eppes (Rob Morrow) receives assistance on criminal investigations from the math expertise of his brother Charlie (David Krumholtz). Charlie is a professor at a California university called "CalSci" (read "CalTech" or "Stanford"), who is a genius with numbers. Charlie's background is invaluable. He provides mathematic models to give the agents a dimensioned view of each case. The model helps them develop promising leads to resolve the crime.

The investigators in *Murder by Numbers* and *Numb3rs* represent two sides of human cognition, the "Bi-Part Soul" of Dupin. They "read" clues to discover a priceless treasure, a missing child, or a decades-old killing. By profession, the investigator might be a scientist, empirically directed, but frequently the struggle to solve the mystery proceeds with a blend of clues and skills. Talents of writers and artists complement physical measurements to make sense of the world "out there." Human cognition blends the symbols of both numbers and words to create meaning.

In a footnote, Northrop Frye writes:

> Literature, like mathematics, is a language, and a language in itself represents no truth, though it may provide the means for expressing any number of them. But poets and critics alike have always believed in some kind of imaginative truth, and perhaps the justification for the belief is in the containment by the language of what it can express [Frye 355].

Twenty-first-century communication fosters yet another search for the dual nature of language, its quality of being specific and expansive at the same time. Mark Andrejevic explains "The goal of this ubiquity [communication in the digital age] is to endow physical spaces with the interactive character of the Internet, allowing consumers to retrieve useful information (such as directions or movie listings) while simultaneously narrowcasting information about their movements and preferences to those who own and operate the means of interaction" (Andrejevic 95). Poe's focus on understanding language through narrative will continue to be even more relevant in the future.

Poe's uses of codes break into the fabric of the text as an early self-reflexive intertextuality, now a commonplace with meta-fiction. This insertion or shift in the narrative plane encourages incipient reader interactivity in creating the narrative. The linearity of sentences drops or seems to change elevation. In a sense, it lurches upwards or falls onto a different plane. These two forces break down the authority of the text in a way that questions the role of a single story but illustrates the multiplicity of meaning in language. Far from being a hunt for buried treasure, "The Gold Bug" sets on a much more profound search, the quest for how a symbol relates to its significance.

CHAPTER 3

Poe's City of the Haunted Mind

Bourbon Street. The Big Easy. Mardi Gras. Let the good times roll. Does this city hold too casual an attitude for mystery?

In a 1996 issue of *Mystery Readers Journal* dedicated to New Orleans mystery and crime fiction, critic Harriet Swift assesses the Crescent City's appropriateness as a literary setting. Her conclusion? For mysteries, steamy lassitude is not so good. She mentions works by Julie Smith, Tony Dunbar, and J. N. Redmann, rightly relegating James Lee Burke to New Iberia, which is not strictly New Orleans. Then Swift asks, why so few? Her conclusion is that despite the city's shadows and narrow passageways, "The hard-boiled [novel] with its requirements of exacting justice and harsh definitions of evil and good is the antithesis of the slow-moving, careless temper of New Orleans."

This antithesis is precisely what makes the city prime real estate for mystery fiction. New Orleans's contradictory, ambiguous character seeps into the soul of a mystery narrative. As Poe's Auguste Dupin says in "The Purloined Letter," "If it is any point requiring reflection ... we shall examine it to better purpose in the dark" (Poe 208). Poe encourages investigation in the dark, inner recesses of the mind. From my perspective, Ms. Swift needs to investigate with a smoky lens.

Poe's own settings lack specificity of being on the American scene. Urban crowding and garish lights pervade the cities he does name. "The Murders in the Rue Morgue" is set famously in Paris. The named city in "The Man of the Crowd" is London. The town square of Rotterdam serves as the launching point for "The Unparalleled Adventures of One Hans Pfaal." While carnival season in Venice swirls above ground, Montresor and Fortunato follow the downward journey to the catacombs in "The Cask of Amontillado." For "William Wilson," the besieged narrator flees whispering double through well-appointed manors in Cambridge and Rome. Barren, rural topography frames many tales as well. "The Fall of the House of Usher" is set in "a singularly dreary tract of country." A deserted chateau in the Apennines is where the narrator discovers "The Oval Portrait." Craggy headlands off the coast of Norway set the scene for "A Descent into the Maelström." With these rough-textured foreign locations, Poe severs ties to verisimilitude, instead moving toward disturbances and upsets in the mind. Locale reflects and exaggerates the main character's psychological state.

Margaret Kane, in "Edgar Allan Poe and Architecture," delineates the qualities that Poe outlines for his settings. She notes patterns in his fictional settings of structures that are ancient, crumbling, and decrepit. "Poe found material for emotional effects in the spectacle of dilapidation: ivy on crumbling walls, half-fallen towers and battlements, an air of decay among evidences of former grandeur, antiquity, mystery and remoteness from common experience" (Kane 149). This gradual weakening of physical structure parallels the exhaustion and instability of the narrating personality's psyche. "The features which make the setting vivid are those which the writer supplies from his own imagination — details of fantastic lighting, brilliant colors, startling decorations" (Kane 158). The effect is akin to a man with a hangover waking to a sunny morning. The stark contrast between an anemic sensibility and a too-bright environment intensifies the setting's disturbance to the narrator's vision.

Contradictions and ambiguities make the Big Easy a collective nightmare, the stuff of Poe-inspired fiction. David Geherin's *Scene of the Crime* discusses the role of place in mystery fiction. Inspired by Geherin's study, I define three uses of setting by writers and filmmakers, seeing these as three types of "scapes," each increasing in intensity and widening in imaginative scope. The first level of local color is highly descriptive. The "sense-scape" emerges from dank mold, greasy fried shrimp, or a clinging humidity. At this level, setting is a well-arranged window dressing, similar to what Henry James describes as reading for the senses as well as for the sense of reason.

In "The Philosophy of Composition" (1846), Poe names as an "absolute necessity" that fiction include "a close circumscription of space" to direct the reader's attention: "it has the force of a frame to a picture." Poe's concept of a controlling space that bridges the distance between physical territory and the reader's psyche defines this second level for analyzing a setting. This concept emphasizes terrain as a mirror of the character's mind, a psychological projection to reflect internal upset. A "psychic-scape" mirrors a character's mindset via narrow streets, winding paths, or dark alleys blocked by wrought iron gates. The last level, which I call "myth-scape," is a unified trope encompassing a broader idea, mind and body reflected in the individual in a situation, which in turn resonates with a theme. Geography transforms into metaphor, gaining intensity and significance from this unity. This is the concept of myth similar to what Henry Nash Smith addresses in his study *The Virgin Land*, on the American West as setting, a collectively perceived meaning casting a long shadow. Topography serves both literally and metaphorically to reflect character, situation, and deep-seated human reality.

Given these features of landscape, New Orleans offers as a fictional backdrop that seems made to order from Poe. The city has a haunted history, not only regarding voodoo, a concept of the "walking dead" played up for tourists, but a more serious soul haunting, stemming from a cursed land, the prolonged human suffering of slavery.

Poe's themes striate this city like the narrow byways of the French Quarter. The city's signature festival of the Mardi Gras is built on masquerade, role playing, internal splits, and dichotomies. The city's hidden dark side is on shadowy display. Masquerade implies a multiplicity of identity creating moral, racial, and psychological ambiguities.

New Orleans is a city of corruption. With a long history of payoffs and kickbacks, the atmosphere is ripe for moral ambiguity. In *Unorganized Crime*, Louis Vyhnanek writes about crime in the 1920s. He notes that the primary crimes cops handled were against persons, and vice crimes were let go. With a wide gap between rich and poor, opportunities for corruption abounded. Whispered deals went down in seedy bars.

Although Poe conceived of this aesthetic for a short literary form, his design expresses many of these "scapes" that continue in more recent popular entertainment set in the Big Easy: *Skin Deep, Blood Red* (1997), first of a six-book series (1997–2002) by Robert Skinner, and *Tightrope* (1984), a film featuring Clint Eastwood. Both these works are cases in point of how the imagination fusing Poe's non-specific settings finds ongoing expression in modern narratives. We discuss Skinner's novel first, because even though it follows the film chronologically, it is set in the late 1930s.

Like New Orleans itself, the book's protagonist, Wesley Farrell, has a haunted past. Wes owns a few small-time shady businesses, bars, pool halls, a club in Storyville, and the Café Tristesse, or "sadness." Wes has a deep sadness of his own. He is Creole passing for white, raised by his great aunt. He never knew his father and wanted to distance himself from his Creole background. Now he lives in fear of being discovered, knowing that in the racist atmosphere of the Depression, he would make many enemies, if not have to run for his life. He's a master with a switchblade and legendary at winning fistfights.

Wes is involved in a search for stolen diamonds. Who will find them first, the big-time gangster or the crooked cop? Frank Casey is the Irish police detective investigating the case, a relatively honest man, who enlists Farrell's help. Later, Farrell learns that Frank Casey is his father. The gangster discovers Farrell's secret and blackmails him with the knowledge.

Several features of the city make appearances in the novel and the film.

Labyrinths create confusion and disorientation. Serpentine roads, dark alleys, and the shadowy night life are city landmarks that intensify moral ambiguities. "The big Lincoln snaked along Tchopitoulas until [it] reached the Public Health Service Hospital; then Pirelli cut down Henry Clay Avenue to Magazine Street.... As Pirelli negotiated the hairpin turn that signaled the change from Magazine to Leake, he failed to slow down, and didn't see a Ford roadster stopped ahead until it was almost too late" (145). The labyrinthine city streets serve to intensify the circuitous plot turns of a suspenseful chase. Wrought-iron gates block passage into grimy alleys. The narrow alleyways also portray a psychological expression of Wes' inner turmoil. Wesley Farrell is familiar with the serpentine streets, but the confusing maze of New Orleans relates to the dangers and unpredictability of Wesley's marginalized life as a mulatto.

The city generates a thriving nightlife. The darkness represents not only Wes Farrell's life making his living off vice, but the urgency for keeping this identity hidden.

> Even though [Farrell] had passed for white for more than twenty years, the word *nigger* had never lost the power to shock him. Because he moved in a shadowy world between the races, he had trained himself not to react.... He was always conscious of playing a meticulously concocted role [19].

Shadows and alleyways conceal him, but they also carry fear. The investigator-protagonist in a *noir* novel typically exposes others, but in this case, Wesley Farrell also worries about his own exposure. The detective's penetrating gaze is cast inward in shame and fear. Again, New Orleans serves to mirror distraught psychological states.

Lee Horsley notes in *The Noir Thriller* that the *noir* detective becomes "more tainted by the corrupt milieux they are investigating" and therefore "marginalized by their criminal connections" (40). The Big Easy exudes a toxic cloud of this corruption. In addition, sitting in a bend of the river creates an outsider status for the Crescent City. The city's isolation suits the loner detective. Its location intensifies both the detective trope and Wesley's outsider status.

New Orleans has a reputation for exuding life and colorful celebration. Even before Katrina, however, another of its nicknames was "city of the dead." In the 1700s, previously buried bodies floated to the surface due to the high water table, giving new meaning to the phrase, "You can't keep a good man down." New Orleans is above all a place of contrasts. With this flurry of kaleidoscopic color, New Orleans is particularly apt as a film backdrop. The downtown regularly plays host to movie companies. A tourist cannot point a camera without finding an aesthetic building or artistic square doing double duty as a movie set. Not far from that movie-set appeal, the Ninth Ward continues in poverty and ruin. The history and destiny of New Orleans is writ on water.

It is a city of storms, as we learned all too well from Katrina. Uncontrollable nature also reflects uncontrollable human nature.

New Orleans seethes with garish, *noir* atmosphere. *Noir* in the Big Easy has a distinctive psychological undercurrent as shown through this comparative analysis of the crime novel *Skin Deep, Blood Red* by Robert Skinner (1997) and the film *Tightrope* (directed by Richard Tuggle, 1984), starring Clint Eastwood. Along with protagonists who have matching names, both narratives depict New Orleans as a city of Lacanian mirrors reflecting each man's precarious balancing act. Setting is more than backdrop as the two Wesleys navigate this mythically re-constructed space in a struggle to resolve crime and psychological trauma.

Skin Deep, Blood Red is set in 1936. Protagonist Wesley Farrell owns a brothel, bars, and a pool hall. A mob boss discovers Farrell's secret and threatens to divulge it if Farrell doesn't help him find a cache of stolen diamonds. The mobster blackmails Farrell into finding the murderer of a crooked cop. Pressures rise as Farrell is forced to acknowledge his life caught between worlds and attempts to resolve the conflict. "Farrell drew smoke into his lungs and let it trickle back out his nose as he looked at himself in the long mirror behind the bar" (Skinner 20). He is meditative about his position between two worlds, but for the moment, he refuses to enter into introspection. "As he put on his hat, Farrell cast one backward glance into the mirror, but the face he saw there now told him nothing" (46).

Over the course of this chase for the diamonds, Farrell crosses paths with a white police detective, Inspector Frank Casey. Farrell and Casey team up against the thugs holding the city, and in the heat of the pursuit, Frank admits to being Farrell's father:

> Farrell felt he must be dreaming. As he looked the other man in the eye, some dim memories of his father begin to mesh with the reality of Casey's long, graceful hands, the mustache, his very smell. Somehow he knew the older man was telling the truth, a truth that nevertheless drove him into an unreasoning fury [160].

By recognizing his father, Wesley also legitimizes the white man's law. As a second act of contrition, he also acknowledges his mixed racial heritage, a secret now known, at least to his family. Accepting his role as a conveyor of Creole culture, in the book's closing pages, Farrell makes promises to his troubled mixed-race cousin Marcel: "'Let's just talk about what your life's going to be like from now on.' He lifted his glass and gave Marcel a wink. 'And by the way, I'm your cousin. Just call me Wes from now on, okay?'" (221).

The author of Wesley Farrell's story and six-volume series is Robert Skinner, a librarian at Xavier University Library. The library was hit hard by Hurricane Katrina, and was closed from August 2005 to January 2006. Skinner's work has not yet received the audience it deserves, and due to Hurricane Katrina, it may not. In a post–Katrina interview, Skinner says, "I'm not so much a writer as a librarian who sometimes writes when he's got the time and leisure to do it — in other words not lately" (*Library Journal*, 31 January 2006).

Reflected in this New Orleans mirror of masquerade and walking dead is the film *Tightrope*, released in 1984, directed by Richard Tuggle, and starring Clint Eastwood. To contrast with Skinner's books, this film set in New Orleans has gained in popular reputation.

When *Tightrope* first came out in 1984, Janet Maslin wrote in the *New York Times*, "Kinks or no kinks, Mr. Eastwood does his usual turn as the most hard-boiled, relentless detective in town." When the film was released on DVD almost ten years later, Peter Travers of *Rolling Stone* called it "one of Eastwood's least known films and one of his best" (128). With its intense narrative of an emotionally dead man coming back to life, this movie deserves close scrutiny. "The New Orleans locations do a lot of the work for the film, because the locations aren't the star, just the locations, which is always how New Orleans works better" (Wickliffe).

Clint plays Wes Block, a New Orleans homicide detective investigating the murders of prostitutes by strangulation. The lab unit finds red fibers around each victim's neck. The murder weapon is a red ribbon. A woman police psychiatrist (Janet MacLachlan) briefs Detective Block about the killer's motivations: "There's a darkness inside all of us, Wes. You, me, and the man down the street. Some have it under control. Others act it out. The rest of us try to walk a tightrope between the two."

Is Wes walking along that tightrope, or has he fallen off? By day, Block is a hard-working cop, a divorced father raising two young daughters, but the divorce has hit him hard. In one poignant scene, Wes's older daughter, played by 12-year-old Alison Eastwood, Clint's actual daughter, finds her father dead drunk on the floor, clutching a picture of his family as they used to be, together and happy. A pile of chewed-up limes lies next to him, a tally of his night's intake of vodka tonics. When Block is not drinking, he roams the same dark world as the killer. He is a regular visitor of strip bars and back rooms at massage parlors. Could Wes Block be the real killer?

At first, the audience is led to believe that he is. The murderer approaches the victim as Officer Friendly, wears running shoes, and keeps the cuffs ready to use. Wes Block wears similar running shoes, and the camera lingers on his handcuffs. Wes also visits a prostitute for his own entertainment. The same woman is later hauled out of the Mississippi, a victim of the strangler rapist. When officers ask if Wes knows her, he recognizes the woman but lies.

In a study called "The Black Hole of Trauma," Van der Kolk and McFarland discuss "the compulsive re-exposure of some traumatized individuals to situations reminiscent of the trauma" (Rivkin and Ryan 493). People severely affected by emotional trauma seek to re-enact the same situation that caused their psychic pain. An example is a wounded soldier eager to heal and return to battle.

Van der Kolk and McFarland refute Freud's idea that a traumatized person repeats the trauma to control the situation or to "gain mastery" of the upset. Instead, their clinical evidence shows that the person recreates trauma to act out against others with violence, either as victim or victimizer, or as an act of self-destruction. By visiting the hookers and ending up drunk every night, Wes directs his hatred against the ex against himself. He is half bent on revenge against the ex, half bent on self-destruction. He seeks the company of women, obviously, but not one who will remind him of what he's lost, or who has the possibility for a real relationship, so he visits prostitutes. Before long, the audience sees the face of the real killer, who is not Wes. Still, the film shows viewers that Wes has the potential for violence and perhaps even murder.

The film's love interest is Beryl Thiboudoux, a rape crisis counselor, played by Genevieve Bujold. Beryl encourages Wes to go public with news of the killer so women can protect themselves. Block refuses, saying, "Women all over this city will be terrified." Beryl responds, "Well, maybe they should be."

At first Beryl calls him Detective "Blot," as in Rorschach, and he gruffly corrects her. Both names "Blot" and "Block" suggest the film's psychoanalytic dimension. During the day, Wes wears a mask of professionalism to block off his actual self, but after hours, he wears another mask to hide from himself.

Their romantic attraction begins when they discover they belong to the same gym. We see them working out on machines opposite each other in a mechanical, erotic pantomime. Then he asks her out, using his version of a suave pick-up line: "Wanna hoist some oysters?" The setting for this date is actually romantic, a riverboat cruise on the *Creole Queen* paddlewheel, and, yes, they order oysters. Despite the overt romantic atmosphere, Wes has fallen into dangerous territory with this water voyage.

Previously for him, water has meant death. One dead hooker was discovered in a hot tub, another was floating in the river under the Crescent City bridge, a third was in a fountain on Canal Street. But being with Beryl buoys him, almost unnaturally. She asks what he was thinking about in the gym, and he trusts her enough to be honest: "I thought what it would be like to lick the sweat off your body." When she fails to recoil in horror, he sees that she's a keeper.

Beryl's challenge that she needs a tough man encourages Wes when he needs it, and he begins to court her. The scenes of Beryl and Wes smiling in the sunshine exude the excitement of a couple in love discovering each other.

They shop in the Market off the French Quarter, and he helps her put groceries in the car. But when she tries to touch his face, he backs away, startled. Clearly, Beryl knows men afraid of commitment, and she recognizes that Wes is one.

Now that Beryl really does get to him, Wes Block is terrified that the emotional block he uses to fend off his feelings is not enough. That night, Wes has a dream. He pulls a hood over his face, approaches Beryl as she's sleeping, and tries to strangle her. He wakes up sweating. His subconscious has released the William Wilson side of himself into the city of nightmares, and he is fearful.

Once Wes opens himself to Beryl, he also opens possibilities for caring again. In a not-so-subtle way, the film tips us off to this concept of Wes tentatively coming back to life. Wes, Beryl, and his daughters attend a Bourbon Street parade at night marching with the Rebirth Jazz Band. Even if Wes is not literally the killer, his self-destruction and the killer's violence are two sides of the same coin. The destinies of the hunter and hunted are entwined.

Eventually Wes learns the identity of the killer. As in Skinner's work, which links authoritative police with an absent father, *Tightrope* also places blame on the police, even if the connection is fraudulent. The killer who disguises himself as a cop to gain entrance to women's apartments actually had been on the force. He is a crooked ex-cop Wes had arrested eleven years before. He personifies the dark side of Wes Block. For Wes to live again, he has to sever this tie to his double, the past, and the part of him still trapped in an emotional morass.

In an essay called "The Double as Immortal Self," Otto Rank notes, "Originally conceived of as a guardian angel, assuring immortal survival to the self, the double eventually appeared [in our culture] as precisely the opposite, a reminder of the individual's mortality, indeed, the announcer of death itself" (76). This function is also consistent with our culture's view of New Orleans' situation after Katrina. According to Rank, after receiving a warning of oncoming destruction, the individual seeks to resolve the split and move toward a rebirth. Even though we received plenty of advance notice about the potential killer status of the monster hurricane, actions lagged and people died. In some manner, our country may have harbored a collective guilt. We mourned while watching news reports of the city drowning; we celebrated when the New Orleans Saints won the Super Bowl in 2010.

The killer's evil presence, a double for Block's released id, is now out of prison and setting up Detective Block for the prostitute murders out of revenge. Another comparison to Skinner's book is not merely revenge but its self-perpetuating nature. Wes Farrell seeks revenge on the world for his outsider status as a mulatto; Wes Block wants revenge on his wife and, in a sense, all women; the killer wants revenge on Block for having put him away eleven years earlier. The cycle continues, not merely on an institutional level, with the authority figure treading on both sides of the law and morality, but on a personal one as well.

In the film's final sequence, the killer breaks into Wes's home and terrorizes his daughters. Then he moves to Beryl's house and attacks her. Plucky heroine that she is, Beryl relies on her previous gym workouts and fights back, stabbing the killer with scissors.

The killer essentially stamps out that tiny sprout of happiness just starting to open in Block's home life. This home wrecker repeats the damage left by Block's wife. Thwarted once more in an attempt for fulfillment, Wes bursts into a rage. Like Wesley Farrell, Block faces himself in the mirror and prepares to confront his alter-ego. The scene is reminiscent of "William Wilson," in which the enraged narrator screams out his challenge to his double: "'Scoundrel!' I said, in a voice husky with rage, which every syllable I uttered seemed as new fuel to my fury; 'scoundrel! imposter! accursed villain! You *shall not* dog me to death!'" (Poe 640).

As Wes runs out of his house to follow the attacker, a thunderstorm ratchets up the suspense.

Wes chases the masked killer through a cemetery to do away his "other" for good. However, the weapon the killer wields by way of a counterattack on Wes is a shovel; the killer is ready to bury Wes again. When the shovel doesn't work, the masked double flexes the red ribbon, a potent symbol of guilt, perhaps on a par with the pink ribbon in Hawthorne's "Young Goodman Brown."

The red ribbon calls up many associations, a gift to a loved one, bondage, or an umbilical cord. When the cord is cut, a new life emerges. This scene predicts that Wes will undergo a bloody, painful birth. However, before new life can emerge, one more severing has to occur. The potent final scene lends itself to intriguing Freudian interpretation. The two men struggle on the train track. The train thunders toward them, running over the killer, and leaving only a wriggling amputated arm, analogous to castration. Wes Block looks at the arm's last twitches in horror. He sees the offending arm as an object, apart from the person. But of course, Beryl, strong runner that she is, catches up to console Wes at this horrific scene and touches his face. Now he finally can accept a human touch. This final confrontation packs a psychological wallop as well as a powerful reconciliation as Wes is unBlocked.

Another striking feature of Eastwood's character is that he diverges from his previously constructed hyper-masculine film personality. The arm amputation essentially summarizes the entire film. In the film's context, Wes Block has to rid himself of lust, but from a broader perspective of Eastwood's career, his portrayal of Block represents that he is casting off his "Dirty Harry" *per-*

sona, clearing the way for *Unforgiven* (1992), *In the Line of Fire* (1992), *Mystic River* (2003), and *Million Dollar Baby* (2004). *Tightrope* conveys much more than a Dirty Harry–style cop chase. It buries a man's soul and shows that he has strength to crawl out again. What better city to present this theme than New Orleans?

Both Wes Farrell and Wes Block integrate the divided selves by acknowledging the existence of the lost self. But each man is a work in progress. As Jung notes in "Concerning Rebirth": "The 'other' may be just as one-sided in one way as the ego is in another. And yet the conflict between them may give rise to truth and meaning — but only if the ego is willing to grant the other its rightful personality" (66). Coincidentally, with both characters named Wesley, the nickname of Wes conveys an unfinished quality. The name stops short of "west," or "going west," that is, dying. Both men have resumed living, and we assume the process does not end there.

New Orleans as a setting for fiction and film offers a potent brew. Like Joyce's Dublin or Faulkner's Yoknapatawpha County, Crescent City achieves a mythic status through a dynamism of psychological damage and imagination. The entire city reflects the human psyche. Through contradiction, paradox, and ambiguity, the settings of these two works reflect a psychic struggle with the deepest mysteries of morality, trauma, and identity. Further, water both heals and poses danger, setting out an ambiguous balance of death in life. Ultimately, in Harriet Swift's article, she concludes that the origin of Mystery Street is, well, a mystery: "New Orleans is not a place, a state of mind, an attitude, that fits with the idea of literary mystery.... The inexorable forward movement of investigation is alien to the unreflective, unchanging nature of New Orleans."

As Poe has illustrated with his airy settings from the Storyville of his own imagination, a lack of forward motion fosters a stasis, which prompts depth and introspection to deepen hard-boiled fiction and film narratives.

CHAPTER 4

Identity as the Divided Self

C. Auguste Dupin has a helper who tells the story. Poe's tales of detection move due to two separate persons, each seemingly with free will separate from the other. Although the characters appear on the page in the same realm, Poe provides each with enough mimetic differences in voice and behavior so the reader concludes that this consciousness is in fact two men. Dupin understands information that the narrator may not have yet put together. Each may have divergent points of view, but because they spring from Poe's mind, the two represent the tale-teller relationship, different sides of the same narrative construct. Dupin's mind processes the story, and the narrator relates Dupin's shaping of this story to the reader.

Many of Poe's characters who speak with more than one voice or who manifest alternative selves do not hold together as a single character. One narrative presence may seem to split into warring and then blended personalities, as in "William Wilson" (1839). Another example occurs in "Morella" (1835). One character dies and returns to assume another's identity. The concept of a literary doppelgänger is inadequate in describing these personalities. The situation with William Wilson goes beyond a clearly divided duality. The transmigration of a soul or self from a dead body to a living one carries more ramifications than a "secret sharer" construct. Poe's flickering representations of the self on the page suggest the need for a dynamic model of character analysis.

Such a model comes from Derek Parfit's theories of personality in which the terms "fission" and "fusion" describe the evolving aspects of identity. Parfit is a British philosopher and psychologist. His articles in the 1970s made an impact in academic circles, but it wasn't until his book *Reasons and Persons* came out in 1984 that he drew attention.

Basically, Parfit emphasizes the near impossibility of pinpointing actual identity. He notes the kinds of choices that the self makes in continuing its identity. His query sets out to answer two questions about the nature of personal identity and its importance. "What I shall try to describe is a way of thinking of our own identity through time which is more flexible, and less misleading, than the way in which we now think" (18).

The concept of a divided self in literature can be awkward to wield for analysis. An example occurs in Eliot's "The Love Song of J. Alfred Prufrock" (1971): "There will be time to prepare a face to meet the faces that we you meet" (ll. 26–27). A performing self hides the actual self. This idea, of course, presupposes that there actually is one actual self behind the role playing. Parfit says that in many situations, that is not the case. A Freudian tri-part analysis is another way for critics to access a character showing a divided self. While the categories of ego, superego, and id have their uses, this method also can be unwieldy in forcing an artificial compartment onto a changing self.

Parfit's model of the self has many ramifications in philosophy, psychology, and theology. He also has written about social connectedness and future Malthusian survival. Many of these impacts are too broad for us to consider here. However, parts of his theories serve to limn the complicated issues of identity emerging in Poe's fiction and finding expression in contemporary novels, television, and film. Parfit's model provides us with a means for discussing and distinguishing among fractured and merged selves.

An amoeba divides for survival, says Parfit, so why not the self? Basically, a personality under stress creates a situation "in which one person can survive as two" (Parfit, "Personal Identity," 10). Rather than perish as one, the doubling gives the self a new lease on life. "We suppose that my brain is transplanted into someone else's (brainless) body, and that the resulting person has my character and apparent memories of my life. Most of us would agree, after thought, that the resulting person is me" (5). Parfit's discussion of identity even covers science fiction–sounding concepts of dividing the brain's hemispheres. What happens to the self when a split occurs physiologically? According to Parfit, the division establishes "two separate spheres of consciousness" (6). This idea is somewhat akin to Dupin's Bi-Part Soul in "The Murders in the Rue Morgue."

Since survival drives the self to split so there can be ongoing life, what tie exists between those selves after the split? The two do not stop communicating. According to Parfit, the relation between those divided selves is another aspect of identity that needs to be included in the concept. Parfit labels this ongoing relation as "psychological continuity." Again using an organic metaphor consistent with the amoeba, Parfit sees the connection between selves in the form of a tree branch. "So this case helps to show that judgments of personal identity do derive their importance from the fact that they imply psychological continuity. It helps to show that when we can, usefully, speak to identity, this relation is our ground" (12). Parfit lays out this idea in logic that Dupin might appreciate: "X and Y are the same person if they are psychologically continuous and there is no person who is contemporary with either and psychologically continuous with the other" (13).

Parfit also provides a term useful for discussing a literary character's cognition, "quasi-memory" or q-memory. Memory has to play a role in this model, as the self contains memories of a dimly or incorrectly remembered past that continues into the present. "My apparent memory of *having* an experience is an apparent memory of *my* having an experience. So how could I quasi-remember my having other people's experiences?" (Parfit 15). One instance might be a college student who recalls a story about a haunted dorm, but cannot recall accurately which version of the tale he had heard or who had told him. A more serious example involves the false memory of believing that one was abused as a child. Another instance is the q-memory of a person characterizing an action as "I did that, I think." Parfit says, "Someone — probably I — did that" (16). Parfit's model allows for these kinds of phenomena, which are common in experience, as well as appealing and fascinating when used to dramatic effect in fiction and film.

Literature includes many characters with selves shaped by vague memory or false dreams. One example occurs in Hawthorne's "Young Goodman Brown" (1835). As the story's narrator asks the reader, "Had Young Goodman Brown fallen asleep in the forest and only dreamed a wild dream of a witch-meeting? Be it so if you will...." Hawthorne works this ambiguity into the text intending the premise to hover between two possibilities. Not-quite memories and others' dreams show up in the Christopher Nolen's *Memento* (2000) and the recent *Inception* (2010). Characters are trapped in states of amnesia or dreaming, feeling as if they are removed from a centralized self. Despite being severed from their own personality, they experience layers of other people's memories and dreams. Parfit's concept of q-memories and q-dreams, then, explains how the mind experiences these thoughts after the fact or non-fact. His vocabulary opens up a critical appraisal and description of these mimetically "false" experiences, which the psyche perceives as a blend of reality and falseness. The self feels the impact of hovering possibilities as truth.

A fundamental beginning to the "evil twin motif" is the narrative of Cain and Abel. Two opposing members from the same family replicate in story form two opposing sides of the same psyche. A significant meaning of this split is the dramatization of a human truth. The impulse toward evil or destructive behavior is integral to the civilized self.

The annals of literature are filled with arch-villains, Lucifer, for instance, Judas, or Shakespeare's Iago. Through most of "Othello," the title character's virtue balances out Iago's evil. In Poe's "William Wilson," the self banishes this force. The reader witnesses how the gradual perception of evil seeps into the core of a personality.

To illustrate how Parfit's model of identity might be useful in literary criticism, we can apply the theory of fission, or division of the self, to Poe's story "William Wilson." The doppelgänger or evil twin of literature does not start with Poe, but he gives the motif a strong impetus by leaving patches of moral ambiguity that defy easy categories of a divided self.

In "William Wilson," a first-person narrator recreates psychological imbalance for the reader. Through this de-stabilizing view of events, the story forges a halved character more daring than the identity divided in Robert Louis Stevenson's *Strange Case of Dr. Jekyll and Mr. Hyde* (1886). In that novel, transformation comes from an agency outside the self, a potion. In Poe's work, the split in the consciousness of William Wilson exists as early as his childhood. In the end of *Dr. Jekyll and Mr. Hyde*, Jekyll makes an altruistic sacrifice of committing suicide to rid the world of Hyde. At the conclusion of "William Wilson," the narrator makes the stunning choice to rid himself of the bothersome whispering conscience forever.

Poe develops Wilson's personality by showing the distance Wilson has moved away from his other "self." The narrator objectifies part of his personality as a separate, fissioned identity. An objectified self makes the opportunity for revelation about morality more likely, but in this case, the narrator ultimately rejects that epiphany. We move away from the redemption of a "good self" toward the evolution of a villain.

William Wilson's narrating identity gradually senses that an identical presence is mimicking him. Because of the first-person narration, the reader absorbs an unbalanced split, a kind of cloning of a duplicate self from what appears to be single character.

Even as a boy, the self called William Wilson, since he refuses to cite his real name, experiences inner instability. As a student at a boarding school, he encounters psychological confusion and disorientation. Poe depicts this imbalance through the structure of the school:

> But the house!—how quaint an old building was this!—to me how veritably a palace of enchantment! There was really no end to its windings—to its incomprehensible subdivisions. It was difficult, at any given time, to say with certainty upon which of its two stories one happened to be.... During the five years of my residence here, I was never able to ascertain with precision in what remote locality lay the little sleeping compartment assigned to myself [628].

With its intricate corridors and impossibility of locating the self, Poe conceptualizes the house as a metaphor of the self, some fifty years before Freud makes this same connection from dream analysis. Interestingly, J. K. Rowling's *Harry Potter* series employs this same motif. Harry's room in the cranny under the stairs defines his marginalized position with the Dursley family. The literal labyrinth of Hogwart's School, with its shifting levels and seesaw-style staircases, mirrors Harry's psychological development. Poe's concept for William Wilson differs in this point: if the school is emblematic of Wilson's psyche, how serious is the fact that he cannot find its center? He cannot fit into the house of his own mind.

The whispered voice of the fissioned personality provides the reader with an early hint that the voice comes from very close quarters. "[The other William Wilson's] cue, which was to perfect an imitation to myself, lay both in words and in actions.... My louder tones were, of course, unattempted, but then the key, — it was identical; *and his singular whisper, it grew the very echo of my own*" (Poe 632).

A Freudian reading of this story leaves unresolved questions. Ruth Sullivan's article "William Wilson's Double" notes that the story's conclusion signals a kind of personality integration. "At the tale's climax, the two selves merge, for both voices blend and speak as one person: the part that survives is the superego-dominated part of the ego" (Sullivan 263). I would argue that Wilson's blended personality represents less a merging and more a branching away from previous selves. This concept helps to eliminate the ambiguity that Sullivan seems to find through much of the story.

Examining the moment of Wilson's tense confrontation with the sleeping alter ego, Ruth Sullivan asks, "What do his anguished words mean?" (258). Parfit's idea that the self has to divide to survive explains this mystery passage that refuses to yield to Sullivan's Freudian analysis. This division into two apparent halves ensures continuity, as the character's fluid changes illustrate.

Sullivan also admits being puzzled by the fact that Wilson never explicitly expresses remorse for his bad behavior. "If the superego-dominated ego is telling the tale, one would expect guilt" (259). Wilson may be relegating his whole experience to what Parfit would call a q-memory. The narrator tries to believe and draw sustenance from his past, but he fails. Part of the horror of his situation comes from his inability to connect with actual memories. All he can summon is the sense that he has lived the "sublunary horror of a dream."

In explaining the divided self of "William Wilson," Parfit's theory of personality takes in more of the story than the Freudian view applied by Sullivan. Wilson says that virtue dropped from him in an instant. When was that instant? As a schoolboy when he confronts the self who is not himself, as Sullivan seems to contend? Or does this immediate drop into depravity happen at the story's end, after the "superego-dominated self," as Sullivan terms the interaction, emerges?

I maintain that for this character, horror starts at the ending. If we read

Wilson's story assuming that the narrator's worst psychic struggle occurs *after* the final confrontation between the two selves, then the severity of his death in life makes sense. Now that we know the entire circuit of Wilson's journey, as readers we should reread the initial passages to witness his barren life. His awareness of a life without a self is horrible to contemplate. When he refers to his own lack of virtue, he means much more than cheating at cards or attempting to lure a flirtatious married woman into a tryst. He refers instead to a complete slip sideways that has made his life a living nightmare.

Poe's story primarily deals with a fission of personality that fails to fuse the divided self back together. In this sense, the fragmented Wilson represents a q-intention to be a self. This development is predicted by the narrator's fears of being weak expressed throughout the work. The narrating self loses his center by growing weaker beneath the whispers of the other. Rather than the two halves coming together for a final battle of wills, it seems as if this final self branches into another, one that suffers even more from the loss of the whispering other. The two voices of Wilson's halves, the whispery voice and the narrative voice, shriek as one: "It was Wilson; but he spoke no longer in a whisper, and I could have fancied that I myself was speaking" (Poe 641). This phenomenon represents a profound split of identity: "all virtue dropped in an instant" (626). This is the torment that the narrator alludes to at the beginning of the story, that he is living a "sublunary horror."

In a psychological thriller, the mystery to be solved is not a crime or murder, but how the mind constructs the narrative of the self. The "evil twin" has made myriad appearances on television shows and in films. It has a career that Meryl Streep or Kevin Bacon might envy. Parfit's model of indeterminate personality provides ways to scrutinize characters manifesting a divided or ambiguous self in classic films such as *Double Indemnity*. A more recent film, *Fight Club*, demonstrates fission as a force dividing identity.

Double Indemnity (1944) features several fissioned identities. Directed by Billy Wilder, this classic film is told in a flashback with narrator Walter Neff emphasizing how he had to fragment his personality in order to survive. The narration provides a frame around his uncivilized self.

Insurance adjuster Walter Neff (Fred McMurray) falls for the flirtatious Phyllis Dietrichson (Barbara Stanwyck). Neff eventually yields to her pleas to help murder her husband. The two can then be together and collect from the insurance company's payoff, a double indemnity in the event of accidental death. Lured by the sensuous Phyllis, Walter agrees to help. To survive in his q-dream of being with Phyllis, he has to split the sense he has had of himself up until now.

For the plan to work, Walter must follow Phyllis's crippled and much older husband, throw him from the train, and then pretend to be the husband to avert suspicion. This plan allows the crime to take place with enough of a time delay so the two can arrange reasonable alibis. Once the deed is done, Walter can collect half of Phyllis's insurance money from her husband's death. He can also collect Phyllis. Neff's adaptation into Mr. Dietrichson represents a split for him. But he is split as well from his previously stable, if not completely virtuous, self.

In Walter's narrative, he finally realizes the futility of his efforts. While he thought he was only temporarily playing the role of Phyllis's limping husband with the cane, he ends up essentially becoming the husband, wounded and cast off by the train, which represents the thundering destruction of Phyllis.

Neff learns from the dead man's suspicious older daughter that Phyllis had originally been the husband's caretaker. Phyllis had been a nurse and the nature of her "dark angel of mercy" persona reflects the subverted, if not perverted, role of a medical caretaker. In *The Dark Mirror*, Marlisa Santos examines patterns in narratives of classic noir films. Santos notes the high incidence of characters' psychological breakdowns onscreen. Doctors fail to cure these mental illnesses. Numerous onscreen psychiatric frauds reflect the public's lack of confidence in psychiatrists' powers to resolve our culture's deeper disturbances in a postwar era. As *The Dark Mirror* says of Hitchcock's *Spellbound*: "The film asserts resolution but is filled with doubts ... meant to provoke an unstable mood in the viewer about the world at large" (xxii). Santos also notes that "the war's aftermath creates an environment of unpredictability, especially in human behavior" (97–98). Both individual and cultural disorientation play out before a "backdrop of psychological instability" that is a hallmark of classic *noir* (Santos 97). *Double Indemnity* gains power from this same imbalance.

Before the advent of Phyllis, Neff has a fairly close relationship with his Barton boss Keyes (Edward G. Robinson). In addition to Walter's role-playing as Phyllis's husband, another split occurs. He has abandoned his previous moral guidepost, wrenching his personality away from that self mentored by Keyes. Walter had intended to become an insurance investigator to meet Keyes' high standards. This intention is not part of the self he holds now.

Parfit's model accommodates this concept of intent as it changes with a person's future selves. "It may be a logical truth that we can intend to perform only our own actions. But intentions can be redescribed as q-intentions. And one person can q-intend to perform another person's actions" (17). Now that Walter has altered his moral compass, he has changed from the man he was. His q-intentions are no longer relevant for the person he has become. Walter has enough respect for Keyes to leave on a Dictaphone a narrated record of what had happened. Neff's first-person narration of events illustrates many splits between his own voice and its spate of good q-intentions.

The relationship between Keyes and Neff follows the contours of father and son. The character of Barton Keyes also shows a split, since he emphasizes that a "little man" of his intuition keeps telling him that the Dietrichson case is suspicious. The suspense rises as Keyes ironically describes his suspicions to Neff, the very person responsible for the fraud in the case.

A split occurs inside Walter because Keyes had seen potential in him. Neff's slip into criminality continues to widen the rift from Keyes' previous awareness of him. By speaking into the machine to Keyes about the whole story of duplicity, Neff attempts to reunite his broken selves through the constructed narrative. His voice, however, is weak. The effort is too little, too late. In the end, like William Wilson, Neff collapses from the weight of acknowledging his divided self. Still, his words have the power and force of a constructed narrative about "a loss of innocence in the consciousness of American society from which it could not retreat" (Santos 163). Neff's narrated story has longevity.

Forty years later, Lawrence Kasdan's remake of this story as *Body Heat* (1981) asserts a character's similar slide from innocence into corruption. The story's focus is on Ned Racine (William Hurt), an attorney. A spoken story is not a key aspect to the narrative, although words and their implications in legal documents represent various truths that the characters cannot fathom.

The film achieves a powerful aesthetic effect through thematic images of heat. The setting is small-town Florida in summer. The adulterous lovers' affair seethes in the Florida humidity. The method of murder is a fiery explosion. Still, Racine's fall from grace, his descent into a different moral plane, is not as striking or definitive as Neff's. The film speaks more about an audience's collective uncertainty about the legal system than about a postwar psychological instability that can affect anyone at any time. In addition, Kasdan uses closeups and zoom tracking shots to emphasize the lovers' physicality rather than using a voice of a narrator telling the story from among the ruins. Poe's tale-telling, first-person style of narration is partially ceded to the objective camera.

However, the ambiguity of point of view that infuses "William Wilson" and other stories powers the narrative of *Body Heat*. Matty's manipulation of words in her husband's will create her own narrative and cause Ned to wonder about her devotion to him. Heat comes to the fore again through Ned's escalating temper. When Ned murderously questions her, the confrontation ends in an explosion that kills Matty. Vision, in the form of the betrayed husband's missing eyeglasses, plays a strong role here. The missing eyeglasses suggest sagacity and literacy, spheres of behavior in which a lawyer should excel. Ultimately, the eyeglasses signal Ned's blindness, his failure to understand the depth of Matty's depraved identity.

The film's resolution of a jailed attorney expresses an ironic touch, and could wrap the film into a neat package, except for a final revelation. From prison, Ned learns that Matty had earlier switched selves with a woman resembling her, a close physical double. Matty's identity switch tosses into Ned's face the identity shifts he had to undergo to be with Mattie.

A striking instance of a modern William Wilson division of self occurs in *Fight Club* (2002, dir. David Fincher). This film is based on the novel by Chuck Palahniuk. Like Walter Neff, the originally nameless narrator (Edward Norton, called "Jack" in the script), is an investigator of fatal car accidents, a specialized insurance adjuster. He drops out of a high-stress life to follow the high-testosterone style of Tyler Durden. The narrator ends up moving into Tyler's broken wreck of a house and participating in a secret organization led by Tyler to restore men to their past glory as leaders. The rebellious group applauds the men beating each other up to break through the shell of non-feeling. Eventually the group escalates its agenda into Project Mayhem, a broad campaign to wreak havoc on a controlled culture.

In "Out of the Past, Into the Supermarket: Consuming Film Noir," Erik Dussere connects *Fight Club* to *Double Indemnity* and the ethos of *film noir*. Dussere notes that Fincher's film "has few of the obvious plot elements we associate with classic noir: no detective, no murder, no heist gone wrong. Rather, Fincher gives us the alienated mood, the stylized 'realism,' and the skepticism about the American mainstream that we recognize as noir, translated into the context of the 1990s" (23). Dussere emphasizes the filled aisles of purchases and overwhelming choices available to the narrator and Tyler from the American marketplace that Tyler has rejected. Before Tyler arrives on the scene, we hear the narrator's voice expressing eager consumerism. He is happy with his single-serving meals on the plane, satisfied with his IKEA furniture, and distraught when his apartment goes up in smoke. Dussere notes the problems coming from America as a land of plenty, but the film asks, plenty of what?

Fight Club gains a major part of its dark mood of alienation from the fissive split running through the personality of the narrator. Viewers learns relatively late in the film that Tyler Durden is a construct of the narrator's psyche. The film also makes clear that the crisis in the narrator's consciousness comes from a terrible psychic deprivation. He is overwhelmed by emotional frustration and grief. Tyler Durden wells up from the narrator's consciousness as a way for him to survive.

A ramification of Parfit's philosophy of the self is that identity has tremendous fluidity. It may not even have a solid reality that one can pinpoint but instead is indeterminate. The concept has caused ongoing controversy. In a 1993 response to one of his challengers, Parfit further explains his ideas about the impossibility of defining identity.

As a man of empirical observation, Parfit rejects critics who characterize his theory as positing a black hole at the center of every individual. Rather, the essential underlying facts that define a person are missing or in constant flux: "At some level, most of us continue to assume that our identity is a deep further fact, which must be indeterminate" (Parfit, "Reply" 28). Despite an extensive catalog of biographical details, pictures, stories, and the most minute accounting of details about our lives, we still cannot fathom ourselves. We typically perceive ourselves as greater than the sum of those parts.

According to Parfit, a determinate identity is not what matters. One person is capable of being psychologically continuous and gaining definition through two or more different people (32). At any one time, a personality is at once divided and fused with that of others. Over the course of one's life, this fusion-created identity changes. The awareness can help a centered self to "let go," and live through the relational selves rather than fearing life that may alter a perceived, singular identity.

Derek Parfit's model of personal identity has ramifications for literary criticism. It moves beyond the doppelgänger construct and the three-part Freudian model of personality. Psychoanalytic theory of personality relies on threes. Dividing a doppelgänger or split character into superego, ego, and id has a sameness about it, even if the analysis allows for dynamic exchange. Paraphrasing a literary text into these compartments has a rhetorical clarity and flows smoothly into the tri-part structure of a classic essay. The methods we use to describe character in postmodern literature and media are still rooted in past critical stances and conventions from the early 20th century. Ambiguities in characters from Poe and adapted for today's popular culture warrant an updated approach.

Literature has long explored this same truth of human experience metaphorically through the awareness of many selves. This concept of the divided self may have begun with the mortal conflict pitting Cain and Abel, but Poe continues the idea with a re-constituted view of what losing a moral self actually means.

CHAPTER 5

Identity as the Enclosed Self

As the current flood of vampire books, films, and television programs reminds us, vampires have lurked in the popular mind for hundreds of years. Vampires were not new in Poe's time. It was a concept that Poe had thought about and embedded explicitly into a tale called "Morella" (1835). An unnamed narrator mourns the loss of his intelligent, learned wife. A loved one believes that the spirit of a dead person comes to inhabit the body of their child, who grows at an unusual amazing rate. The narrator believes that the spirit of the dead Morella comes to inhabit the living child. Although many of Poe's tales provide graphic images of spilled blood and decaying flesh, "Morella" focuses on a different aspect. Poe uses vampirism to explore a deeper question of whether identity can persist apart from the physical body:

> That identity which is termed personal, Mr. Locke, I think, truly defines to consist in the saneness of a rational being. And since by person we understand an intelligent essence having reason, and since there is a consciousness which always accompanies thinking, it is this which makes us all to be that which we call *ourselves*—thereby distinguishing us from other beings that think, and giving us our personal identity. But the *principium individuationis*—the notion of that identity—which at death is or is not lost forever—was to me, at all times, a consideration of intense interest [Poe 668].

This model of what constitutes a person connects strongly to Derek Parfit's theory of the self and how the essence of a person may be shaped by other selves, or the force of fusion.

According to Parfit's concept of personality indeterminacy, fusion plays a key role in defining what makes up the self. The force to bundle up more than one self is at the opposite end of fission. "Physically, fusion is easy to describe. Two people come together. While they are unconscious, their bodies grow into one. One person then wakes up" (Parfit 18).

Parfit notes the example of the mind continuing in another's body as an example of fusion of the self. This construct, which was still in the realm of science fiction when Parfit imagined it over thirty years ago, has now become more imaginable. Advanced techniques of cloning and minimizing rejection of organ transplants through sophisticated drugs have made two bodies in one, in a sense, possible.

Author Michael Connelly gains dramatic intensity from this situation in *Blood Work* (1998). The usually grounded former FBI agent Terry McCaleb wonders how his transplanted heart may have changed his personality.

After transplant surgery and a long recovery, McCaleb becomes involved in a case of a woman killed in a store robbery. The dead woman's sister, Graciela Rivers, comes to visit him. Before he knows who she is, he has a strong sense of familiarity that repeats as a kind of *déjà vu*, a vague sense of memory that he cannot catch. He watches her reflection. "The sense of familiarity came over him again" (7). He connects immediately with Graciela Rivers, since he had seen her sister in the store surveillance tape recording her murder. Gradually, Terry learns that his transplanted heart comes from Graciela's sister.

To deflect the awfulness of this revelation, McCaleb shows empathy for Graciela. He also sees her as someone without an identity. She is the relative of a person who has been killed, a victim who would likely never learn who had killed her sister. "McCaleb had known hundreds of people like her. Loved ones taken from them without reason. No arrests, no convictions, no closure. Some of them were left zombies, their lives irrevocably changed. Lost souls" (9). When Graciela asks for his help in locating her sister's killer, McCaleb senses an otherworldly tie with the deceased. "For the first time he felt the undertow in the emotional current. There was something else at play but he didn't know what. He looked closely at Graciela Rivers and had the sense that if he took another step, asked the obvious questions, he would be pulled under" (10).

Later, McCaleb goes for a medical follow-up. He asks his woman cardiologist about the living with survivor's guilt. "Sometimes I feel like the modern Frankenstein, other people's parts in me." His logical doctor begs to differ. "One other person, one other part," she says. "Let's not be so dramatic." Terry answers, "But it's the big part, isn't it?" (17). The change Terry notices in his personality comes from his perceived fusion with another self. While he knows literally that this merging cannot happen, his renewed sense of obligation drives him into agreeing to Graciela's request.

Parfit discusses how, when identity fusion occurs, the characteristics of each self can continue. What, for instance, does each self remember? "For any two people who fuse together will have different characteristics, different desires, and different intentions. How can these be combined?" (18). This situation resembles that of two people moving in together, merging two households and placing some belongings in storage. The one surviving entity emerging from this melding might have memories or intentions from the original two, but some might be quasi-memories, q-memories.

Parfit emphasizes that "the compatible beings will blend, the others that are incompatible will fight it out and the stronger ones will prevail, or the stronger will weaken" (18). Memories and ambitions that one had will manifest in the other as q-memories and q-ambitions having an impact on personality and identity. We have heard of eHarmony for creating relationships. This compromise to blend and shift personality traits to accommodate two personalities could be a type of q-harmony.

Does fusion bring death for one self as it gives life to another? Parfit considers that some might consider the merging a kind of extinction, in that one person's quirks might be muted in the new relationship. The person has changed in some ways to accommodate the blended "being" that is both, as in a marriage. Parfit says that in most instances, the fusion change of personality is not an all-or-nothing proposition but a matter of degree (19).

In a fusion relationship, one self might q-remember the other's life and vice versa, and these elements are a part of the branched personality. An example may emerge when people who have been together or married for a long time collaborate in storytelling through an alternating method of narration. When the husband's memory falters, the wife picks up the story line without missing a beat.

To Parfit, selves are "relational," existing in matters of degree. "And these selves then become something like members of one's family, either a distant self, like a distant cousin, or a more recent one, as a close relation" (22). After a fusion, the self invests more either in the previous self or the newly grafted self. Parfit further divides the concept of fusion into qualities of psychological continuity and connectedness. Continuity from fusion goes one way only, as in a series of personalities developing for an individual over time. However, continuity requires overlapping and reciprocity (20). Continuity is the spread of a personality's network at any one time. Parfit proposes that fusion may occur due to a person taking in all these q-memories and q-ambitions from another. "Q-memories will weaken with the passage of time. Q-ambitions, once fulfilled, will be replaced by others" (21).

Parfit's model supposes the metaphor of a tree. The trunk or varying lines off the trunk represent continuity, and branches on the tree represent connectedness and variety for the selves as they change over time. "To imply psychological connectedness, I suggest the phrases 'one of my future selves' and 'one of my past selves'" (22). The notion of self is amorphous, not delineated or outlined. "The word 'I' can be used to imply the greatest degree of psychological connectedness" (25). It is perhaps more than a coincidence that in Parfit's theories and articles, he uses the acronym "PI" as an abbreviation for "personal identity."

Fusion is a useful way for narrative to deal with a serial killer's point of view, frequently incomprehensible in actual life. Forensic psychologists working with people convicted of many killings over time speak of the "Mind of Evil." The extremes of a Jeffrey Dahmer or Ted Bundy represent a black hole of the self that poses an indecipherable question.

Martin Roth, scriptwriter for television crime shows, shares his research about the profile of a serial killer. "Their patterns usually call for sexual contact, followed or preceded by murder or mutilation" (Roth 10). Mutilation seems to suggest division, but the initial motivation for cutting up a body is often the damaged self's eagerness to fuse with the victim. The mutilation to follow hardly makes sense as a way to prevent the victim from "talking," to prevent victim identification. Frequently, the male serial killer wants to boast about the act. Instead, mutilation comes more from the killer's unreasoning rage over failing to have complete control over the murder.

Control is a hallmark of repeated homicide. The male serial killer has a need to stop time, as shown by the frequency of taking trophies or pictures of the crime scene and of arranging the victim into an artistic position. This extremity of control shows up in the killer's yearning to overpower and enclose, to achieve fusion in the form of suffocation or even necrophilia. However, in literature the drama has to be shaped. Fusion offers a pattern of merging that shapes the killer's madness. It also gives a kind of reason to the serial killer's behavior of wanting to take on another self. Hannibal Lecter's interest in consuming, for example, presents an extreme case of fusion, giving his cannibalism a bizarre logic.

The profiles of serial killers in fiction and onscreen have overshadowed the random unpredictability of these actual homicides. Forensic psychologists warn against actual criminal investigators becoming too certain in creating a list of expected behaviors in serial killers. For instance, the idea of a repeat killer taking a trophy or acting out the same ritual behavior from killing to killing has recently been discredited. One study conducted by Louis Schlesinger at the John Jay College of Criminal Justice in New York examined cases of 38 serial killers with over 160 victims. The study found taking trophies from victims is highly variable in these criminals. The study urges criminal investigators not to rule out a certain suspect if the crime shows no evidence of ritualistic behavior. Lack of evidence is not solid evidence.

Another study contradicts the common perceptions about male serial killers and intelligence. Subjects examined in a MacArthur Violence Risk Assessment Study showed an "inverse relationship between verbal intelligence and psychopathy" (DeLisi et al. 169). Ultimately, these men as characters do not fit a set narrative. Ultimately, the psychology of a real-life serial killer is complicated, paradoxical, and unpredictable.

Still, empirical studies cannot override the mythology surrounding the repeat killer. Taking trophies or having genius-level intelligence pervades fictional representations of serial killers as characters. Creators of drama featuring serial killers have, like Poe before them, found these qualities fascinating. The trophy/art/shrine motif that a killer creates to commemorate a victim counters the pathetic impulses that lead one human being to destroy another. This supposed "pattern" gives a reason, however inaccurate, behind meaningless murders. A super-intelligent killer suggests a preternatural level of control and deviousness. A genius character could also play into an anti-intellectual mindset striating popular culture.

The motif of a super-intelligent killer makes sense to undergraduates suffering tortuous assignments from their professors, to ill patients afraid of their doctors, or to people mystified technology or seemingly nonsensical academic studies. In our culture, positions of control require people with intelligence. The stereotype of an intelligent serial killer feeds into most people's frustrations over being dominated in a college class or at the office. Plus, a smart villain makes a prolonged chase more likely. As Sherlock Holmes exults, "The game's afoot!" If the killer can outsmart police or authorities, then he can be anywhere. A killer on the loose prolongs the suspense to build dramatic intensity.

Women serial killers have a different profile from their male counterparts. They are much more likely to murder people close to them, with victims being husbands or lovers, family members, "patients entrusted in their care ... roomers, [or] tenants" (Roth, *Strictly Murder!* 49). Therefore the elaborate fantasy necessary for psychological recreation of a fused personality with the victim is unnecessary.

According to a study of 100 women serial killers, most of the time, with estimates at around 74 percent, the woman killer's motive is money. Covering up a crime is the next most common motive at 24 percent, with murders due to drugs or as part of pressure from a cult comes in at around 13 percent (Philbin and Philbin). For women killers, the methods of murder put considerable distance between killer and victim. The top two methods are poison or shooting, requiring less personal contact.

Two films present striking portraits of distorted characters representing extreme examples of fusion at work on the self. The trunk and all its branches strain to fuse with another. Norman Bates's appropriation of "Mother's" identity in *Psycho* (1960) represents fusion in the extreme. The son inhabits the dead mother's persona to retain the belief that she still lives.

Hannibal Lecter's cannibalism provides a version of fusion in *Silence of the Lambs* (1991). He seeks to consume and therefore fuse and enclose the victim. Lecter's familiarity with the methods of serial killer "Buffalo Bill" provides another manifestation of fusion. Buffalo Bill kills so he can flay the victim and enclose himself in her skin. In these cases, the killer's personality is already "split" before the narrative occurs, so talking about the killer's divided self at this juncture is irrelevant to the action and does not advance the discussion. Fusion, however, focuses our attention on the main thrust of the narrative, the character's ongoing attempts to fuse more personalities.

Fusion as a concept in fiction and the media presents the unbalanced killer as one who kills so to take on the identity of another. In Poe's story "The Tell-Tale Heart" (1843) as an inside look at the mind of a psychopath, we detect a network of images conveying fusion.

From the outset, Poe's disturbed narrator seemingly presents the reader with a divided personality. What he says is at odds with what he does. "True!— nervous — very very dreadfully nervous I had been and am; but why *will* you say that I am mad? The disease had sharpened my senses — not destroyed — not dulled them" (Poe 303). I propose that the consciousness of the narrator of this tale represents more the struggles of a fused or enclosed personality. Because Poe's fiction works toward a "unified effect," as he notes in "The Philosophy of Composition" (1846), fusion is an overriding organizing principle of "The Tell-Tale Heart."

In this well-known story, the narrator obsessively plots the murder of an elderly man, because he cannot bear the man's eye looking at him. After weeks of planning, he suffocates the old man with a mattress, cuts him up, and buries him under the floorboards. The police arrive to investigate the noises reported by neighbors. The narrator invites them in, and they all sit in the very room where the narrator had done the deed. For a short time, all seems well, until the narrator hears thumping from under the floorboards and shrieks out a confession. He thinks that the old man's heart has resumed beating to give him away.

But the narrator, as is clear, is actually in full control. He knows what he needs to achieve his own satisfaction. As Daniel Hoffman notes, "To portray the methodicalness of a madman is the work not of a madman but of a man who truly understands what it is to be mad" (Hoffman 227). Fusion carries its own urgency.

Again, the crime is motiveless, as the narrator tells us, except for that unsettling Eye. While the narrator thinks he is shutting off the eye of a father-figure, for all purposes, he is actually meeting it head on, fusing with it.

Using Parfit's concepts of personality fusion, we view more corners in the dark room of this tale. The narrator senses the penetrating beam from Eye watching him. After the killing, the fusion of identity occurs almost seamlessly. As proof to the police that the old man is away, the narrator shows them the dead man's "treasures, secure, undisturbed" (306). No theft of any kind has occurred. Of course, the deceased's life has permanence and continuity. The narrator-killer has fused with the old man's personality and picked up where the older man has left off. Does the narrator, our point of view, have a strange eye now? Or has he had one all along?

The sound effects of a thudding heart could be a sign of the supernatural, that is, the spirit of the dead man coming back to life to avenge his own murder. It could also be the overwrought narrator's anxiety betraying his guilt. Through the idea of fusion, both concepts are possible. The thudding under the floorboards is out of sight and uncanny, the unknown. From the unfused policemen's perspective, the more likely option is that the narrator's own beating heart sounds the alarm, prompting him to confess. Still, the narrator believes in the materiality of both possibilities. He has essentially absorbed the life of the old man into himself.

Another way to gauge this personality fusion is in terms of strength and weakness. The tale begins with a disparity of strength. The old man, who should be weak, keeps a terrible stranglehold on the narrator. To break the grip, the narrator has to exert more force through the strength he wields as a single personality, his refined sense of hearing.

If the old man has been the figure of authority, under a Freudian model, the narrator is well rid of him. The narrator's sense of self drains away as the police, also figures of authority, sit smiling. His perception is that they are taunting him.

The pace and rhythm of this story provides an extended example of how Poe recreates the psychology of a killer with chilling exactness. The only saving grace is that the old man, as far as we know, is the narrator's only victim. That this action takes place with excruciating slowness dramatizes the gradual transition of personalities from the old man to the narrator. Even if the diegetic time is not actually long (the story itself is among Poe's shortest), the perceived action seems drawn out, based on Poe's repetitions, "the lantern, closed, closed," dashes, and exclamation points. The speaker's q-intentions of being kind to the old man for an entire week before the killing exacerbate the tension of holding in his hatred. "I heard all things in the heaven and in the earth. I heard many things in hell" (303). With this phrase, Poe sets the narrator deeper into an excruciating, tortured existence. "One of his eyes resembled that of a vulture — a pale blue eye with a film over it. Whenever it fell on me, my blood ran cold" (Poe 303). Ironically, to the narrator, this blind eye shoots out a beam like a death ray.

When a vulture consumes another, it enacts fusion. A living person has no need to fear a vulture. An already dead person is beyond caring. Only a dying person needs to worry about being ripped to shreds. The narrator knows that he is already dead, psychologically, and the old man's plan for him is underway, so, according to the narrator's twisted perception that the Eye is an aggressor, he launches his plan of psychological self-defense.

His strategy is the following: if the old man plans to use fusion on me, I will use it on him first. The lantern is the first phase of his plan to counter the Evil Eye. He shines this light for a week, the same week, one assumes, that he is inordinately kind to the old man. Every morning, he goes into the room to trick the old man into thinking that he cares. He pretends to be nice, playing a role.

The narrator feels more powerful after a week of failed "lantern" competition. However, the old man has cannily adapted countermeasures against the narrator's campaign. When the narrator slips into the room and remains still, the old man does, too. And when the man groans, the narrator knows about it ahead of time. The moan is a "low stifled sound that arises from the bottom of the soul when overcharged with awe. I knew the sound well" (304).

Poe laces the narrator's tale-telling with figures of fusion and absorption in describing the pending murder: "Death in approaching him, had stalked with his black shadow before him and enveloped the victim" (304). In a Freudian interpretation, the bed is possibly the site of the narrator's own creation, if the old man is the narrator's father. Certainly, the narrator's projection that the Eye carries a relentless judgment suggests a rebellion against the father. In addition, the crime has the intensity of a patricide. As with *Psycho*, the story plays out the long-smoldering resentment of a caretaker son who must pretend to ply an aging parent with kindnesses. There even may be a suggestion of sexual abuse with a bed being a place of guilt and shame. But we do not have to go that far into a figurative appraisal of the murder weapon. With a fusion model of identity, the literal weight of the enclosing bed as a weapon suffices.

Because the method of murder is suffocation, Poe again gives the narrator's actions an enveloping pattern. Suffocation with the pressure of a mattress achieves a premature burial. Murder by virtue of the weight of a bed emphasizes the fusion effect. The narrator achieves his plan to surround the old man, to fold an outer layer against the living being and silence it.

Once the old man is still, the narrator refers to "stone" three times in assessing whether the victim is actually dead, evoking qualities of being hard and insensate. What the old man perhaps had been in life continues after death. The heart continues to beat. We watch in morbid fascination as the narrator continues to overwhelm the man by force, like a boa constrictor squeezing the prey it intends to ingest.

Ironically, in this pattern of fusion, the narrator cuts the body into pieces. Still, there is no hint of blood spatter or errant tissue. The narrator is too careful for that. "A tub had caught all — ha! ha!" (Poe 305). Collection, gathering, and encircling continue to mark events.

Studies of serial killers have noted that the killer is frequently eager to stop time. The murderer is likely to take trophies from the victim or arrange the body into an aesthetic pose to taunt and unsettle the person discovering the body. Poe presents these same gestures but in metaphor. Stopped time occurs as the narrator describes the dead man's heartbeat: "a low, dull, quick sound, such as a watch makes when enveloped in cotton" (305). He repeats the phrase as proof of the old man's emergence from the fusion. Later, when the policemen visit, the narrator sits on a chair placed over the exact spot where the corpse rests (306). Does the chair placement show the killer's arrogance in taunting the officers? Is the placement a deliberate artistic construction, a kind of a trophy, a wish to enclose pieces of corpse? As profilers of male serial killers have pointed out, more eerie tableaux have been constructed to commemorate a killing.

As the narrator blurts out a confession, his original identity as clever killer disappears. His heart and the old man's are now fused. The hallucinatory nature of the old man's beating heart makes no difference. The old man's ongoing reality blends with the narrator's own. Fusion had been his murder weapon, and ironically, it returns to claim him.

Poe wrote sixty years before Freud. At times, critics might patronize early writers by using a Freudian method. Look how smart we are, peering into an artist's innermost thoughts. But Poe was writing with an awareness of a broad spectrum of experience, taking in varied perceptions. A Freudian analysis fails to understand the material that doesn't fit. It's like a theory on the life of stars that seems to provide an accurate understanding until extraneous observations enter the picture. Evidence surfaces that the theory cannot account for. Therefore, the situation requires a re-vamping of the previous theory.

Parfit has his detractors. Still, his theory of personality continues to have numerous followers, including the development of this two-dimensional model by Simon Prosser. Prosser picks up Parfit's efforts to open up theories of personality and consciousness. Prosser's model of two-dimensional consciousness model attempts to pry concepts of cognition and apperception away from a dual Cartesian, mind/body perspective and toward a more open, fluid idea taking into account more alternative states of perception. Prosser's argument explains ideas from G.E. Moore, Bertrand Russell and others about objects "representing" others.

Prosser finds this model of perception limiting. He illustrates Moore's thinking through an example of a red tomato. "When one sees a red tomato one can focus one's attention on the tomato, or on its redness, but one cannot focus one's attention on the experience itself.... Representationalists take this to suggest that all that is encountered in an experience is its content" (321). Prosser addresses ways in which "standard representationalism" in philosophy, after Bertrand Russell, fails to address perceived experiences of identity such as "blurry images, after images, hallucinations, [and] aspect switches" (324). To include these states in perception, Prosser develops a concept of horizontal, vertical, and diagonal perceptions, resulting in this "two-dimensional consciousness" model. These extend the "centered self" of a personality into the world and into its self-perception. Prosser notes, "Experiences are true, false, or neither" (334).

Prosser's argument using phenomenology and linguistic analysis goes into more detail than is relevant here. It suffices to say that several concepts from Prosser apply to Poe's fiction. Prosser's model includes a method of awareness that takes into account hallucinatory experiences. The horizontal and vertical ideas help to clarify the purpose of vertical and horizontal references in Poe's work, and isolate the quality from Poe that makes his narratives so relevant to viewing experiences from other media.

Despite ensuing controversies over theories of mind from Parfit and Prosser, these ideas offer concepts that help in viewing Poe's fiction. In a sense critics are stuck in a rut with the concepts of identity in the media being representational, Freudian, or Lacanian. Constructs about the continuity of personality and connectedness make sense for popular culture in the dynamic interplay between material and reader/viewer. If we consider media as having its own consumer-centered personality seeking connectedness and continuity to ensure its survival, this theory can pinpoint how the energy of Poe continues to dominate our culture in recently published novels, television programs, and films.

Two books are Laura Lippman's *What the Dead Know* and Linda Fairstein's *Entombed*. Laura Lippman, originally a journalist in Baltimore, has learned lessons from Poe, her fellow Baltimorean. Lippman is author of a mystery series about Baltimore journalist Tess Monaghan, and student of Poe. She writes about Poe in *The Shadow of the Master*, "In a Strange City: Baltimore and the Poe Toaster" (107–111). She knows the lessons of Poe are ultimately indecipherable.

Lippman was keeping watch for the Poe Toaster, a shadowy figure who left roses and cognac annually at Poe's grave, on January 20, 2000. "I was the one who saw the Poe Toaster first." Then she reluctantly admits that everyone there undoubtedly lays claim to the honor. "All I can say is that I've never known of a true Baltimorean — outside of an elderly man in a nursing home — who wants to unmask the visitor. The mystery is what makes it special." With digital surveillance being more precise and harder to escape, the midnight visitor may have stopped the practice out of concern for maintaining the mystery. For two years in a row as of this writing in 2011, the Poe Toaster has been a no-show. Lippman asks a number of questions about her experience and purports to answer them. "This much I will tell you — yes." (Connelly, ed. 110–111). Lippman, then, knows the value of keeping an identity mysterious. And this is basically the theme of her novel.

Lippman's *What the Dead Know* (2007) revolves around the fusion principle of identity. She develops the formula with nuance and insight into adolescent psychology. Two young sisters, Sunny and Heather Bethany, disappear from a suburban mall. Decades later, a car accident in that same town lands a young woman in a hospital. Forced to give her name, she claims that she is Heather Bethany. "Floating on pain killers, she fantasized about the morning, what it would be like to say her name, her true name, for the first time in years. To answer a question that few people had to think about twice: *Who are you?*" (10). The damaged young woman's thoughts equivocate through the entire narrative. Is she actually Heather Bethany returned and alive? The woman has so many facts down about the cold case of the missing Bethany sisters that she either has to be who she says or she knows what happened to the girls. The reader knows from the outset that all is not what it seems with the young woman. The unexpected turn in this heart-wrenching narrative is that the missing girl who has turned up is really Sunny, the older sister. She has assumed the identity of her younger sister, Heather, who is dead from an accident Sunny could not prevent. Out of pressing guilt, the older sister resurrects the dead younger sister, taking on her identity. This plot hinges on a different kind of fusion, as Sunny tries to cover up for what she had failed to do, protect her younger sister. By delicately balancing ambiguities over who the girl actually is, Lippman keeps the reader in suspense over the extent of this identity transplant.

Despite eventually revealing the sister's identity to the reader, Lippman sustains the underlying mysteries of what makes up an identity to the novel's end. The conclusion reiterates the "nevermore" answer to the book's cryptic question of the title, *What the Dead Know*. The dead might know answers to these questions of personhood and how events change and rob us of our identities. Certainly, those living have no idea.

Lippman's uses of the enclosed-self theme dramatize the power of guilt. Heather's lost life smothers Sunny's ongoing one. Lippman also probes the dramatic impact of fluid identity on others in the family. After the girls' disappearance, their parents' lives came to a standstill. Their father Dave tried desperately to locate them, without success. Miriam, the mother, suffered tremendous guilt, since she had embroiled herself in an extramarital affair when the girls were taken. The Bethany marriage ended in divorce.

Dave is now dead. The mother, Miriam, has moved to Cuernavaca, Mexico, to escape her painful past. She almost revels in the high-end hotel, lush courtyard and a manicured lawn, with white peacocks, but her immediate reaction is wondering what the girls might think about such grandeur. "Amazing, the levels of pain, the subtle variations, even after more than a decade" (290). She weeps. "She was here to learn new words, a new way of speaking, a new way of being. She had already learned a few things today, and been reminded of others she already knew. She would now have hunger, not be it" (291).

Lippman presents a sensitive handling of a girl's psychology. Sunny Bethany has stayed away out of guilt over what she has done. The depth of her absent self-esteem is profound. She cannot fathom that she should return home by herself. After her sister's death, she cannot believe that her parents would care to have her back, that she alone is enough. She has undergone severe damage, having been kidnapped and held a psychological prisoner of an older boy she thought she loved. The scar of her experience cuts not only through her but through everyone in the family.

Another recent novel making inventive use of the fusion principle of identity is Linda Fairstein's *Entombed* (2005). In the book's acknowledgments, Fairstein discusses the impact Poe had on her as a young reader:

> My first encounter with Edgar Allan Poe's *Tales of the Grotesque and Arabesque* made an indelible impression on my adolescent imagination. A dead man's heart beating beneath the floorboards, the huge pendulum descending on a prisoner in the pit, the Red Death invading the festive masquerade, and the repeated torment of premature burial and entombment behind cellar walls — each of these narratives was responsible for youthful nightmares, and all of them have lured me back over the years to delight in their dramatic power and poetic elegance [501].

Fairstein's protagonist, Alexandra Cooper, unravels two cases through a careful structure of motifs representing enclosure. This emphasis carries out the "entombed" theme from the title, which repeats phobic motifs from several of Poe's stories. In addition, Linda Fairstein sets crime scenes where Poe had lived in New York City. *Entombed* situates itself directly in the shadow of Poe, not merely in subject matter, but in locale, type of crime, and in the thematic unity of the self being suffocated.

Author Fairstein is well acquainted with fringe identities. For twenty-five years, she led the Sex Crimes Unit out of the Manhattan District Attorney's office. She has had a wealth of experience dealing with and prosecuting individuals with distorted personalities.

In *Entombed*, protagonist Alexandra Cooper faces a puzzling unsolved crime. A skeleton has been found standing upright in a wall. As in many recent titles of detective fiction, Fairstein's work places the investigator protagonist in the position of processing two cases at once. This sets up a model for a double-strand of narratives in which one case resonates against the other.

The design partially reflects a reality of the incredibly busy crime labs.

It is unrealistic for investigators to have only one case to solve. To have only two cases is barely more accurate, since even rural crime labs have a heavy caseload. For instance, journalist Irina Cates reported that forensic labs in Billings, Montana, processed 5700 cases in 2009. That load averages to around 15 cases a day. Crime lab facilities in less densely populated cities are stressed perhaps even more so than those in heavily populated metropolitan areas due to budget crunches forcing case re-distributions (Burns). So the idea of Alex running several cases at once gives the narrative authenticity.

A double-strand plot also sets a brisk pace for the narrative. Each storyline vies for attention in its own right. The principle of fusion, therefore, is at work on the level of the entire work, as one tale competes with the other, and neither story thread takes precedent.

The Silk Stocking case of an ongoing contemporary silk stocking killer case blends with the cold case of the skeleton labeled as A.T. From the fusion of the two emerges the entire text. In addition, the double-helix type of structure is a strategic move by a writer in that it builds a rapid pace for alternating chapters to deal with the different cases.

On the one hand, Alex and her squad deal with the panic over the Silk Stockings killer, a rapist who assaults women at knife point, gagging them with a silk stocking. The squad takes a number of hits in the press and bad publicity over allowing this killer to strike again. "SNAG IN SILK STOCKING—Prosecutor's Promise to End Serial Attacks Gets Hosed" (23).

The chase for the silk stocking rapist is thematically connected to the upright skeleton cold case, indeed, the entire aspect of the investigation for the Poe mimicker, masquerader. Characterizing the crime by way of the silk stocking emphasizes the image of an enclosed female form. This image in turn mirrors the cold case crime involving the upright skeleton as victim. The crime of suffocation and rape represents a fusion of identity as a result of an enveloping, claustrophobic enclosure.

Clues to the identity of the skeleton come from a bag of rat poison dated in the late '70s, and a ring inscribed on the inside with the initials A. T. Again, the circle suggests an enclosure of identity, along with connection to a loved one or a contiguous personality in Parfit's sense.

The Poe copycat represents another fusion of personality. The murderer's identity draws definition by subsuming features of Poe's life and work. The FAQs on Fairstein's author website provide details of Coop's back story: "Alex majored in English Literature at a great liberal arts college before making her decision to go to law school." So Alexandra Cooper is well poised to fathom the criminal's references to cases from Poe.

Alex's own suffocated feeling comes into play as politics pressure her to be quiet about additional cases that might possibly be the work of the Silk

Stockings rapist. She is an impassioned public servant, so Alex holds the public safety in high esteem, and this gag order does not sit well with her. She undergoes her own version of suffocation:

> I thought of another eight crimes that rested in my case folder, which had not been connected by forensics but which had the same nuances of language and order of sexual acts the rapist performed to make me certain it was the work of the same man. The mayor had ordered the PC not to heighten the public's fear by including those other cases [65].

The investigators get a break when one of the victims of the Silk Stockings killer survives. The procedural machinery works to interview Annika Jelt in her hospital room and to notify her parents, who live overseas in Sweden. This seemingly tangential fact about the injured girl's family gains the reader's attention in that the pattern of fusion fails to close.

This lack of fusion, essentially a broken circuit, occurs when Annika's parents try to get into the country and cannot get through immigration. In this way, Fairstein comments on the restrictive post–9/11 bureaucracy that dispassionately prevents the parents from reuniting with their seriously traumatized daughter. The parents are from a farm in Sweden, and they lack all the proper documentation for being allowed into the States. "Rules is rules and I don't break them for anybody," the immigration supervisor tells Alex and her team. "'Welcome to America, post nine-eleven" (83). In these passages, Fairstein suggests an even broader concept of being entombed, of an entire population and culture insulated from the rest of the world.

While Alex's team deals with problems in the Silk Stocking case, a tense Alex feels the need to reduce her stress level. She decides that attending a law school event in Greenwich Village with friends is just the ticket. Undergoing renovation, the law school's dean has launched the equivalent of a ground breaking. The event will commemorate a new project to renovate the old building. As the ceremony gets underway, screams and shuffles signal that the renovation has exposed an unusual find: "Perfectly smooth ivory-colored bones framed the empty orbital sockets that met my horrified stare. I was face-to-face with a human skull buried behind an ancient wall" (30). Earlier, Alex had characterized her excursion to this building as a "girls' night out" (26). Once investigators examine the skeletal remains, the event has indeed turned into a girls' night out. With the dry wit almost required when dealing with death, investigators from Alex's team, Mike Chapman and Mercer Wallace, label the skeleton "The Thin Man." Before long, the array of bones has to be renamed, since the remains are those of a woman.

Forensic anthropologist Andy Dorfman determines that the woman had been bricked up behind the wall under dramatic circumstances, a premature burial. The bones are clean, without tissue. On the ground below the skeleton are her fingernails, "like small caramelized bits" as the forensic anthropologist describes them. Alex imagines the scene: "the hopelessness of her delicate fingernails scraping against the stones that had been cemented in place" (43–44). The conclusion is far from sweet, and Alex is haunted by the reality conveyed by the pieces.

The detectives discover that Poe himself had lived in the gloomy brownstone where the skeleton was found, the Poe House. Other clues to the nature of this crime are lines from Poe's verse. The reference is an obscure Poe connection but Alex is savvy enough to pick up the allusion. The killer is recreating crimes from the works of Poe.

The team is called to another crime scene of a murdered doctor. Alex exhibits *q*-memories of Bronx River Park: "My childhood memories of sunfilled gardens with vividly colored flowers bore no resemblance to the vast, darkened park that we entered. There were occasional streetlamps along the route, but the roadway was surrounded on both sides by a tall, dense growth of trees. The wind caused tall shadows to dance in front of our headlights, and the sprawling grounds seemed an eerily sinister place" (199).

The groundskeeper's name is Sinclair Phelps. He is a shell, not connected with people. His workers do not even speak English. Phelps is described in animal terms, animals that are predators. He has an aquiline nose, the hide of a gator, and he is ready to pounce. He pays attention to Alex, being solicitous about her comfort and suggesting that they move inside (200–201).

The team tracks down yet another literary mystery. A call to the Raven Society is the last message on the murdered doctor's cell phone (206). One of the suspects in this second murder of the doctor has accused Poe of plagiarism. The accusation is that Poe has lifted lines from Elizabeth Barrett Browning to construct "The Raven." Many members did not take kindly to the accusation.

Essentially plagiarism is yet another crime of entombment, with a poor writer cloaked by the words of an artist. Entombment characterizes the Raven Society as well. It is a closed group, due to a shooting a decade before (311–312). As Alex learns, the Raven Society is extremely exclusive, with very special rules (384). One rule is that the prospective member must have killed someone in the manner of a crime laid out in Poe's fiction.

On the grounds of the Bronx River Park is another Poe House. The cottage has a "low sloping ceiling" and contains the bedroom where Virginia Clemm had died. It was also where Poe wrote "Annabel Lee," "Ulalume," and "The Bells," the guide tells Alex and Mike (318–319). During a brief moment alone, an unknown attacker bashes Alex on the head. She awakens in a box, a literal premature burial:

My pain was dwarfed with fear. I was in a box smaller than a coffin. I didn't need to look back. I could feel the wooden boards beneath my back, close to my arms on each side, and knew there was not enough space above me to allow me to pick up my head.

Panic prevented me from doing what I needed to do most—regulate my breathing and conserve whatever oxygen there was available [322].

Haunting images from Poe's stories rush through Alex's mind. She thinks of Poe's "The Tell-Tale Heart," with the policemen above the corpse unable to hear the beating heart that the killer narrator hears. A wriggling against her leg calls to mind Poe's "conqueror worm." She is trapped in what she later learns is the root cellar. She is literally gagged this time, so she cannot call loudly enough to alert her colleagues above, who wonder where she had gone.

Once Mike and Mercer her colleagues rescue her, the next step is a modern entombment, an MRI machine which she gives her pause, although she realizes its necessity.

Alex learns in an interview with Kittredge, one of the Raven Society scholars, that Poe himself was a suspect in the real-life murder that resulted in Poe's story "The Murder of Marie Rogêt." At the time, journalists misunderstood Poe's intent, since crime writing was a new subgenre (380). From this connection, the possibility lurks that one of the literary scholars, students of words, has turned words into actualities.

Suspicion prompts Alex to return to the Botanical Garden in the Bronx. The murderer's lair is an enclosed *topos*: "The road looped around a fenced-in area of several acres in which buses were covered with a large tarp to ward off the frost ... an urban oasis" (470). While visiting a house on the grounds of the Botanical Gardens, she takes in photographs and unusual signs that the house does not seem lived in. When Alex explores a renovated part of the house, she discovers what appears to be a brick crypt. The murderer's identity is now exposed, and Alex struggles to escape.

The book's final scenes present a montage of allusions to Poe stories. The murderer uses gangs of teenagers to create a diversion the same way Dupin enlists his band of irregulars to create a distraction when Dupin visits D—'s apartment in "The Purloined Letter." Separated from her colleagues, Alex ends up in a cave filled with bats. The murderer tracks Alex down with dogs and forces her into the cave. He forces her at gunpoint to re-enact the final scene from "The Cask of Amontillado." Her attacker taunts her with obscure quotations from Poe (484). The murderer knows that Alex prides herself on her sharp recall. As Montresor taunts Fortunato by appealing to Luchesi's expertise with wines, the murderer zeroes in on Alex's Achilles' heel.

In another parallel between Montresor's torture of Fortunato, the killer of A.T. from the previous case watches Alex build her own tomb. He forces her to begin cementing herself into the stifling enclosure, "eyeing me as I ferried heavy rocks from the hillside into the cave" (486).

The killer is successful in mirroring Poe's crime, because he makes Alex believe in the power of Poe's fiction. She listens him spout a litany of reversals in his life. He has a long list of reasons for seeking revenge and hating others. Alex then starts to fuse the personality of the killer with Poe's life.

> I thought about the tragedies that had overwhelmed Poe's life from infancy. He had all the psychological torment that could have created a monster, a serial killer. Aaron Kittredge believed he might have been one. It seemed more plausible to me with every second in [the killer's] presence [489].

The killer prepares to bind Coop so to lead her further into the cave, the modern parallel of Poe's catacomb. Alex rescues herself, jamming thorns from the garden into his eye to blind him. With this attack, Alex mimics the crime from "The Tell-Tale Heart," in the same way that the narrator murders the old man due to his offensive Evil Eye. When the attacker collapses in agony, she grabs his shotgun, fires it into the sky, and flees.

Once the killer is captured, Alex and Mike Chapman congratulate each other on the successful resolution to both the Silk Stockings case and the Poe copycat crimes. Images of enclosure persist even in this afterhours confab. The two mention how the murderer appeared in court swathed like a mummy, "his shattered skull packaged in layers of bandage and gauze wrap" (498). Coop then hopes that she is off the hook, but Mike tells her she has to "get back in the ring" (496).

The phrase "back in the ring" connects Alex to the upright skeleton from the novel's early chapters. With the skeleton, crime lab investigators had found a ring inscribed with the initials A. T. Victims in the two storylines each had similar initials, A.T. for Aurora Tait, and A. J. for Annika Jelts. Yet a third set of initials rounded out a trio of victims, A. C. for Alex Cooper. Alex is alive, but she faces the paradox of being back in the ring, stifled and enclosed in her professional position. Yet another Poe reference comes into the story before the novel ends. Alex stands up and knocks a table, nearly upsetting a "porcelain bust" of the poet (497). With this gesture of table rattling, Fairstein may be alluding to her own status as a writer.

The Edgar Award is the highest honor for mystery writing. The trophy is a bust of Poe similar to what Coop nearly knocks from the table. Fairstein has not yet won an Edgar Award. The fact that she rattles the Poe statuette characterizes Coop's attitude toward the award. Does the character's gesture say that Fairstein does not care about the award? Or is she suggesting that eventually she will knock the Edgar-awarding community off its established pedestal? Regardless of the answer, Coop's action links her to the killer who also rattled Poe's image.

The murderer follows in Poe's footsteps, re-creating crimes from the master's work. Similarly, mystery writers re-combine elements from Poe's detective narratives to form their own stories. They don the guise of crime fiction tradition. Whether Linda Fairstein ever wins an Edgar Award, as a writer, she is enveloped in the writing genre that Poe developed.

Television programs also utilize this model of enclosure. *Law and Order* and *Dexter* are two popular programs putting fusion to work. Personality fusion is a central principle structuring *Law and Order*. Even though the show seems to belong to a category of fact-based docudramas, or "police procedurals," the informing principle of *Law and Order* is enclosure. The two halves of the crime-solving community, police and district attorneys, represent a unified legal immune system that envelopes the disease-causing virus that is the suspect. To uphold legal codes, the justice system swarms onto the anomalous evildoer.

In this model, the system is a set narrative construct. Actors come and go, characters' names change, and people are merely placeholders in the story. The random, arbitrary element in the organization comes from those "ripped from the headlines" cases. The criminals are indeterminate identities, distorted and idiosyncratic, finding an infinite number of ways to breach morality. Regardless of the myriad motives the program has revealed over the years, the defendants are rarely recognizable as us. Jack McCoy's adversarial role makes us empathize more with his interest, and the system's, in putting the defendant away. The final outcome is usually order. Even if McCoy and company lose a case, the older and wiser supervising district attorney urges them to get over the frustration and move on to the next offending virus attacking the body politic.

The television program *Dexter* (Showtime) also incorporates a principle of fusion. The structure of this program is the obverse of *Law and Order*. Instead of showing a stable system confronting an unstable personality, *Dexter* dramatizes how the system itself is out of balance. To right the wrong, Dexter must take extreme measures to put away killers. He has to become a serial killer himself. The television series began in 2006, based on the novel *Darkly Dreaming Dexter* (2004) by Jeff Lindsey.

Two ends of the personality wire fuse in several ways. First, Dexter himself leads a double life. One is as a respectable blood spatter pattern analyst, a professional forensic worker, and the other manifests in his interior life, populated by his "Dark Passenger." Eventually he learns that this figure is his foster father Harry Morgan. Harry had been a police detective who had acted as a tutor and mentor for his sociopathic son. Harry tried to urge his son to channel his homicidal impulses for good. These are the rules of Harry: Dexter must vet his victim carefully and be very clean in his execution, leaving no clues. Dexter still has no idea of his real father's identity.

Fusion shapes Dexter's interest in revenge. Dexter's principle is a kind of consumption, similar to Hannibel Lecter's. He wants to overwhelm and enact upon the killer what he or she had originally done, to repay unreasoning malice with even more powerful evil. Dexter follows up on his inchoate impulse to do the right thing but he obviously selects a wrong context. The ghostly figure of Harry works out his tendencies on Dexter, to make him do his bidding. Even so, the deformed elements in Dexter's personality are indicative of inequities in the justice system. The system will not rectify the wrong; therefore, Dexter is left to tidy up.

In contrast with the narrator of "The Tell-Tale Heart," this character has a father figure shaping his behavior, although Dexter does what this father says. He doesn't resist. He is as compliant, most of the time, as Pinocchio is to Gepetto. In fact, Lindsey's book is based loosely on the story of Pinocchio, with Dexter being a puppet of his creator. The Pinocchio narrative is decidedly based on identity stemming from fusion, since the creator impresses a mark onto his creation. *Pinocchio Bleeds* was an early title Lindsey had wanted in lieu of the alliterative *Darkly Dreaming Dexter*. That much preferred title resonates with echoes from two phrases of Poe's "The Raven," "deep into the darkness peering" (opening of stanza 5, line 26), and then toward the end, "And his eyes have all the seeming of a demon's that is dreaming" (last stanza, line 3). Both these allusions convey the controlling self, or the narrator who looks for the raven, and the piercing perspective of the raven as the fused secret sharer of the inner self.

By the end of the fourth season, the scales of justice swing back at Dexter. His nocturnal murders catch up with him. In an episode entitled "The Getaway" (aired on December 13, 2009), Dexter loses everything he had worked for after he finds his wife dead in a pool of blood in their bathtub. Arthur Mitchell (John Lithgow), a psychopath Dexter had pursued throughout the season, wreaks revenge and kills Dexter's wife Rita Morgan. Dexter's position as a crime spatter analyst/serial killer illustrates an arbitrary fluidity within a system that should be stable. In critiquing the bureaucracy of the legal system, *Dexter* questions the effectiveness of American justice.

Poe's narrator in "The Tell-Tale Heart" changes his personality by killing and fusing with the murder victim. *Laura* (1944), directed by Otto Preminger, dramatizes this same theme metaphorically, except three suspects fuse with this victim, who is actually not dead. Based on Vera Caspary's 1942 novel, *Laura* has consistently been on the list of "The Top 100 Mystery Novels of All Time."

The story of Cain and Abel is the *ur*-text for a self created by fission. A woman's fused self traces back to the narrative of Lilith and Eve. According to *midrashic* legend, Lilith manifested a power and fertility that challenged Adam's supremacy. After a dispute with Adam, Lilith was replaced by the more obedient Eve. Shaped from Adam's rib, this second woman helpmate was more dependent on him.

In *Laura*, the title character Laura Hunt (Gene Tierney) has been murdered, her face obliterated by a shotgun blast. The film's three male protagonists have varying kinds of fusion identities shaped by the dead Laura. Initially, Laura is Lilith, all the more desirable because she is unobtainable. The film asserts Laura's absent identity through her relational fusion of a self through three men.

Two of the men have already met her and been part of her life: her long-time good friend, the writer and astute critic Waldo Lydecker (Clifton Webb), and her fiancé, Shelby Carpenter (Vincent Price). David Shields' article in the *Yale Review* provides a useful summary of the three men (the third being the police detective) and their competition for Laura. Shields calls Shelby Carpenter "a lummox with no interior life whatsoever" (42). As the stereotype of a shallow man of money, Vincent Price creates a contrasting persona to the ghoulish characters he later created on screen. He became a one-man cottage industry starring in films based on Poe's stories, among them *House of Usher* (1960), *The Pit and the Pendulum* (1961), and *The Masque of the Red Death* (1963).

The police detective investigating Laura's homicide, Detective Mark McPherson (Dana Andrews), is unfamiliar with Laura before he is called onto the case. Initially, McPherson's attitude is that Laura's murder is unimportant, a third-rate crime. However, during the course of the investigation, McPherson becomes infatuated with a portrait of Laura in her sumptuous apartment. Her image encloses him. Shields asserts the primacy of McPherson over the action. "It's 1944: there's a war on; the hero can't be an artist or a playboy. He needs to be someone who can just get the job done" (40). That someone, of course, is McPherson. By the time Laura herself shows up in the flesh, McPherson is head over heels. He is in the same psychic place as the formerly sainted woman.

Laura's return to the living reveals that a young model named Diane Redfern, who resembles Laura, was the actual murder victim. Author Caspary explicitly intends to replicate the mythic pairing of Eve-Lilith for Laura-Diane Redfern. Redfern, the actual victim, is modeling for a "Lady Lilith" ad campaign shortly before she is killed. The name Diane Redfern emphasizes an aggressive sexuality, with reference to the huntress, Diana. Unlike the straightforward Hunt that is Laura's surname, the murdered woman is more cunning. She had also been having an affair with Shelby. Redfern suggests a dangerous, primeval, swampy environment. She is the siren, *la belle dame sans merci*. While Laura's portrait may possess the sheer power to make McPherson fall for her, the real, more physical woman, Diane Redfern, has drawn Shelby with her physicality.

Despite Caspary's obvious reference to a predator, Laura Hunt is idealized through her occupation of being an ambitious, successful career woman. Caspery herself had worked in an advertising firm, so she was familiar enough with that world to give Laura's occupation specificity and color.

The murder of Diane Redfern might also reflect the collective anxieties of American women during the war. Killing off Redfern eliminates the sexual threat of women afraid for their men being away. The plot makes it safe for women like Laura Hunt to be independent and ambitious.

David Shields discusses at length the three men who are Laura's biggest fans. Of Laura, Shields says she is the "target of everyone's search, object of everyone's desire" (39). His article addresses the "hunt" symbolism of Laura's surname, but not of Redfern's. Shields also skips the key significance of Lydecker, a writer who turns killer.

This film emphasizes the changing relationship between image and the word. Lydecker's occupation illustrates the waning powers of writing and words. The image has more power to control actions, even if that image is deceptive. Lydecker cannot control Laura the way he wants, so he twice plans to kill her, and he fails both times. Waldo makes the initial mistake of killing Redfern instead of Laura. Later, Lydecker's words broadcast over the radio do little to fool McPherson and fail to provide Lydecker's alibi. Author Caspery's own background in advertising gave her experience with the upcoming surge of graphic arts on Madison Avenue. She uses this weakness in Lydecker to parallel a cultural shift. Images were soon to supplant words. Since the mid-thirties, films had grown in importance, and television was soon to replace radio as the medium of choice. The word constructions of stories become embedded and enclosed by the image.

By the 1950s, the fused-woman motif in mid-century America had changed. We can measure the extent of this change by juxtaposing Preminger's *Laura* with Hitchcock's *Vertigo* (1959). The first film has a resolved ending. Laura and the police detective McPherson unite for a happy ending. In Preminger's narrative, the uncontrollable Lilith siren is killed off, leaving the idealized woman who comes back to life. In Hitchcock's *Vertigo*, the reverse is true, with the idealized, ethereal Madeleine Elster being killed and the blowsy Judy Barton/Diane Redfern emerging in her place. Male control tries to contain and shape the story, with limited success. The ideal woman falls from the male grip.

Since *Vertigo* was released on restored DVD in 1998, the film has gathered a vast following of commentators. Critics have encircled the rich work to represent a 360-degree sweep of viewing angles. Many have offered their meanings on Scottie Ferguson's winding, circular experience. Robin Wood, Donald Spoto, and Dennis R. Perry provide insightful explications of the film in terms of gender roles, Hitchcock's influences, and biographical psychoanalytic criticism. This essay proposes that the fusion model of the self tilts emphasis of the film away from physical attraction and more on a tale's near-magnetic power to draw in a listener.

The fusion patterns in Poe's "The Fall of the House of Usher" present several striking parallels to the complex stories embedded in *Vertigo*. Each work proceeds by a similar narrative progression jump started by a traumatic, near-death plunge. For the narrator of "Usher," the trauma occurs by the tarn; for Scottie, the slide down the roof shakes him to the core. Then each storyline unfolds in a similar pattern. A puzzling summons brings each character to the "case." Various characters represent forces of vague attempts at healing. An unsettling chase leads toward an ever-receding truth. Events escalate to question the self's ability to discern between illusion and reality as well as life and death. Poe's narrative sets in condensed form the same emotional subtleties probed in Hitchcock's film.

"The Fall of the House of Usher" dramatizes the dangers of a mind's immersion into a story. The story's unnamed narrator has recently received a disturbing letter from a long-time acquaintance, Roderick Usher. How the letter itself has reached him poses something of a mystery, since the narrator has been "in a distant part of the country." He approaches the Usher estate, a "dreary tract of country," feeling depressed and disoriented. Hoping to shrug off the mood, he approaches the shore of a small lake. "I reined my horse to the precipitous brink of a black and lurid tarn that lay in unruffled luster by the dwelling, and gazed down — but with a shudder even more thrilling than before" (231). Instead of providing clarity, the tarn's opaque water upsets him further. The inverted reflection of Roderick's ramshackle mansion alarms him. A few moments later, "shaking off from my spirit what must have been a dream" (233), he looks at Usher's actual house. This view only reinforces that "a pestilent and mystic vapor" surrounds the house. Vision stays foggy even once he opens his eyes. He descends into a nightmare abyss, an alternative reality that both seduces and terrorizes.

Jump-starting the imagination, the tarn is at once a wellspring of creativity and a drowning pool. The body of near stagnant water with no visible bottom represents a flailing epistemological gesture of seeking a grounded self and finding only darkness.

The narrator's near fall is center of attention for this story. The name

"Usher" clarifies that Roderick and Madeline Usher are the means of conveying the narrator to the brink of the tarn. They "usher" him to witness this danger of the tale at close range.

This paradox of both desiring and dreading a fall to destruction occurs several times in Poe's fiction. Pym thrills to his imagined plunge into the bottom of a cliff. The narrator of "A Descent into the Maelström" (1841) envisions the swirling power of the whirlpool and collapses. "The Imp of the Perverse" (1845) lays out the paradox: "And because our reason deters us from the brink, *therefore* do we the most impetuously approach it" (282). Poe uses these textured moments of paralysis for more than horror. Each tangle of conflicting sensation comes before a shift in the storyline. The emblem wrenches the narrative from one level into another.

Critics have called this reallocation of narrative from one framing tale to another embedded story a *mise en abîme*, translatable as "set into infinity." As noted earlier, the phrase describes an enclosed, inset image on a shield in emblems of French heraldry. The figure also may appear as a reflection in the center of a piece of jewelry, or a painting that replicates condensed patterns of the outer structure via reflections or mirrors. In a journal entry, André Gide first applies the term to literary criticism to characterize stories within stories. He compares these to "the heart point" in the center of a shield that give a quality of infinite regression to a narrative. Mieke Bal labels this same phenomenon of story within a story a "mirror text" (Bal 57–58). However, Bal's phrase seems inadequate on two counts. A mirrored image duplicates the original view exactly. Poe's emblems shrink the view, displaying the main narrative's essential elements in condensed form. Secondly, a mirror reflection is static. In Poe's work, a descent into swirling water or plunge from a cliff dramatize an abrupt drop, an enhanced energy that shifts direction, almost literally, of the ongoing story line.

Poe's funnel or dizzying configurations of falling seem a more accurate metaphor of the momentum needed to shift the speeding train of a story. These emblems dramatize consciousness tumbling and whirling into a vision. Arthur Gordon Pym thrills to the force of this terror as he clings to a sheer cliff: "[P]resently I found my imagination growing terribly excited by thoughts of the vast depths yet to be descended, and the precarious nature of the pegs and soapstone holes which were my only support." He tries to stay focused on the climb but is unsuccessful. "The more earnestly I struggled *not to think* [original italics], the more intensely vivid became my conceptions, and the more horribly distinct." Eventually, he surrenders to the imaginative recreation of what could happen: "to picture to ourselves the sickness, and dizziness, and the last struggle and the half swoon, and the final bitterness of the rushing and headlong descent. And now I found these fancies creating their own realities, and all imagined horrors crowding upon me in fact" (*Pym* 875). The force of imagination called upon to bridge the gap between materiality and illusion comes alive in these passages. The self flirts with danger and pending fear to create both an aversion and a welcome plunge toward destruction in "The Imp of the Perverse." Imagination and terror prompt a moment that is almost masochistic. "We stand upon the brink of a precipice. We peer into the abyss — we grow sick and dizzy. Our first impulse is to shrink from the danger. Unaccountably we remain" (282). The appeal of the dangerous stirs a frenzy of attraction and aversion. The rackety slide down a pitched roof that galvanizes the opening sequence of *Vertigo* carries these same connotations.

The well-known narrative of what is perhaps Alfred Hitchcock's finest film has burned a groove in the consciousness of everyone who has ever viewed it. Police detective John Ferguson (James Stewart) nearly plummets to his death while chasing a criminal across the rooftops of San Francisco. A crippling acrophobia, or fear of heights, ensues. In this psychologically damaged state, Ferguson, nicknamed Scottie, resigns from the force. He receives some solace from his woman friend Midge (Barbara Bel Geddes). Gavin Elster (Tom Helmore), an old college friend from the past, contacts him and requests a favor. Will Scottie please conduct unofficial surveillance on Elster's wife Madeleine (Kim Novak)? Her behavior is strange, as she lapses into trances and disappears for hours at a time.

Scottie follows Madeleine along a circuitous route and ultimately saves her from drowning when she jumps into the water under the Golden Gate Bridge. By this time, Scottie realizes that saving Madeleine from her drive toward self-destruction is crucial, since he has fallen in love with her. Scottie's increased vigilance is useless, however, against the woman's rush toward death. She climbs a church tower and falls. Scottie's fear of heights prevents him from saving her, and he blames himself. After a court inquiry that exonerates Scottie, he himself falls into catatonia.

Emerging from an uncertain recovery a year later, Scottie notices a woman on the street who in profile resembles Madeleine. He proceeds to introduce himself to Judy Barton, and the two go out a few times. He then tries to remake her into the image of his lost Madeleine. Once she reluctantly agrees, Scottie has seemingly rolled back the past, and the two lovers are happily reunited. But another piece from the past is that this new woman was actually Elster's mistress. He had engaged Judy to play his wife in an elaborate drama to murder his real wife.

A slip from Judy reveals this information to Scottie. In a rage, he forces Judy/Madeleine up the tower, the scene of Elster's and Judy's original crime. With this second chance, he can restore his balance and resume living. In the film's final moments, Judy/Madeleine falls again to her death, this time in reality. Scottie ventures onto the high ledge, arms extended, the light wind ruffling his tie.

The film's basic plot comes from the novel *D'entre les Morts* (*From Among the Dead*, 1954) by Pierre Boileau and Thomas Narcejac. These two authors had a fascination for detective fiction, and knew well Poe's contributions to the genre. Hitchcock also felt a strong influence from Poe's suspenseful narratives. In "Discovering the Poe/Hitchcock Connection," Dennis R. Perry notes that the director felt a kinship with the author in being drawn to suspense. He was also moved by Poe's dissatisfaction with his art: "the sadness of his life made a great impression on me" (Perry 399).

The brilliance of *Vertigo* has radiated the cinema coming after it. Nearly every strong film in the past thirty years owes a debt to its storytelling techniques. Many *auteurs* have paid homage to its power, from Truffaut and the French New Wave directors to Scorsese, Oliver Stone, Brian de Palma, and Christopher Nolen. In turn, Hitchcock owes a debt to Poe. The architecture of Poe's "The Fall of the House of Usher" casts many shadows across the psychological landscape of Hitchcock's film. The dizzying subjective/objective experiences of "Usher" come alive through Scottie's acrophobia. From the outset, the unsettling tarn that upends Poe's narrator parallels Scottie's near plummet from the rooftop. Both scenes represent the self's fusion with an alternative reality, an abyss of insoluble mystery.

Scottie's "tarn" moment of disequilibrium stirs him to his marrow. His acrophobia traces more than a linear drop. It's a fall shaped by a headlong descent into a vortex, a swirling downward rush, accompanied by the self's perception of flying away from a center.

Hitchcock visually recreates this rush of feeling through story and camera technique. He says, "I thought about the problem for fifteen years. By the time we got to *Vertigo*, we solved it by using the dolly and zoom simultaneously" (Truffaut 187). Deborah Linderman describes Hitchcock's technique as "a POV shot articulated by a simultaneous forward zoom and track out that together convey the effect of everything rushing out from center" (Linderman 54–55). The shots simulate the state of being pulled toward and away at the same time or an attraction/aversion conflict. This dynamic *mise en abîme* image recreates the tightly knotted, paradoxical perception that the narrator of Usher calls "a mystery all insoluble."

When Scottie almost falls, an authority figure offers assistance ("Give me your hand"), but the helper turns into victim. Scottie watches stunned as the cop plummets to his death. Karen Hollinger frames the intensity of this scene as an Oedipal trauma, because Scottie witnesses the "death of the Father (the policeman in uniform as representative of authority)" (Hollinger 20–

21). The Freudian explanation partially explains the power of this scene, but the experience is traumatic enough in itself. Robin Wood describes Scottie's situation: "to live he must hold on desperately to the gutter, his arms and body agonizingly stretched, his fingers strained, his mind gripped by unendurable tension; to die, he has only to let go" (110). In addition, the fall of the policeman is virtually Scottie's own, as he perceives that his career is destroyed along with his life's ambitions up to that point. He fails as a lawyer before he even tries.

Poe's influence on Hitchcock's storytelling has received the most extensive discussion from Dennis R. Perry's insightful *Hitchcock and Poe* (2003). Perry writes, "'Usher' and *Vertigo* bear a singular resemblance, almost as distorted doubles of each other" (176). Further, he notes that each work echoes the "reduplicative structure of dreams" (178). While this juxtaposition is useful, Perry's analysis lasts only a few pages, and he drops the "Usher" connection to wander into ties between the film and "Ligeia." The concept of the telltale art highlights grounds for an extensive comparison between "Usher" and *Vertigo*. Poe and Hitchcock connect through their studies of the power and limits of the imagination in constructing and responding to a story.

Parfit's fusion principle of the self provides a lens to focus on these similarities. Just as the narrator of "Usher" is drawn into Roderick Usher's theatricals, so Scottie is the willing audience for the story that Elster and Judy have concocted. He fuses into Madeleine's story, suffers along with her, and then tries to recreate it. Only when he learns the truth behind the story does he emerge from its spell, as the narrative dissipates in the couple's final ascent up the tower. In "Obsessed with *Vertigo*," Lawrence Shaffer comments that Judy's "death finally brings the film to its knees. The loss of her ordinary reality is even more disastrous than that of Madeleine's ideality" (395). I empathize with Shaffer's reaction here. However, if we move away from emotion, a focus on the film's narrative structure refutes this opinion. Given the film's central valorization of an imaginative fusion through story, it almost does not matter that Judy/Madeleine falls. Madeleine's story has vanished since it never existed. Judy's demise is relevant only to those viewers and obsessed critics who might have hoped for a happy ending in the story of Scottie and Judy. Meanwhile, in the context of a fused storyline, the connection between tale and teller continues with film and viewer happily reunited.

A critical perspective of fusion encourages a unified construction of the film's many embedded stories. The entire film-viewing process is part of Hitchcock's storytelling. In "'The Look,' Narrativity, and the Female Spectator in *Vertigo*," Hollinger expands on critic Laura Mulvey's definition of film analysis in terms of visual elements. Mulvey's "place of the look" is but "one element in a larger narrative and visual whole that represents the rich and variegated experience that is film" (27). Hollinger suggests that the gaze from the viewing audience on the other side of the camera needs more emphasis in the film's critical appraisal. "*Vertigo* places its spectators, both male and female, in a visual position of submission to its creation of the fantasy of Scottie and Madeline/Judy's Oedipal transformations ... and creates fluid, multiple, and mobile spectatorial positioning" (Hollinger 27). Hitchcock's film works its cinematic power on the audience through the same fusion of imagination and romance that engages Scottie.

After the characters' initial upheavals in "Usher" and *Vertigo*, the story process attempts to heal the rift. Inside the Usher mansion, the narrator wanders, still profoundly unsettled. "On one of the staircases, I met the physician of the family. His countenance, I thought, wore a mingled expression of low cunning and perplexity. He accosted me with trepidation and passed on" (Poe 233). The unsettling quality to this stock Gothic character, already "on the scene," seems akin in many ways to that of Scottie's Midge.

Many viewers find the grounded, commonsensical Midge a comforting presence for Scottie. Initially, she is. However, Hitchcock's camera captures many of her subtleties, through "mingled expressions" of unreadable looks and shifty glances. She is not entirely on the up-and-up. While the Usher family's doctor is a more obviously negative force, Midge later brings Scottie into the presence of such a force when he is in the sanitarium. In *Hitchcock's Films Revisited*, Robin Wood notes that Midge was not even in the original novel by Boileau and Narcejac (109). Her character is inserted into the Taylor and Coppel screenplay, and Hitchcock's influence is apparent. The development of Midge's sturdy feminine presence carries the damaged Scottie through the film's exposition until the more stunning Madeleine arrives. As women, Midge juxtaposed with Madeleine presents a study in stark contrasts.

Fusion, rather the failure to fuse, characterizes Scottie's relationship with Midge. Midge's story is one that Scottie is not willing to listen to. Even though Midge is an artist, she makes a poor fit as creator for a narrative to stir Scottie. Midge is, in a sense, an updated Laura Hunt.

Like Laura (and her creator Caspary), Midge works for an ad agency. Midge and Scottie went to school together, have known each other for years, and were briefly engaged until she broke it off. He claims to be too available to her, but the resistance is his. Scottie already knows her story, and he has passed it by.

The view of the Golden Gate visible through the window of Midge's apartment encapsulates the film's initial scene of Scottie hanging from the gutter. Christopher D. Morris considers a "hanging figure" as emblematic of the suspenseful dynamic driving most of Hitchcock's films. Certainly, Scottie is figuratively in that same precarious situation through the entire narrative.

His life has been upended. He leaves his career as a police detective, and he is "on the bum," wandering about, searching for a fusion of self with another. This fusion is to be expressed not just sexually but imaginatively. He tells Midge, "I look up, I look down, I look up, I look down." He is hanging, not moving forward, but he worries that even dropping a pencil could cause him to lose his grip.

So Scottie resigns from the force because he feels that his acrophobia compromises his ability to do the job. His reasoning for throwing in the towel so soon seems hard to fathom. Logically considered, the circumstances triggering his trauma are a one-time event. How many more times in his investigating career would he ever be forced to chase a thief across rooftops? Still, like Adrian Monk, the obsessive-compulsive detective, Scottie's trauma at the film's outset drastically changes the story he had planned for himself. He is therefore vulnerable to receiving the tales of others.

After Scotty's initial fall, Midge suggests a number of remedies for him. He could run away. Scottie scoffs, claiming that he has no plans to "crack up." He is correct. A split self in the fission sense does not happen to him. Instead, his personality becomes distended when he attempts to fuse his personality as a listener into Madeleine's story.

Another remedy Midge proposes is that Scottie try to rise above his acrophobia. She provides him with the step stool that helps toward a resolution of the vertigo. He is grateful for her contribution, but he falters on her "three-step solution." Again, Midge's narrative is abortive.

With its three steps, the stool presents a metaphor for the three-part structure of the film's narrative arc, as critics have noted (Linderman 53). The first step marks his connection with Madeleine and the ostensible story of her haunted past. The second is his discovery of Judy. The last step is the highest, marking his attempt to resolve the two, which is where he fails, ending up cradled in Midge's arms.

European censors pressured Hitchcock to shoot a final reconciliation scene for the film's foreign distribution. This coda shows Midge alone in her apartment listening to radio reports on the location of the film's villain. Elster had escaped to Switzerland and was now "somewhere in the south of France." According to the report, authorities expected Elster to be extradited "once he is found." The door opens and Scottie enters Midge's apartment without a word. She pours him a drink, and the two stand without speaking.

That conclusion definitively puts a wrong stamp on the film. The main thrust of Hitchcock's story is an individual's discovery of previously unknown aspects of the psyche in dealing with loss. By film's end, Scottie may or may not have successfully climbed onto the third step of the stool and transcended his trauma. Still, if he merges with Midge's fused identity of "Mother," he ends up in the same place he has always been. That ending negates most of the rest of the film and was never part of an official American screening.

Although Midge has worked her way up in a man's world, she is totally unsuccessful as a "story" to rouse Scottie's starved imagination. Her employment with an ad agency suggests her compromised position as an artist. Midge recognizes the futility of herself either as a creator or subject of a "story" that Scottie would join. She berates herself after she paints her parody portrait, putting her head on Carlotta's body. When Scottie shakes his head, refuses to join in on the joke, and quietly leaves, she is hard on herself. The script reads as follows: "'Oh! Marjorie Wood!! You fool!!' ... And she picks up a brush and with three vicious daubs paints a moustache and a beard on her image. Then she throws the brush out the window" (Coppel and Taylor). In the end, Midge masculinizes the painting. She cannot summon up the idealized artistry that Scottie sees in Madeleine's absorption of "Portrait of Carlotta."

Midge's realistic "mothering" is why Scottie resists her in the first place. When she goes to visit him in the sanitorium, she delivers a line that falls like the proverbial lead balloon. "Johnny, try! You're not lost. Mother's here." Midge is the un-idealized story, lacking the substance and color to satisfy Scottie's impoverished imagination.

Madeleine's beauty is luminous, but Scottie is additionally drawn by virtue of her story. She would be nothing without it. The tale of Madeleine taken over by Carlotta and pulled toward the grave in a sense parallels Scottie's own fascinations with falling and losing oneself in the tarn.

Both "Usher" and *Vertigo* includes numerous "stories within the story." These represent the *mise en abîmes* that disrupt the central protagonist's sense of self. The flat surface of the central narrative is pockmarked with dangerous narrative pits. Initially, each character tries to resist giving in. However, before long, each man feels the pressure for fusion and falls into the story.

An ambiguous summons filled with questions and uncertainties draws both the narrator of "Usher" and Scottie to the case. The narrator vaguely remembers Roderick Usher: "A boon companion in boyhood; but many years had elapsed since our last meeting.... Although, as boys, we had been even intimate associates, yet I really knew little of my friend" (Poe 232). Roderick has changed so much since then that the narrator "doubted to whom I spoke" (234). In *Vertigo*, Scottie comes onto the mystery when Gavin Elster first contacts him. Scottie asks Midge if she remembers Gavin from their college days, and she is no help, either. Given the depth of falsity in Elster's other stories, we have to wonder if he had ever actually known Scottie at all.

At this point, Scottie is so vulnerable to the powers of storytelling that Elster's tale merely lays down crumbs for Scottie to pick up, Madeleine herself being one of them. For both the narrator of "Usher" and Scottie, their visions of a beautiful woman take on more urgency once they learn the woman is ill and in need of rescuing. Madeline Usher has a wasting disease. "A settled apathy, a gradual wasting away of the person, and frequent although transient affections of a partially cataleptical character were the unusual diagnosis" (236). Elster tells Scottie about his wife's times away, that she goes into these staring fits. "I'm not making it up. I wouldn't know how." However, clearly he does know how.

Aside from the name similarity, the Madeline/Madeleine figures share many of the same developments. Initially Madeline Usher is ethereal. "While he spoke, the lady Madeline (for so was she called), passed through a remote portion of the apartment, and without having noticed my presence, disappeared" (Poe 236). The narrator begins to fall into a state of being immersed: "I regarded her with an utter astonishment not unmingled with dread; and yet I found it impossible to account for such feelings. A sensation of stupor oppressed me as my eyes followed her retreating steps" (236). Madeline Usher flits across the scene in the same way that Madeleine Elster passes Scottie at Ernie's. The script calls for this action: "Her eyes come to rest on Scottie for a moment, then move an [sic] with the small smile."

Scottie follows Elster's wife through many disembodied, asymmetrical spaces. On the first day of surveillance, Scottie sits in his car reading the newspaper, waiting for his "mark" to appear. The camera swings upward to simulate Scottie's glance at the tower, Madeleine's ostensible residence. Eventually she descends from what Scottie may imagine as the elegant high-rise apartment and starts her car. Scottie follows her first to Podesta's department store. His view of her through a crack in the door is filled with light, color, and flowers, extremely romanticized. At the Mission Dolores, Madeleine disappears into the chapel, but her figure escapes to the side. She is never centered or framed by the shrine. Outside, she stands over the grave, separate from death, clearly in the sunlit path.

According to Dennis Perry, the compulsion driving Scottie to chase Madeleine is a "return to the womb" (179–180). Perry asserts that this primal connection emerges as Scottie moves from light to dark. However, the film's images do not support Perry's thesis. Throughout the chase, Madeleine is lit, and Scottie is the one standing in shadows. The camera's view to simulate Scottie's perspective emphasizes that Madeleine is framed by lit spaces too large for her. She only half inhabits these spaces, at the flower shop and in the chapel. Similarly, in the gallery, she sits alone in the large room contemplating Carlotta's portrait. Scottie watches with a partial view from behind the door frame to the gallery.

At the McKittrick Hotel, Scottie discovers that "Carlotta Valdez" has never slept there; she just sits. Playing detective from the street below, he sees

Madeleine framed by the window, but then according to the inn clerk, she is not in the room. An emptiness surrounds Madeleine. Scottie's attempts to figure out these spaces hardly represent a "return to the womb." Instead, Madeleine's story leaves many spaces for him to join in. Scottie's POV from a darkened vantage point fuses with the camera's so that his perspective is the same as that of the film viewing audience, also sitting in the dark watching a lit space too large for the people it encloses. Hitchcock's camera technique to cement Scottie and viewer could partially explain the film's intensity and people's near-fanatical obsessions with it.

With Madeline Usher in the background as a ghostly presence, Roderick and the narrator pass the time with music, poetry, and art that play off this intangibility. The seventh stanza of Usher's poem "The Haunted Palace" sets an eerie figure of spectral shapes dimly perceived: "Through the red-litten windows see/Vast forms that move fantastically/To a discordant melody." Usher reacts excitedly to the poem, and the narrator cannot grasp the reasons: "I lack words to express the full extent, or the earnest *abandon* of his persuasion" (Poe 239). Patricia Merivale attributes this same elusiveness to the object of a pursuit in Poe's sketch "The Man of the Crowd." The narrator looks for "a person sought for, glimpsed, and shadowed, gumshoe style, through endless, labyrinthine city streets, but never really Found — because he was never really There, because he was, and remains, missing" (Merivale and Sweeney 105). This futile search aptly describes Scottie's journey as he tails Madeleine Elster through the San Francisco alleys and one-way streets.

As in "Usher," every time Scottie and the film viewer glimpse Madeleine Elster, she becomes more disembodied. She fails to fill each of the framing spaces completely. Madeleine never fully inhabits any space until she worms her way into Scottie's subjective consciousness, when she jumps into the bay from a supposed suicide attempt. Her deadly fall occurs in a liminal space, under the bridge, between reality and illusion.

At this point, Scottie takes the plunge into her narrative. She gains even more definition when she enters his space, his apartment. She is in his place, his bed, before his fireplace, drinking his coffee. The next morning, she comes again to his place as he follows her directly to his own apartment door. As she draws closer, her story grabs hold of him more tightly, and he internalizes her distress. He takes another step toward fusion.

While spending time with Roderick, the narrator emphasizes the "stupor," "sulphureous lustre [sic]" and phantasmagoric miasma affecting his senses (236–238). Listening to poetry such as "The Haunted Palace" adds to the "wild fantasias" disrupting his reason. He concurs with Roderick about the "sentience of all vegetable things" (239). *Vertigo* presents a landscape glowing with this same fog.

When Scottie and Madeleine journey to the redwoods, colors grow hazy. He worries that she might disappear. A vaporous effect encloses Madeleine, there among "the *sempervirens*, the oldest living things." Following her role, Madeleine defines herself in the sequoia's chunk of wood. She says, "There I lived and there I died," encased in the wood as firmly as she is encased in Madeleine Elster's suits and severe coiffure. When the two embrace and kiss on the shore, the fusion is complete, in both body and imagination. She is finally wrapped by Scottie. He promises to stay with her forever. Ironically, she is the one who leaves, but the power of her story remains with him for much longer.

For both works, various types of art form a series of *mise en abîme* disrupting the story's linear surface. In "Usher," the narrator and Roderick hold their own private arts festival, with poetry, music, and narrative. The narrator falls into it, swooning as Roderick moves him away from a sense of reality. "We painted and read together, or I listened, as if in a dream, to the wild improvisations of his speaking guitar" (236). Gradually Usher draws the narrator into "the recesses of his spirit" (236). The narrator and Roderick peruse the Usher library. Many dusty volumes are of arcane topics, "in strict keeping with this character of phantasm ... the manual of a forgotten church" (239–240).

Similarly, Elster tells Scottie the richly embroidered story of Madeleine and Carlotta as proof that "someone dead" has a hold on Madeleine. The fine arts are also part of Elster's narrative, as Madeleine leads Scottie to the museum and portrait of Carlotta. Books also augment the history. When Scottie wants to know the "small stuff" of local history, arcana from the past, Scottie and Midge head to Pop Liebl's used bookstore Argosy at her suggestion. The lights dim, and Pop Liebl regales them with the information Scottie yearns to know to create his own story. They stand among the old volumes as the shop owner recites from memory the tale of the betrayed woman, "walking through the streets asking where is my child? The sad Carlotta, the mad Carlotta." The scene connects with Scottie's previous experience with Madeleine among the redwoods. The story gains sentience through the bookstore's dusty, atmospheric effects. The name "Pop Liebl" suggests a cross between "evil" and "Liebe," the German word for "love." Pop is a fatherly raconteur, an expert, not chosen by Elster, but by Midge, that touchstone of commonsense and practicality, except for this slip-up. When Scottie presents the Carlotta story to Elster, the man plays up his role as protective husband. He alleges that Madeleine knows nothing about this disturbing story of her past. Scottie, therefore, now possesses the power of the word over Madeleine, as he tries to heal her. From this point on, Madeleine rushes to the tower to destroy her own image.

In "Usher," Roderick reports on Madeline's demise and conveys another startling development: "When one evening, having informed me abruptly that the lady Madeline was no more, he stated his intention of preserving her corpse for a fortnight (previously to its final interment) in one of the numerous vaults within the main walls of the building" (240). This need to preserve the dead without burial literalizes what Scottie does psychologically after he loses the story of Madeleine.

Roderick and the narrator view the dead Madeline together. Usher's sister shows up with a faint smile. Like the iconic Mona Lisa, she shows "the mockery of a faint blush upon the bosom and the face, and that suspiciously lingering smile upon the lip which is so terrible in death" (241). Poe's Madeline is like Hitchcock's portrait of Carlotta. After the trial, Elster approaches Scottie and Elster continues to draw Scottie in with his own false story of who killed Madeleine. Then in Scottie's nightmares, he and Elster stand before the window, with Carlotta from the past fused with Madeleine. Scottie's mind has accepted Elster's story as his own. The fusion is complete. Scott Ferguson, the previously reliable everyday Joe, has become Elster, a broken man who will let nothing stop him to get what he wants.

Poe describes the narrator's terrors as Madeline Usher rests in the vault under his own room.

> Sleep came not near my couch — while the hours waned and waned away. I struggled to reason off the nervousness which had dominion over me ... my efforts were fruitless. An irrepressible tremor gradually pervaded my frame: and at length, there sat upon my very heart an incubus of utterly causeless alarm. Shaking this off with a gasp and a struggle, I uplifted myself upon the pillows ... overpowered by an intense sentiment of horror, unaccountable and unendurable [241].

This striking passage closely applies to Scottie's hysterical nightmares after he loses Madeleine the first time. He tosses and turns to escape the crushing nightmares and hallucinations. He rises from his pillow in terror, but he cannot wake from the disoriented state. The resting place of Carlotta/Madeleine is below him, and the sequence ends with his plummet into it.

After Madeleine's story ends, the double who remains is the slattern, the easy woman. Judy is Diane Redfern, the essence of unbridled fertility. Nothing about Judy suggests enclosure. She has curves, as opposed to the closed-in manly suits that Madeleine Elster had worn. She wears too much eye makeup and her hair down. She is blowsy, wearing purple and green dresses, and low-cut blouses. When Scottie tells her that she reminds him of someone, she appears to take his comment in stride. "I've heard that before," she tells him, "and to be honest, I've been picked up before." Then when he asks her out to dinner, she is suspicious, expecting to pay for her dinner in ways she undoubtedly has in the past.

Originally from Salinas, Kansas, Judy is the naive, corn-fed girl who has arrived in the big city of San Francisco to make her way. She is trapped as a shop girl working at I. Magnin's. Forced to rely on looks as her only resource, she soon falls afoul of powerful men, her dreams ruined. Her only route for being upwardly mobile is to latch onto a man with money, like Gavin Elster or even Scottie.

In the audience's accepted perception of the fifties, men were trying to reassert themselves, to find the positions of authority they had abandoned to fight and run the war. They worked to reassume the reins of power in postwar 20th century, not just as individuals, or on the level of a power struggle between the sexes, but on the level of media. The film industry of the 1940s and 1950s was fending off a drubbing from other entertainments, especially television. The resurrections of iconic women Laura Hunt and Madeleine Elster on the large screen represent a masculine resumption of freedom and power, a challenge to the small screen newly centered in America's living rooms.

Unlike the aspiring Laura Hunt, who maintains poise and social mobility, Madeleine Elster/Judy Barton is stuck in her appointed social class. As Elster's wife, she has no dimension outside Elster's definition of her. Compared to her former role as Madeleine Elster, Judy Barton has simple tastes. When Scottie selects a corsage to buy for her, she points out a simpler preference, but his choice prevails. She has no power to resist what Scottie wants for her. As Judy, she is ill at ease when Scottie takes her out in the park or on the dance floor. Apart from the Madeleine persona, she is clearly out of her element and has few ways of coping. Although distressed over Scottie's plans to re-make her into the image of a dead woman, a woman Judy helped to murder, she agrees, she says later, because she loved him.

The process during which Madeline/Madeleine comes to life follows the same trajectory in both narratives. During a horrific storm surrounding the Usher mansion, the narrator tells Roderick the story of Ethelred to distract him. He detects the slight scratching below that indicates Madeline's movements. The scratching grows louder. Scottie essentially hears the same scratching when he snaps the link on Carlotta's necklace.

Usher announces his awareness of guilt. "Is she not hurrying to upbraid me for my haste? ... *Madman! I tell you that she now stands without the door!*" (245). Elster had likewise buried his wife alive in a story, but no one rushes to upbraid him.

Just as the bloody form of Madeline Usher presses at the door, the ghost of Madeleine Elster emerges from the tomb. The Usher narrator had recited the Ethelred tale, and Scottie retells Madeleine/Judy her sordid history as they ascend the tower stairs the last time. His narrative moves from a coarse motive to another. He tells a tale of the creation of Elster and the reality of Judy in all her imperfections. "You were his girl, huh? He trained you ... remade you the way I remade you." The idealized stories juxtapose against these *mise en abîme* narratives relayed by both the narrator and Scottie. Degraded and patched together, the shoddy imitative stories predict total collapse. Illusion of ideality breaks down in the glaring light of struggle, guilt, and blood on the robes. Scottie tells Madeleine/Judy, "I loved you so." His fervent passion for creation is in past tense. The tales are not the valorization of art but a testimony to the wounding power of life.

Madeline Usher falls "heavily inward upon the person of her brother" (245), while Madeleine/Judy plummets to her death on the roof below. The script reads that from Judy's point of view, "The black figure moves forward, seems to merge with the shadow and become part of them."

In the aftermath of Madeline Usher's re-emergence from the crypt, the "Usher" narrator flees: "From that chamber and from that mansion I fled aghast" (245). After Madeleine/Judy's fall, Scottie stands atop the tower ledge with an unreadable pose. He either faces the heights with transcendence or is perched on the edge of an abyss. "The shaky structure of the house now collapses into the polluted tarn."

Donald Spoto marks loss as this film's primary theme (280), and among the many losses that Scottie incurs is that of story. A comparison between Poe's tale of the fallen Ushers and Hitchcock's revelation of imagination ruined sheds light on the high cost of disillusion over the self's ability to tell itself a tale. The house ends up in the tarn, and no other observer will find a story in its muddy reflections.

Remember that final alternative ending in which Scottie ends up with Midge? After she clicks off the radio announcement, no other word is uttered by a human voice. Scottie steps in and onscreen action takes place in silence. The word is degraded and disappears altogether. While the sequence is wrong in so many ways, this coda caps off the film as an entire work freighted with loss beyond what language can express. Given the many emotional upheavals and dramatic reversals recreated through word and image in these two narratives, that loss is indeed profound.

CHAPTER 6

Masks of Time

Poe's bloody fingerprints mark many walls of today's entertainment, especially in the thriving subgenre featuring gruesome horrors of bodily decay. A prime exemplar of this narrative is "The Masque of the Red Death" (1842). The story begins like an Ebola virus, with blood oozing from human pores:

> The "Red Death" had long devastated the country. No pestilence had ever been so fatal, or so hideous. Blood was its Avatar and its seal — the redness and the horror of blood. There were sharp pains, and sudden dizziness, and then profuse bleeding at the pores, with dissolution [Poe 269].

Literary gore hardly started with Poe. The Bible, classical Greek and Roman literature, and Shakespeare make up whole libraries of blood-stained pages. Blood as a literary metaphor traditionally carries messages of disbelief or guilt over a completed violent act. Poe's fiction is different in that blood in the text carries a time element. It conveys uncertainty over when and where death will happen. The protagonist quivers from the suspense of this pending destruction. D. H. Lawrence calls this quality in Poe a "disintegrative vibration," part of the author's "vampirism."

Lawrence faults Poe for this dance of love and death that is missing the redemptive "love" partner. However, America's entertainment culture, with its myriad displaced metaphors of sex and violence, has thoroughly embraced Poe's take on the formula. In translating blood to the screen, contemporary storytellers mute suspenseful vibrations and amp up the disintegration.

Today, Poe-charged narratives gush bodily fluids through high-def images in films, TV shows, and video games. These entertainments have broad appeal to diverse audiences, although for different reasons. Large screens awash with plasma earn high ratings. As the emblematic "The Masque of the Red Death" makes its transition into the 21st century, the narrative tells a sad story: our culture cannot accept the fact of passing time. Instead, the message that the human body deteriorates comes through an ironic mode.

The "gruesome horror" subgenre has several characteristics. Bodily fluids and a strong "goo" factor stir a pleasurable visceral revulsion in audience. Images of the decaying human form place the reality of death in objective monsters outside the self. In variations of this subgenre, pathology is morality. The deterioration of the body often equals moral disintegration. Audiences view and accept that the patient falls ill because he is doing something wrong. The central conflict of this narrative is between the psyche and physicality. The narrative's embedded mystery involves human incomprehension of workings of the human body.

Science fiction is on the same plane as grotesque horror. The forms differ primarily in how the central character uses empirical ways to fathom these changing biological processes. For instance, Mary Shelley's *Frankenstein* (1818) incorporates elements of both science fiction and horror. It begins on the empirical end of the spectrum. While the novel's opening chapters have no shortage of graphic charnel house references, its central consciousness is a doctor, a man of science. Victor Frankenstein ostensibly lines up his well-reasoned knowledge to spark life into his ghastly creation. The novel ends with gruesome horror, as the monster is an oversized homunculus which most observers view with revulsion. The actual horror, however, is that the creature of stitched together flesh and bone ends up acting too human. It is the mirror image of us.

In *The Philosophy of Horror*, Noel Carroll analyzes what constitutes a monster: "The objects of art-horror are essentially threatening and impure" (42). The monster may be impure in form, with combined human and animal parts, or in place of origin, as in a being from another planet.

Threat comes from unusual size or number. A threatening monster has to be huge, like Godzilla, or the screen has to be swarming with them, as in *Arachnophobia* or *Snakes on a Plane*. The monster does not have to be large to evoke shudders and revulsion. Horror can also propel a narrative toward revealing a tiny inside monster that comes out. Over thirty years ago, audiences were stunned by the sudden emergence of internal monsters, like the satanic vomit in *The Exorcist* (1973) or the infant-sized fetus creature that pops out of John Hurt's chest in *Alien* (1979).

"Slasher" films, such as *The Texas Chainsaw Massacre* (1974) or those directed by Wes Craven, like *Nightmare on Elm Street* (1984) featuring Freddy Krueger, appeal to a youth demographic. A huge shudder factor is a major reason that teens enjoy these films. In dark theaters, the spectacle of people enacting horrific violence onto each other causes young couples to hug and hang on tight to their dates. The films objectify violence, and keep it out in front of the viewers, sometimes with an "in your face" proximity. Still, the process is itself a safety valve. To be scared in the movies allows the teen viewers to ignore the actual terrors of growing up.

A key element to Poe's horror is the suspense that holds it together, but what is suspense? Is it like pornography, in that we know it when we see it? Or can we analyze it objectively?

Theories about narrative suspense fall into several basic categories: reader or viewer identification with the character being threatened and a question demanding an answer, that is, an unfinished narrative pattern. Christopher D. Morris summarizes the conventional wisdom about suspense as being "an emotion resembling anxiety induced in a reader or viewer through the experience of a narrative work of art (one that unfolds a story in time) concerning what will happen next, particularly to admired protagonists" (3). This theory exemplifies the behavioral model of stimulus and response. When a reader or viewer identifies with the onscreen character, the text or film stimulates the reader/viewer toward a reaction. The connection sounds logical, but does it leave any gaps?

To examine the character-identification theory, consider the situation of a rock-climber dangling from a cliff. Does suspense come from the fact that we put ourselves in his place and feel that we, too, are on the verge of falling? The empathy connection here is tenuous, experienced on the surface only, if at all. How can we become one with that rock climber? We know nothing about him. He could be strong enough to pull himself up and avoid plunging to his death.

The character identification theory has another shortcoming obvious in this scene: A girl drives her car at night with a lunatic in the back seat wielding a meat cleaver. The audience has knowledge that she lacks. Here we as the viewers know nothing about the girl except her vulnerability. Our empathy is less with her and more with her situation. Can an audience's identification with a character fully explain the power of suspense in these situations of the cliff-hanger or lunatic in the back seat? Aren't the circumstances of the situation the key suspenseful elements?

Another drawback to the character identification criterion is what has been called the Suspense Paradox. A repeat experience of a book or film should hold no suspense, since the reader or viewer already knows what will happen. Still, people want to undergo the experience anyway. For instance, a movie buff might see *Vertigo* at least a hundred times, and each time he has to resist urging Judy to back away from the edge of the tower in the closing scene. So, character identification cannot be the sole reason for the effect of suspense on a viewer. In *The Hanging Figure*, Christopher D. Morris explains:

> Behavioral and cognitive psychologists, perhaps influenced by Aristotelian categories of mimesis, tend to understand suspense as initiated and terminated ... in the events of the discourse structure; their work pays less attention to suspense that accompanies the political and philosophical questions raised by literary or cinematic texts [21].

Clearly, the model requires re-configuration.

A second theory of suspense is that the narrative sets up a structural pattern moving toward resolution. Suspense, then, is the difference between something happening and not happening, the tension between knowing and not knowing. Donald Beecher identifies this element with suspense embedded in the text as "patterns craving completion, problem-solving situations, and much else that places the mind in a state of epistemic quest" (257).

The key obstacle to that knowledge is time. As Emma Kafalenos mentions, suspense stems from the "temporary gaps [in knowledge] that arouse desire during the process of reading" (56). Add to that the concept of a reader's anticipated assurance for the well-being of a character and we have a more complete definition.

A text has its own properties of suspense created by the clock set ticking in the fictional world and the writer's manipulation of this time. This model of the character enmeshed in the gears of events is a better representation of how suspense works.

Poe fully grasped the differential between a reader's perception of time lived and time in a text. He shaped it to great advantage. In "The Murders in the Rue Morgue," Dupin and the narrator live an inverse time. The two shutter the windows by day and cruise the streets at night. In "The Tell-Tale Heart," the narrator tries to control time, slowing it down — taking forever to put his head into the old man's room. "Oh you would have laughed to see how cunningly I thrust it in! I moved it slowly — very, very slowly" (303). As he prepares to murder the old man, time speeds up: "the hellish tattoo of his heart increased. It grows quicker and quicker and louder and louder every instant" (305). Once the narrator kills the old man and the police make their visit, time resumes its control. The guilty narrator detects "a low, dull, quick sound — much such a sound as a watch makes when enveloped in cotton" (306).

In "Philosophy of Composition," Poe measures the effectiveness of short fiction by emphasizing that a text should only be long enough to be read in "one sitting." Clearly, Poe thought that the fictional universe should have its own time, moving according to the story's own design. Design in this case does not mean a visual or spatial pattern but rather a temporal pattern associated with the rhythm of events, plot, and causality.

"The Masque of the Red Death" is neither a detective story nor a tale of a character's loss of inner control. Most critics see this story through a biographical lens. Benjamin Fisher writes that during Poe's life, "epidemic illness was not unfamiliar in American cities" (22). Fisher makes the case that Poe exploits the situation to sharpen the story's edge of paranoia.

More poignantly, Poe knew the symptoms of tuberculosis firsthand, his mother and stepmother having died of it. January 1842 marked the beginning of the consumption that took the life of his wife, Virginia Clemm. She was singing at the piano, and a blood vessel broke in her throat. Shortly after that, she was diagnosed with tuberculosis. Five months later, Poe published the tale of Prince Prospero in *Graham's* in May 1842.

The sporadic progression of Virginia's illness finds a parallel in the approaching figure of the Red Death. As Poe later wrote to his friend George Eveleth, the uncertainties of her slow decline brought him to the brink of insanity:

> I took leave of her forever and underwent all the agonies of her death. She recovered partially and I again hoped.... The vessel broke again. I went through precisely the same scene — then again — again — and even once again at varying intervals.... It was the horrible never-ending oscillation between hope & despair which I could *not* longer have endured without the total loss of reason ["The Letters of E.A. Poe," 4 January 1848].

Virginia died in 1847.

"The Masque of the Red Death" progresses according to several distinct time rhythms showing similar swings between hope and despair. From the start, the plague works a quick destruction on the countryside: "the whole seizure, progress, and termination of the disease, were the incidents of half an hour" (Poe 269). To escape the plague that spreads, well, like the plague, Prince Prospero flees to his country chateau, taking with him a thousand members of the aristocracy ruling an unnamed country. The nobles are safe.

The revelers break from the profane, mortal time of the broader human community to gather with Prospero. By removing natural light, they set themselves apart from rhythms of seasons and communal social rituals. They seal themselves in. Just as Prince Prospero creates a perpetual hermetic existence, Poe creates a fictional time internal to this text.

In the text, time comes to such a standstill that the march of time shows up in the palace architecture. Poe goes to great lengths to describe each successive room as a partially obscured space. The reader's perspective comes into focus as sequential moments, a strip tease of gradual revelations of color and dim light. As one proceeds along the hall, each room is only partially revealed. Each chamber is lit by flickering braziers in the adjacent corridor, creating an uncertain perspective. During this time, no grief or thought can enter. The march of time eases, as the secluded nobles entertain themselves for "five or six months" (269). Then Prospero dreams up the masked ball that allows entry to their destruction.

The monstrous ebony clock in the last, sable chamber plays a central role. Martin Roth's discussion on this story's "inside and outside" dimensions fixes the clock as the "heart of the abbey," noting that Poe's "The Tell-Tale Heart" makes the same equation of time and basic rhythms of human life (Roth 50). When the clock chimes on the hour, the "giddiest grew pale, and the more aged and sedate passed their hands over their brows" (270). The clock's voice silences the musicians, and the revels stop; "dreams are stiff-frozen as they stand" (271). Death approaches.

The word "Masque" is perfect for the story's title. It serves as both a pun on "mask," meaning to hide an identity and the "masque" as dance, for which time is also especially crucial. As a dance, "masque" alludes to the stately rhythm followed by the revelers, as well as the two-figure dance/confrontation of the Prince and the Stranger who shows up in a blood-spattered costume.

The costume is a reminder of mortality. Outraged by this affront, the Prince draws his dagger and chases the stranger through the seven dimly lit, different colored rooms in the palace. The pursuit is on, although at two different time schemes. The masked intruder moves with a "deliberate and stately step" (Poe 273) and walks "uninterruptedly," while the Prince "rushe[s] hurriedly" and "in rapid impetuosity" (273). He lives in a frantic flurry of moments.

Eventually, the Prince catches the intruder. It happens in the seventh chamber, "closely shrouded in black velvet tapestries ... [where the] window panes were scarlet — a deep blood color" (270). The two dancers face each other. "There was a sharp cry — and the dagger dropped gleaming upon the sable carpet" (273), and the Prince collapses and dies. Time ends. As with his namesake from "The Tempest," Prospero's magic slips through his fingers like hourglass sand. He had held the revelers, as well as the reader, in his spell. With the main character's death, the reader experiences the *frisson* of seeing reality in death's vacant face.

Prospero is the first to fall, with his retinue following him into death as they did in life. In a fit of panic, the revelers cross the previously forbidden border into the ultimate red and black room. They seize the disguised intruder, or try to, as they "gasped in inutterable horror at finding the grave-cerements and corpse-like mask which they handled with so violent a rudeness, untenanted by any tangible form" (273). They die in contorted positions, with pools of their blood spattering the hallways. At this point, the blood spurts again call to mind hourglass sand, marking time until the hourglass is empty.

The narrative template of "The Masque of the Red Death" appears on television under many masks, most pronouncedly on the popular show *House*. For each episode, the patient of the day manifests some bizarre or horrible condition, graphically bleeding or vomiting onscreen. This person essentially shows up as a blood-costumed stranger, like Red Death itself.

Prince Prospero has his analogue in Dr. Gregory House, played by the British actor Hugh Laurie. House is a brilliant diagnostician who ultimately solves the case of the puzzling disease. However, before that happens, he creates trouble for everyone at Princeton-Plainsboro Teaching Hospital. He tricks patients' relatives into signing forms. He walks in on doctors interviewing patients. He performs unnecessary surgeries. Like Prospero, he is secure in his arrogance. Comparisons between Prince Prospero and House abound. Like the Prince, House leads a group of surgeons, medical aristocrats, who mostly entertain themselves, except when the clock of mortality chimes with groans from their question-mark patient. In Poe's story, the Prince's palace reflects a time frozen in the architecture. On *House*, temporality is likewise altered, due to the artifice of shifts, with medical caregivers working around the clock in fluorescent lights of operating rooms. Like the sealed-in revelers of "Masque," House and his team of medical specialists retreat from mortality by being in the middle of it.

Prospero dies. Similarly, House suffers when confronting the Red Death patient, since he has the worst condition of all. He's a miserable human being. Due to a leg injury, he's in constant pain, which he uses as an excuse to be obnoxious, but he claims that his injuries and addiction to painkillers help him understand the sick. If it does, his empathy is not on immediate display.

Ultimately, the show provides an incredibly cynical view about health care, its limits in understanding the human body and impotence in curing it. Bodily processes are shown in graphic, and sometimes impossible, detail. In one case, a young mother secretes milk from cells on her leg. In some episodes, the corpses are more alive than drugged or depressed main characters. The dead pop up from morgue tables or out of drawers and speak to the living characters about what not to do, to show them how to live. With this graphic focus on fringe cases of disease, the show reinforces our beliefs in our own robust health. The show's pitch is to aging baby boomers coming to grips with their own mortality. Appealing to an older demographic, *House* emphasizes our need to objectify processes of body breakdown, rather than to understand this process as a part of life.

A collection of essays entitled *House and Philosophy* (2009) examines the moral dilemmas confronted by the doctors of Princeton-Plainsboro, House in particular. Among these ethical issues is that niceness is overrated, the fact that everybody lies, and the morality of murdering a murderer. David Goldblatt notes similarities between House's methods of arriving at a diagnosis and Sherlock Holmes's approaches to case solving (Goldblatt 33). Certainly both are forensic drug using, antisocial, arrogant geniuses. However, I see House more as a Dracula figure. If we spell his name as "H-A-U-S," it has a middle European, Transylvanian air. Certainly he drains off more than his share of blood. He sets his own rhythm to the day. He is handsome and, like a vampire, he uses women, feeding off them to keep his ailing ego alive.

House first aired in 2004. The popularity of its suspenseful uses of gruesome horror has led to imitators. To ride the dragging leg popularity, so to speak, of *House*, *Mystery Diagnosis* began the following year. That show was even marketed as a "true to life" version of *House*.

Mystery Diagnosis has all the formulaic elements of a mystery narrative, but unlike *House*, it purports to be "true." The title scenes emphasize the idea of medical "vision," through a microscope, therefore giving us the idea of understanding or gaining vision about the workings of the human body. The opening sequences emphasize the masked surgeon or medical care practitioner in a position of authority ready to dispense "the truth" about some bizarre condition. Each episode is set up with a compelling title. Who wouldn't want to find out the mysteries behind "The Woman Who Saw Pink" or the "Girl with Holes in Her Jaw"? The patient endures unusual symptoms that go undiagnosed for years, sometimes decades. We have the same limited knowledge as the sufferer, so we have full immersion into the mystery. Even so, there's a suspense implicit in the show's structure, apart from the person who is ill. We stick with the case even if the main "character," or focus of the case study, is whiny or unwilling to help himself.

Each hour-long show braids together two cases posing a medical mystery. Inevitably, the story proceeds through initial unusual symptoms, times of the patient being symptom-free and then facing hope of a new diagnosis, which turns out to be wrong. The viewer's knowledge, like the patient's, comes in bits. The show is set up so each segment ends with yet another bizarre symptom or the teaser promise of a miraculous cure that we know will be a dead-end, because the show's hour is not yet over.

The website for *Mystery Diagnosis* shows four cases proceeding in wave-like narrative arcs, documenting the roller-coaster progression of John's illness, eventually diagnosed as Meniere's Disease or Sean's "deadly sore throat," as being a rare symptom for Lyme disease. (The shows always use "deadly" in describing conditions or symptoms.) The viewers suffer, along with the patient, horrid embarrassments or inconveniences, the shame when doctors accuse them of faking or malingering, and then the distress of hoping for deliverance and not finding the true answer.

Like clockwork, at the hour's end, the specialist delivers the news, confirmed by the latest technology, that the patient has a missing enzyme or a relatively well-known ailment with unusual symptoms, or a genetic structural anomaly leading to a bizarre condition, as in the case of the man whose brain was growing into his sinus cavity. The show makes liberal use of Poe's formula of uncovering the mystery of the human body. An emphasis on death and its processes diverts us from the facts that these shows, whether fiction or so-called "reality," remove us from the ways we are not alive.

Both Prospero and House evince qualities of vampires. The revelers and the hospital followers of House are more like zombies.

A cloaked figure roams at night, compelled to drain life from people to survive. While Polidari wrote his sketch about "Dracula" in 1819, Poe's concepts of the altered time and life rhythms of Dupin and Prospero seem play off elements of the Dracula figure. Bram Stoker's version came out in 1897. Since then, each age has reworked the vampire figure to fit a specific meaning for that time. Dracula is essentially a metaphor of the opposite of sexuality. Bodily fluids are taken out, rather than put in. Underlying this metaphor are central mysteries about sexuality, creation, and the workings of time on the human body. Vampire books are huge sellers, as witnessed by Anne Rice's multi-volume *Vampire Chronicles*. *True Blood*, originally books, is now an HBO series, and the best-selling *Twilight* books have been made into a film. Television shows are also flapping with vampires. *Buffy the Vampire Slayer* was a long-running series, currently in syndication, but the new *Vampire Diaries* illustrates that vampires have long legs.

Following the huge success of *Twilight* and *True Blood*, onscreen vampires continue to be wildly successful. A film released last fall, The *Vampire's Assistant*, is based on the first three *Cirque du Freak* books by Darren Shan. The series appeals to a youth demographic and is a huge franchise. Unable to cope with rapid physical changes, teens already feel like freaks in their own bodies. Being a vampire gives a teen an excuse to be a monster. The movie's motto is "Meet Darren. He's sixteen going on immortal." A disrupted time element is key.

Vampires are creatures out of sync. They shun natural light, dwelling only in darkness. Dripping blood, they live forever, past the bounds of a normal human lifespan. We know that the only way to kill a vampire is with a wooden stake through its heart. Theoretically, a stake through the heart pins the creature to the ground and prevents it from rising up (Barber 157). Why a wooden stake? Wouldn't a steel spike be more effective? Perhaps a wooden stake gains lethal power from its function as the vertical gnomon of a sundial, a primitive time keeper. The connection makes symbolic sense. A vampire's worst enemy is ultimately the inexorable march of time, the same as for mortals.

Why so many vampires? Does this figure, like the caveman of the GEICO commercials, make it more politically correct to revile a scapegoat? Or do we need this figure to fear in the wake of 9/11? Is the current vampire craze due to our unresolved feelings about terrorists and other "evildoers" pointed out by politicians?

If Prospero is a vampire, the revelers who follow him are the zombies. Interestingly, both vampires and zombies are structurally asynchronous, removed from an organic sequence. Being undead, zombies are also creatures born of time derangement. Time has stopped, but they keep coming. Unlike Victor Frankenstein's creation or other monsters, zombies are usually human-sized, but represent a conflation of nature and human organic processes gone horribly wrong. Their bodies lack symmetrical form and balance, as a walking zombie might list to one side like a drunk on Saturday night. Their motor neurons fire out of sequence, and the resulting herky-jerky motions give them a monstrous asynchronous quality.

Zombie cannibalism reflects another facet of being out of sync with nature. As human beings, we eat to build up our bodies. Zombies jump over the usual schedule of bodily energy. They skip food altogether and move directly to flesh and blood.

Zombies continue to capture our imagination. The film *Zombieland* is a parody earning rave reviews. Its motto is "This place is so dead." Are zombies trying to tell us something?

Zombies are a prominent feature of role-player video games. *Silent Hill* and its sequels depict zombie as mutants, created due to toxic waste. These gruesome figures are terrifying, a menacing premonition of an ecological disaster. *Resident Evil* and *Dead Rising* likewise illustrate an apocalyptic upset with the natural order. These episodic, film-length scenarios place the viewer front and center with first-person role-playing. They give the impression of a condensed time and plunge the player into his or her own time universe. The goal is to kill the greatest number of evil creatures before time runs out. The illusion of control, even via a remote control, emphasizes that we have, in fact, no influence on events at all.

It's not only on our entertainment screens where zombies pop up. The iconography of the living dead and concepts of mindless followers are everywhere. In the 2008 national election, both political parties exploited the zombie *zeitgeist*.

These mysteries of reality are delivered via the latest technology. The medium is appropriate for the message. Blu-ray is the latest optical disk storage system. It has six times the capacity of the standard DVD format. The name Blu-ray comes from the fact that a violet laser reads the data. The laser uses a shorter wavelength, which leads to the high capacity of data. Now that HD television is standard, Blu-ray use is expanding exponentially, not only for TVs but for video games, on consoles like Xbox 360, Nintendo Wii, and PlayStation 3. Sony marketing campaigns label Blu-ray as "the ultimate in high-definition experience," but the technology also tips its hand with another Sony slogan: "Make Believe." Clearly, the point is to dazzle us with the so-called reality of this simulacrum. Distractions from graphic blood and gore seal the deal.

These images narrow, focus, and recreate the press of mortality in even brighter detail. But in some sense, this refined way of seeing is like pictures from the Hubble telescope. Even if we glimpse eternity with sharper clarity, do we truly understand what we're looking at? The answer only emphasizes the truth at the heart of Poe's story: By immersing ourselves in high-definition gore, we protect ourselves against it. We are still powerless against the invasion from the Red Death.

Despite our illusions of being armed with the latest vaccines, all that arsenal of medicine may be as useless as Prospero's gleaming dagger against an unknown intruder. An article in 2009 in *The Atlantic* poses a troubling question: "What if everything we think we know about fighting influenza is wrong?" (Brownlee and Lenzer 46). After examining the often flawed studies of swine-flu vaccine effectiveness, the article notes that "vaccines and antivirals must be viewed as only partial and uncertain defenses against the flu. And they may be mere talismans" (54). The article considers the solution to this widespread health problem as mostly smoke and mirrors, connected to politics and fostering the illusion of government competence. Recent reports about shortfalls in vaccine availability give credence to this article's central premise.

This story about the flu vaccine working due to superstition undercuts our hopes for the certainties of science. Irrationality continues to shape our thinking about time's effects on the body. For us, as for Prince Prospero, death is still a monster to be kept outside.

With the development of Blu-ray, high-definition images render each blood droplet, each vomit spewing, in glorious, focused, three-dimensional detail. On small and large screens, along with computer monitors, Blu-ray highlights Poe's blood aesthetic and renders it in hyperreality. The images then lose their potency and connection with meaning, if they ever had them. This loss of value prompts a pursuit for more evidence that our own mortality is real.

In "Simulacra and Simulations" (1985), Jean Baudrillard talks about the pervasive nature of hyperreality in today's media, noting that it is "dangerous to unmask images" since they reveal the fact that there is nothing behind them" (3). The essay traces the development of an image through these stages from meaning to meaninglessness:

1. It is the reflection of a basic reality.
2. It masks and perverts a basic reality.
3. It masks the absence of a basic reality.
4. It bears no relation to any reality whatever: it is its own pure simulacrum [4].

In the first phase, the image is an accurate representation, a one-to-one connection between sign and object. Baudrillard calls this "the order of sacrament." The next type of image presents an evil or malevolent appearance. The third level pretends to be reality when it is nothing at all. Baudrillard considers this level sorcery. The last phase shows that an image has moved into total simulation with no correspondence to reality.

The gruesome horror on our big plasma screens seem to fall somewhere between the third and fourth levels of images. The pervasive quality of this reality is not to trick us, since we view and play with an awareness that these narratives are of a different order from our waking lives. However, they manage to work sorcery on us, to lull us into thinking that we can control time. Why do we need a time de-rangement now? It's hard to believe that we are nearly a decade into the 21st century and are still beset with primitive problems. The hopes for a modern, gleaming future have dissipated. We face a sinking economy, war, disease, and more dangers than ever.

Baudrillard pinpoints the dialectical nature of truth: "It is always a question of proving the real by the imaginary; proving truth by scandal; proving the law by transgression; proving work by the strike; proving the system by crisis and capital by revolution" (9). The gruesome horror first visualized by Poe and re-constituted for our consumption on Blu-ray continues to shield us from the vacant face of the Red Death.

CHAPTER 7

Poe's Psycho-Fantastic Voyage into Reality TV

With pioneering narratives, Poe was the first to stake a claim in many literary territories. First detective story? Check. First psychological horror? Check. But first reality TV show? Let's check.

Poe's *The Narrative of Arthur Gordon Pym of Nantucket* (1838) starts a sub-genre of narrative that I call the "psycho-fantastic voyage." The basic formula is simple: Man confronts the elements and goes mad. When *Pym* first came out, it was reviled, and even today, critics aren't sure what to make of it. The story may fall short of attaining a myth-status, like *The Odyssey*, but it is certainly more than an oddity. *Pym* is thoroughly original in reconstructing geographical exploration as psychological discovery and loss. Through a sustained drama of a battle with the environment, both topographic and psychic, Poe explores yet another mystery of human experience, how consciousness negotiates with the world out there. This narrative pattern has set a template for many current reality TV shows featuring half-crazed characters confronting environmental hardships. High-def sagas like *Deadliest Catch, Ice Road Truckers*, and the new *Swords: Life on the Line* set out high-stakes action-adventure with stomach-churning suspense, thus taking a psychological toll on the players. Again, Poe's original narrative leads the way for 21st-century entertainment.

The Narrative of Arthur Gordon Pym of Nantucket (1838) is Poe's longest fiction, his only novel. It's not as well known as his short stories, and it should be. The subtitle claims the story is filled with "incredible adventures and discoveries." Some of these include an encounter with a ghostly rescue ship, complete with on-deck corpses nibbled by gulls; cannibalism, preceded by the nerve-wracking ritual of drawing straws to see who would be the featured entrée; an earthquake creating labyrinthine tunnels lined with black granite in the shape of what could be letters; and a rush of hot, milky ocean being sucked into a hollow South Pole. As if these events are not enough, a giant white figure presides over an incomprehensible ending.

In the work's final pages, the protagonist Pym, his travel companion Dirk Peters, and a local native named Nu-Nu travel headlong in a canoe toward a milk-white waterfall. Their vessel is a made of bark from a "tree unknown." The work's final lines are in the form of journal entries: "*March* 22d. The darkness had materially increased, relieved only by the glare of the water thrown back from the white curtain before us.... And now we rushed into the embraces of the cataract, where a chasm threw itself open to receive us. But there arose in our pathway a shrouded human figure, very far larger in its proportions than any dweller among men. And the hue of the skin of the figure was of the perfect whiteness of the snow."

Poe had a passing knowledge of sea voyages, having made a few himself, although never to the South Pole. Critics have carefully documented that he relied on travel narratives about Antarctic explorations from books he had reviewed by Benjamin Morrell and J. N. Reynolds, sometimes lifting entire passages. While these works clearly served as factual sources, Poe's use of details blending exotic exploration with the mind's terrifying terrain is original with him.

He had long explored mental topography in poetry. By the time of *Pym*'s publication in 1838, he had written several poems using natural features to represent an invaded, confused psyche. He describes a vision in 1829's "Fairy Land," which tells of "dim vales — and shadowy floods — / and cloudy-looking woods, / whose forms we can't discover" (ll. 1–3). "Alone" develops this motif of geography as upsetting psychological trope in that the poet refuses to find "passions from a common spring" (ll. 3–4), but instead soaks up inspiration "From the torrent, or the fountain — / From the red cliff of the mountain — / From the sun that round me roll'd / In its autumn tint of gold" (ll. 13–16). Further, this catalog of picturesque nature evinces more than a standard Romanticism, as the poet's last vision is of a "cloud that took the form / (When the rest of Heaven was blue) / Of a demon in my view — " (ll. 20–22). "The City in the Sea" and "The Valley of Unrest" (1831) blend nature and temperament with phrases like "melancholy waters" and "light from out the lurid sea." He continues to refine this gem to a high polish in verse through the forties, such as "Dreamland" (1844) and "Ulalume" (1847). Clearly part of Poe's technique in *Pym* is to infuse natural features with a poetic intensity that comes unspooled through narrative.

At publication, critics considered *Pym* a hoax, with too many "atrocities and strange horrors." Poe himself may have tried to disown it by calling it a "silly book." He had just been let go from the *Southern Messenger* in Richmond, and may have wondered what he had been thinking. Henry James thought some passages were brilliant, but considered that for the most part, Poe sacrificed careful artistry for gothic thrills. Leslie Fiedler found Poe's foray into this masculine world a bad move from a writer who was best with nervous, cadaverous characters like Roderick Usher and the swooning narrator of "The Tell-Tale Heart." Readers are still not sure how to account for the work's puzzles and odd ending. Most studies focus on thematic developments of life and death, the double, the black/white dichotomy, reality and illusion. Only one study attempts to deal with its entire structure. Curtis Fukuchi considers the work's overall narrative pattern in terms of an inevitable working of Providence.

An explorer confronts raw wilderness and loses his mind. As fiction, Poe's "psycho-fantastic voyage" has had very long legs, like a mountain climber. In 1899, Jules Verne wrote a sequel to *Pym* called "An Antarctic Mystery," and in later works, Conan Doyle launched into this terrain, with *The Lost World* and an intriguing short story called "The Mystery of Blue John Gap," both published in 1912. *The Maracot Deep* (1929) features an exploration to the sunken city of Atlantis and *Edge of the Unknown* (1930) examines the psychic powers of Harry Houdini. Conrad's *Heart of Darkness* owes a huge debt to Poe's version of a mind-blowing wilderness. Action-adventures by Haggard and Burroughs also create a psychological edge for nature. Burroughs' *Tarzan of the Apes* (1914) is a kind of obverse to Pym. Pym loses everything bit by bit. By contrast, Tarzan, scion of an aristocratic line, has lost everything before the story begins. We see the process of imposing order on an untamed world, re-building the self back toward civilization. In this way, Tarzan's progression serves as a source for the successful reality shows *Survivorman* and *Man versus Wild*.

The most recent take on Poe's psycho-fantastic voyage has been on reality television in shows pitting hyper-masculine guys against the environment. The premise of *Deadliest Catch* is that four to six vessels of a crab fishing fleet out of Dutch Harbor, Alaska, compete for the biggest hauls during king crab and opilio crab seasons. While the shows also have this ostensible contest ongoing between the four or six captains of crab fishing vessels, truckers, or sword fishermen, how many pounds of crab, how much value to a haul by the truckers, the secondary contest is between man and nature. The actual underlying competition is between each man talking to himself in the face of unrelenting nature. Who can stay together the longest under these God-awful conditions? Frigid temperatures and high seas create an extreme situation of survival. Poe would approve that these programs air on the Discovery, History, and National Geographic channels, giving a rational gloss to the shows' mad undercurrents.

In *Deadliest Catch* in 2005, each episode travels the edge of suspense with titles such as "Sea of Misery," "Lock-Out," "Shipwreck," "Unsafe and

Unsound," "No Season for Old Men." The show's opening sequence shows a vessel swaying in a disorienting miasma on high seas. Since the middle of season 4, the theme song for this program has been "Wanted: Dead or Alive" by Bon Jovi. This is a theme that was destined for this show; the chorus, especially, is very apt. The song originally appeared on Bon Jovi's 1986 album *Slippery When Wet.*

This program has a very Pym-like setting, with rough men aboard a ship forging through impossible seas and weather. Danger abounds with pitching decks, winds howling in the riggings, and frothy frigid waves washing over the sides.

> Poe sharpen[s] to the point of near suffocating exactitude ... an emphasis on the biology of place ... subterranean tunnels, intertwining passageways, and dimly lit corridors descending toward absolute darkness are standard tropes in the Gothic novel.... But in Poe, the machinery of the haunted castle or mansion always becomes a semiotic parallel to the tortured psyche of the main character [Magistrale and Poger 14–15].

Despite the show's location on wide-open seas, the limited range of the hand-held camera on *Deadliest Catch* recreates this constrained claustrophobic perspective. We wander into the labyrinths below decks, cram ourselves into tiny crew quarters, and witness extreme closeups of the captains' tortured faces in the wheelhouse. The danger-loving camera invites viewers to endure numerous replays of on-deck accidents to the point of obsession. A crane comes loose, a multi-ton crab pot slides sideways, a tsunami-sized wave thunders over the gunnels and nearly washes the exhausted crew members overboard.

These reality shows set outdoors take a postmodernist slant to relate the story. With shaky hand-held cameras and ghoulish lighting at night ,the program recreates the disorientation of the experience onboard a ship. The effect of this narrowed focus is a sense of altered consciousness consistent with Poe's inward explorations. Despite marking the locations of the crab fleet with longitude and latitude readings and chart headings, this transition, like the show being on the Discovery or National Geographic networks, is merely a rational polish of what is essentially a surreal experience. Vision is blurred, and the crew lurches from one illusion to another, with false hopes for successful fishing and hypnotic stretches at sea or across the ice pack.

Magistrale and Poger note in reference to Poe's narrators: "these isolatoes are in rebellion against some restrictive moral or physical law that denies them their high poetic place in the universe" (15). This quality describes Pym, but it applies equally to the ship captains on *Deadliest Catch.* Like Pym, these players are on the edge of survival. They battle the elements and usually lose. Hypothermia, changeable weather, and equipment breakdowns plague their quests.

The *Deadliest Catch* characters fall into two categories: first, seasoned captains, who are generally running a family business, broken and older than their years, dissolute guys on the edge, and second, the new deckhands or greenhorns. The young "horns" either make it or are quickly injured on deck and retreat to their bunks, seasick, homesick, or both. They suffer physical problems and just about lose their minds.

Captain Phil Harris of the *Cornelia Marie* suffers a pulmonary embolism at sea and has to pull out of the season. Ordered to stay on land, he fumes over not being there, smokes a blue streak, and is back within a few months. During the first few days back in the wheelhouse, he loses crab pots in the ice, the ship has engine trouble, and Harris ends up smoking two cigarettes at once. He says to the camera, "You've never seen me this bad."

A worrisome medical problem afflicts another of the men, Sig Hansen, captain of the *Northwestern*. Late one night in the wheelhouse, he twists his face in pain. He grabs his chest. Is it indigestion or a coronary? He has to quit smoking and he's successful for about 20 hours, but he can't stand the withdrawal and is back at it in days. Keith Colburn on the *Wizard* suffers posttraumatic stress over a huge wave that nearly washes some crew members overboard. His brother ends up with broken ribs, and another crew member suffers a shattered cheekbone. Colburn spends much camera time conveying his guilt over the incident.

Pym and *Deadliest Catch* are of the same order, not merely in setting and character, but in how they tell the story. Pym has a first-person narrator adding breathless commentary on each stage of his deprivation onboard ship and the island of Tsalal. Similarly for each captain of the crab vessel, tensions are ratcheted up to the nth degree. There are no tedious voyages out and back. Trouble lurks like landmines on each run out to sea. The narrative structure moves at breakneck pace, with one disaster after another, like a series of explosions in a Jerry Bruckheimer film. The show is a masterpiece of editing. Keen tension accompanies the raising of each crab pot. Will the deckhand snag the buoy line on the first try? Will the cage be teeming with crab, or have only a few forlorn critters clinging to the sides? Will the leaky engine hold? Will the storm blow past? Is the crew member's leg only bruised or actually broken? Answers to these questions come rapidly or not at all. Another contributing factor to keep the pace going is that the sequences on board each vessel are short, with crosscuts to other ships in the fleet hundreds of miles away.

A scene of high tension in *Pym* involves cannibalism. This same element of anxiety over consumption finds its way into *Catch*. Cannibalism makes its appearance in a few ways. One is the time-honored ritual of biting a head off a live fish for "good luck." The greenhorns especially undergo this hazing, with much snickering from the seasoned deckhands as the young man gags and spits out the ripped-off head, glassy eyes and guts hanging out the back.

Cannibalism persists in deeper way, however. Through this choice of livelihood, the men devour themselves. They love the sea, and several of them are only continuing in their fathers' trade. The skippers are meticulous about tossing out crabs that are undersized, at least on camera. Ironically, they bemoan low profits from empty pots, and blame bad fishing on a curse or bad luck. They don't seem to connect the light hauls to their ravenous appetites for devouring the environment for profit. The name of one of the fishing vessels, *Time Bandit*, gives a slight nod to this inevitable irony of the crab fisherman's position. A time bandit never gets away scot free, but must pay in the end. There is no profit in stealing time. Despite their crab conservation measures, the men are hauling themselves into extinction. Every loaded crab pot they winch up means fewer numbers for the next season.

In *The Spy Story*, John Cawelti and Bruce Rosenberg note Poe's role in shaping the spy novel through stories using anagrams and ciphers, as found in "The Gold Bug." Essentially, Poe could be considered the great-great-grandfather to popular books like *The DaVinci Code* and Dan Brown's current *The Lost Symbol* as well as films like *National Treasure* and all its sequels. But with Pym's hieroglyphs in the earth, the signs point to a different order of hidden meaning, an attempt to fathom the semiotics of nature.

Over the course of Chapter 23, Arthur Pym and Dirk Peters navigate a series of ravines shaped almost like letters. At one point, one of the markings resembles an outstretched arm. The landscape holds signs which a human mind can almost discern, but not quite. Ultimately, Pym and Peters disagree as to what the markings mean. In *American Hieroglyphics*, John T. Irwin notes that Pym "denies the markings on the wall are man-made — a denial of human presence that is symbolic of that death of the self to itself ... a death that is not simply the external limit of self-consciousness but its internal limit as well, a death lying at the core of self-consciousness" (Irwin 170). Pym's failure to understand this language embedded in the earth casts doubt on any value or knowledge coming from his exploration. Certainly, the ambiguous nature of Pym's ending that blends all sense of differentiation of self into a vast whiteout of experience bears out this failure.

In a less profound though equally human effort at reading language by way of signs interpreted as metaphors from the human body, the crab fishermen of *The Deadliest Catch* often navigate by way of subtle markings on the ocean pointing the way to their treasure. Skipper Phil Harris claims to know where the crabs are from certain patterns of air bubbles, which he calls "crab farts." In addition, the captains perceive elements of underwater topography in terms of human anatomy. They have to risk a perilous venture into waters requiring tricky navigation techniques. They call it braving the danger "between the butt cheeks." Imposing the human form on the immense body of nature is another way to mediate and control the environment, the non-human.

The huge popularity of *Deadliest Catch* has sparked a veritable carnival of entertainment marketing. The show maintains a huge web presence with numerous sites branching from the home site. In postmodernist fashion, the sites include games, backstage views of webisodes and profiles on the captains, advertising tie-in, and crossovers to other television shows appealing to a golden demographic of young males, 18–45.

"Have you got what it takes to skipper a crab boat on the Bering Sea?" is the announcement for the online *Deadliest Catch* game, available through the Discover Channel's website. The interactive site presents an initial budget of $250,000. The player has to allocate the funds among costs of the boat, onboard amenities, food, medical supplies, and percentage of profits for the men. The game therefore conflates physical survival with economic viability.

Among the "backstage" views are "Catch Confidential": "The season is over, but you can still watch exclusive webisodes here." Included on this site is a Toyota ad for "Tundra, the truck that's changing it all."

To give the viewer the illusion of participating in the fun, we have "Punk'd on the Bering," pranks and tricks, fake-outs, sabotaged pots — welding the crab pot door shut and loading a port-o-potty on one of the buoys, among others. The series also includes the occasional "backstage glimpse" show as when the captains get together in a bar to shoot the breeze. A backstage show ending the most recent season featured the ever-steady host of *Cash Cab*, another Discovery Channel hit, with cabbie and game show host Ben Bailey as facilitator.

Cash Cab is a quiz show á là *Jeopardy* played in a cab as customers travel to their New York City destinations. That most rational of forms, the quiz show, poses a stark contrast with the chaotic, intuitive sense required to travel the jammed traffic in New York City Even so, *Cash Cab* values the power of the mind. The Big Apple is laid out in grids, which the camera shows the viewers to plot out the riders' progress along the route. The cab riders work together to answer the questions, and succeed or fail on their collective brain power. Despite the wild, flashing lights signaling the show's beginning, this show seems extremely comforting. Ben Bailey as driver is no menacing Charon ferrying souls to the land of the dead. Bailey is considerate and polite, quietly resigned after he stops to let out a fare who failed. "And the cash cab rolls on," he says philosophically. On this program, there is no such thing as a harrowing cab ride or impolite driver. Although the tracking camera shots capture plenty of humanity on the sidewalks that stroll by, there is no specter of terror from the streets.

Bailey brings a totally different image to this backstage show. He sits among these rough and tumble character others, almost prim, with no cigarettes or beer in front of him and patiently prompts the raucous stories and tales of harsh decisions from these seagoing men.

The huge success of *Deadliest Catch* has spawned additional eco-reality shows, such as *Survivorman*, and *Ice Road Truckers*. In *Survivorman*, naturalist Les Stroud heads to isolated areas alone and pushes himself to the edge of survival in isolated places like the Canadian northwest, a Georgia swamp, or the Kalahari Desert. It's only him and a camera for a week. Occasionally, he has help, a guide or local inhabitant to tell him about dangerous creatures. Kenneth Silverman has said of *Pym* that it's a book about hunger and the impossible quest for being nurtured, as well as the drive toward self-destruction (Silverman 136). Like Pym, Les Stroud endures extreme deprivation for a week — a canteen of water, no food, no fire, no light, each night the shrieks of animals going berserk. Basically, the show reaches a hairy hand into our living rooms and asks, could you go alone into the wilderness and survive? Collapsed on our cushy sofas, most of us know the sad answer.

Another offspring from *Deadliest Catch* is *Ice Road Truckers*, which had its U.S. debut in June 2007. The show follows half a dozen drivers hauling big rigs across frozen lakes in the Northwest Territories to Yellowknife or from Fairbanks to Prudhoe Bay. In spring 2009, season 3 welcomed Lisa, a woman trucker, to this macho realm at the top of the world. The acceptance of a woman in this context might possibly be due to a post–Sarah Palin zeitgeist. As in *Deadliest Catch*, the episode titles capture a Pym-like, near-apocalyptic tone: "Into the Whiteout," "Lost on the Ice," "Edge of the Earth," "The World Crumbles." There is even an iPhone app for a viewer game of the show. One TV reviewer writes in *The New York Times*, "Watching these guys ... make their runs, it's hard not to share in their cold, fatigue and horrible highway hypnosis, that existential recognition behind the wheel late at night that the pull of sleep and the pull of death are one and the same.... [I]t gets right exactly what *Deadliest Catch* got right, namely that the leave-nothing-but-your-footprints, green kind of eco-travelers are too mellow and conscientious to be interesting to watch. Instead, the burly, bearded, swearing men who blow methyl hydrate into their own transmissions and welcome storms as breaks from boredom ... are much better television."

The most recent addition to these shows about environmental perils is *Swords: Life on the Line*, about sword fishermen in the north Atlantic off Newfoundland. *Swords* charts an already familiar course, thanks to *The Perfect Storm*, both the book by Sebastian Junger (1997) and the film (2000). An additional tie-in with media crossover is that one of the boat captains on *Swords* is Linda Greenlaw, who had been acquainted with the Gloucester men who went down in that 1991 storm depicted in *The Perfect Storm*. In the film, Greenlaw is portrayed by Mary Elizabeth Mastroantonio as the girlfriend of George Clooney's character.

There's no doubt that unresolved anxiety from September 11 continues to have an impact nine years later. *Ice Road Truckers* began on the BBC in 1999, but its popularity soared after 9-11. The media's constant repetition of 9-11 footage did its job to blur the horror of that day, but we have yet to resolve it. These shows keep alive the idea that ordinary people can aspire to extraordinary heroism, and the extreme environment provides that setting.

In these programs about making a living off the land, Poe's psycho-fantastic voyage for our time is ultimately a denial of our need to be more responsible toward the environment. The programs represent an anti-eco-gesture. Environmental deterioration such as global warming is an overwhelming problem with apocalyptic ramifications. In the face of such immense reality, the programs represent a type of denial of our inability to control the environment and ourselves as we interact with it. We should take a cue from Jonathan Schell's argument laid out in the classic *Fate of the Earth* and the more recent *The Seventh Decade*.

Schell discusses the "bomb in the mind," an image evoking a persistent low-level anxiety, then a "bomb out of the mind" as the denial of this reality. What better method of denying the reality of environmental catastrophe than a so-called "reality show," giving the illusion that the environment is still our playground?

> It's therefore as useless to lament our lost innocence as it is for an adolescent to lament lost childhood. The task is to live — that first means *survive*— with our new powers, however troublesome or unwanted they may be. We have to incorporate those powers into our thinking at a fundamental level and learn how, forever after, to live as a species that can destroy itself, but has chosen, through an enduring act of political will, not to [Englehardt].

GPS gadgets and Google Earth may de-mystify the landscape, but the popularity of these current psycho-fantastic television voyages show that we still have a deep need to face vicarious disaster from the outside world. Despite sometimes exploiting cheap and easy thrills, these reality programs make a serious effort toward defining both the potential and limits of the self as it confronts the outside world.

CHAPTER 8

Over the Chopping Block

Programming on the Food Network lays out a massive feast for cable television viewers. The network's array of programs appeals to a wide demographic for every time of day and every taste. Episodes featuring celebrity chefs offer simple elegance from Barefoot Contessa Ina Garten, quick-and-easy efficiency from Rachael Ray or Sandra Lee, muscular sensitivity from Tyler Florence or "naked chef" Jamie Oliver, or down-home appeal from Paula Deen and the Neelys. Most of the shows have a straightforward beginning-middle-and-end narrative structure, as in here are ingredients, here is a recipe, and here is the completed product. Gloomy meditations from Poe would seem an unwelcome guest to this sunny array. While whisking eggs for an omelet or meringues for a tasty dessert, none of the celebrity chefs whip anxiety or depression into their concoctions. However, if we view this network through the Poe channel, mystery and suspense infuse at least one program on the Food Network in ways that Julia Child never imagined. The program *Chopped* makes liberal use of Poe's elements of suspense. Its narrative pattern follows the same story structure as "The Pit and the Pendulum" (1842).

Poe's tale is set at some vague time during the Spanish Inquisition. A man is dragged before a board of judges and before he knows it, he is sentenced to a dark dungeon where he experiences a series of bizarre tortures. At the center of the absolutely black cell is a bottomless pit that he narrowly avoids plummeting into. More than once he loses consciousness. After one of these faints, he wakes to find himself strapped down with his chest exposed under the arc of a razor-edged swinging pendulum. He manages to position himself so the pendulum cuts the strap. No sooner does he escape than heated walls turn the cell into an oven, and the burning steel sides move forward to edge him toward the abyss. In the nick of time, the invading French army rescues him from the abyss.

On many levels, Poe juxtaposed with the Food Network is a contradiction. A close look reveals that Poe's fiction is starving. His style does not include sumptuous feasts as in Richardson's *Tom Jones* or dainty tea cakes conveying memories as in works by Proust. Poe's words are sodden with drink, sherry, wine, and *medoc*. Food is not even on the menu in Poe's writing chamber aside from a few mentions.

A brief culinary reference comes up in "The Murders in the Rue Morgue." A basket of apples demonstrates Dupin's amazing powers of recall, as he reconstructs strings of thought in a virtuoso performance that amazes his narrator companion. A fruit peddler makes an appearance in a flashback as a clue to the narrator on how Dupin had read the narrator's mind. The fruit merchant was the last in the narrator's series of thoughts. "I now remembered that, in fact, a fruiterer, carrying upon his head a large basket of apples, had nearly thrown me down, by accident" (Poe 145).

In "The Fall of House of Usher," Roderick is too ill to be a congenial host. He and the narrator sustain themselves through music, books, and art. The only mention of a provision comes in the story of Ethelred the hero, who gains strength by "virtue of the powerfulness of the wine which he had drunken" (243). Despite the social level of the two friends' connection, the story shows us no real wine, just its evocation on a page, a symbol of a symbol.

When Montresor and Fortunato look for the precious "Cask of Amontillado," the wine is only a phantom, an absence cast in the negative. Montresor and Fortunato launch onto the search in the first place on the basis of a lie. Twice Montresor says about the cask: "I have my doubts" (274). The search is fraught with suspense along the way, ending with a murder and Fortunato's impassioned plea for the love of God, which goes unanswered. Fortunato drinks plenty of an inferior Medoc as Montresor lures him into the illusory search, but the rare Amontillado that Montresor uses to lure him into the catacomb is an illusion. In the end, Montresor poses the question: "The Amontillado!" and Fortunato's answer is paradoxically, "True, the Amontillado" (277).

The catalog of Poe's writing includes one gourmand, Pierre Bon-Bon, "the *restauranteur* of uncommon qualifications" (Poe 522) in "Bon-Bon" (1835). In this little known humorous sketch, food does not compare to the man's philosophies or his literature. "Bon-Bon was responsible for the metaphysics of Kant, a modern Leibniz, in short, Bon-Bon was emphatically a — Bon-Bonist" (523). Bon-Bon maintains an equal interest in powers of the mind and the stomach. He is three feet tall and with an equally wide circumference. No one could perceive "the rotundity of his stomach without a sense of magnificence nearly bordering on the sublime" (524). Bon-Bon is visited one wintry night by the devil, who eerily is missing one feature. "In short, Pierre Bon-Bon not only saw plainly that his Majesty had no eyes whatsoever, but could discover no indications of their having existed at any previous period—for the space where eyes should naturally have been, I am constrained to say, simply a dead level of flesh" (529). The demonic figure goes on to demonstrate that, without eyes, he can see better than Bon-Bon himself.

Bon-Bon proceeds to drink himself into a state of indiscretion, telling the Devil that he is a liar, and a case of hiccups. Speaking in terms that Bon-Bon understands, the Devil talks about having eaten souls, among them Aristotle, Plato, and other Classical scholars. He says, "Long ones are *not* good; and the best, if not carefully shelled, are apt to be a little rancid on account of the gall" (532). Out of rising alarm over the untenability of his situation, Bon-Bon sees an opportunity for a Faustian pact and offers himself to the Devil for money. The Wicked One refuses, however, to take the living Bon-Bon. The rotund restauranteur takes grave umbrage at the refusal and hurls a bottle at the Devil. The bottle disturbs a lamp hanging from the ceiling, and "the metaphysician [was] prostrated by the downfall of the lamp" (534). Through caustic humor, Poe satirizes excessive metaphysics with gluttony. Food may not be connected to life, but excessive intake is an infraction.

In chapter 2 of *The Narrative of Arthur Gordon Pym*, Pym has a well-provisioned compartment as he stows away aboard the *Grampus*—"a host of delicacies, both in the eating and drinking department" (Poe 760). Later these are detailed as "three or four immense Bologna sausages, an enormous ham, a cold leg of roast mutton, and half a dozen bottles of cordial and liqueurs" (761). After consuming the salty food, he suffers, along with the dog, the "torments of thirst" (767). "Salt provisions of the most exciting kind had been my chief, and indeed, since the loss of the mutton, my only supply of food, with the exception of the sea-biscuit; and these latter were utterly useless to me, as they were too dry and hard to be swallowed in the swollen and parched condition of my throat" (769). The food never brings actual relief, only a momentary respite followed by a worse situation.

Pym manages to stave off hunger, barely, until his friend Augustus comes down to rescue him with three boiled potatoes (773). In chapter 6, food is again mentioned in conjunction with the problems of shifting loads of provisions below decks making the ship unstable. The grain swells in the sacks, increasing the danger aboard ship (786). With uncertainty above the deck and an explosive storeroom of provisions below, Pym is caught in the middle. His need for food increases to the point where he must take desperate measures. "The gnawing hunger which I now experienced was nearly insupportable, and I felt myself capable of going to any lengths in order to appease it" (813). He chews leather from a trunk on board. Events move him in gradual steps toward hunger and deprivation.

The most blatant example of food consumption gone amok in Poe's writing is without doubt the cannibalism the starving men are forced to commit while on board the ship. In the most desperate straits of hunger, the three men still on board the brig draw straws to see who will be sacrificed. Pym and Dirk Peters end up eating Parker, who had drawn the shortest straw: "we devoured the rest of the body, piecemeal, during the four ever memorable days" (819–820).

Pym faints over the whole incident of drawing straws, which effectively separates his consciousness from the unholy consumption. This anxiety over food could partly stem from the fact that in Poe's own life at the time of writing *Pym*, he was afflicted with such desperate poverty, obtaining food represented tremendous tension or emotional upset. His treatment of sustenance in the narrative, even if the food is a provision and a life-giver, is regularly fraught with considerable suspense.

Kenneth Silverman's biography *Mournful and Never-Ending Remembrance* (1991) notes numerous specifics about the writer's destitution. While he was writing *Pym*, Poe and family were "literally suffering for want of food," eating only molasses on bread for weeks at a time (125, 137). In supposing too close a connection between life and art, we make the same mistake as early Poe critics concluding that because he wrote about murder he was himself mentally unbalanced. Still, even as a metaphor, food is rarely a symbol of life in Poe's work. For whatever reason, Poe's uses of literary food are paltry, like the few scraps of bread left by rats, as in "The Pit and the Pendulum."

The traditional format of a cooking show was established by Julia Child on Public Broadcasting. The program had an educational mission, as did Julia's book on *Mastering the Art of French Cooking*. Another kind of culinary show challenges chefs to vary dishes with a theme ingredient, as in the programs *Top Chef* or *Iron Chef*. The culinary reality show *Chopped* differs from these in that the narrative is powered from start to finish by a high-wire suspense.

Anxiety over food reaches a peak in *Chopped*. Using the suspenseful design first energizing Poe's fiction, this show works with the concept of a food competition as a suspenseful, psychological thriller. Episode titles play up the mystery element, as in a recent show with the alliterative label of "Quahog Quandaries and Pickle Puzzles."

In this ostensibly real cooking contest, four experienced chefs compete through appetizer, entrée, and dessert rounds, with one competitor being eliminated, or "chopped," each round, until only one is left standing to win the prize money of $10,000. The show airs four or five times a week, in various time slots, usually in the evening.

Each chef enters with a back story and a food passion. "He who has never swooned, is not he who finds strange palaces and wildly familiar faces in coals that glow" (Poe, "The Pit and the Pendulum" 247). The camera follows that chef at work at a restaurant or catering; some even work in the galleys of yachts. The contender explains his or her motivation, food philosophy, or greatest influence. Many contestants want to start a new restaurant. Chef Marcellus is very confident although less specific: "I'm gonna go in there and blow everybody away with my cooking skills."

Another point covered in this brief bio might be a conflict or obstacle that the person had to overcome, a recent family death or adverse medical diagnosis. The information humanizes the chef as a "character" in the drama. Gillian wants the money to take a trip to Spain and run with the bulls for her dad. He died before he had the chance to do this himself. Marcellus has a goal of beating out an ex-girlfriend, who competed on the show earlier and was chopped in the first round.

There also might be a class conflict where a small-town chef wants to out-sauté a high-end restaurant chef in New York City, or set up a big city rivalry, New York versus Chicago. It seems likely that each chef contestant works from a script outlining his or her identity as a type of "brand," perhaps from the application biography that he or she had initially submitted to the show to distinguish him or her from the rest.

The twist to this narrative is that the cooking competition immediately plunges competitors into uncertainty. They open a dark picnic basket of "mystery ingredients." The basket contains three or four disparate foods that would not ordinarily go together. There might also be a huge revulsion factor. One example is that for an appetizer round, the chefs had to work with a rattlesnake ("Rattle and Roll"). On that same episode an ingredient for the entrée round includes a plastic bag containing a pink-bodied, flayed rabbit. This ties in with Poe's prisoner: "After this I call to mind flatness and dampness; and then all is *madness*— the madness of a memory which busies itself among forbidden things" (Poe 247). With the challenging ingredients, the chefs are almost literally fed death, and it's the chefs' responsibility to treat the dead thing as inanimately as possible, as in a high school biology lab.

The judges are strict supervisors, allowing no possibility of being human. No cracking allowed, either of smiles or psyches. Other episodes have presented combinations of catfish, marshmallows, tomatillos, and rutabagas for an appetizer or a dessert made from red chili peppers ("Step Right Up!"). After the chefs take an inventory of the basket's contents, action begins.

The program's setting is dark and institutional. The studio could almost be a prison kitchen, with work stations in a line, pantry items on dull metal racks, and all utensils in monochromatic shades of gray. The chef contestants wear gray or dark blue uniforms, marked with the *Chopped* cleaver as an insignia. The dark blue smocks seem reminiscent of dreary prison jumpsuits. Despite attempts of the show's opening moments to individualize the players, once in the kitchen they are non-individualized in their uniforms, all the same, waiting to be judged.

For Poe's prisoner on the cell floor, time has a dramatic impact: "a very singular figure riveted my attention. It was the painted figure of Time as he is commonly represented, save that in lieu of a scythe he held what, at a casual glance, I supposed to be the pictured image of a huge pendulum, such as we see on antique clocks.... While I gazed directly upward at it ... I fancied that I saw it in motion" (252). Each swing of the pendulum brings him closer to doom.

Chopped also unfolds by the tyranny of the clock. Suspense is a constant. Each round is timed, as is everything in television. However, for most television, a clock is offstage, revealed to the viewers only by the transition to a commercial. Here the march of time is front and center. Food critic and host Ted Allen intones, "Chefs, time starts ... NOW!"

The audience is let in on the nerve-wracking countdown pressure. Elements of suspense increase toward the end of each timed round, as Ted Allen marks the time, counting down the last ten seconds. Will each chef have time to make raw poultry edible? Will time allow an aesthetic arrangement of the food on four plates?

The pendulum swinging over Poe's prisoner is razor sharp. *Chopped* uses the same metaphor of a painful demise. A violent subtext underscores the frenetic action. A meat cleaver is the show's motto, and as the contestants parade offstage between rounds, the audience catches a glimpse of a protruding meat cleaver stuck in a wooden column on the set. For the transitional scenes leading to commercial breaks, the meat cleaver flies unpredictably through the air, a foreshadowing of the drastic fate awaiting one of the contestants.

Conflict is palpable as the chefs race back and forth in the kitchen. They share or fail to share ingredients, cast disapproving glances at each other, or try to psych each other out. On a few episodes, actual blood is spilled, as a contestant cuts a hand or finger slicing onions. One woman chef burned her hand taking a pan from the oven without using a mitt. Another chef was chopped because of running in the kitchen with a butcher's knife. "The sweep of the pendulum had increased in extent by nearly a yard. As a natural consequence its velocity was also much greater. But what mainly disturbed me was the idea that it had perceptibly *descended*.... Its nether extremity was formed of a crescent of steel ... and under the edge evidently as keen as that of a razor" (Poe 252).

Action drips with suspense when the chef contenders face the judges' pronouncements. The moments of highest tension come before the contestants learn who will be chopped and ordered to descend the stairs to the underworld.

Poe's prisoner is relegated to his fate in a similarly oppressive atmosphere. "I saw the lips of the black-robed judges. They appeared to me white — whiter than the sheet upon which I trace these words and thin even to grotesqueness" (246). The *Chopped* competitors are judged by a rotating panel of three expert chefs and culinary experts with extensive experience, executive chefs, restauranteurs, or food editors. They sit behind a wood block table under what seem to be *klieg* lights.

Host Ted Allen introduces the judges. His opening rundown on their backgrounds grants them demi-god status. "Latin cooking superstar Aarón Sánchez" or "executive chef Alex Guarnaschelli" appear frequently on the judges' panel. Along the way, the chefs issue dire predictions, noting that the contestants' downfall will be the oxtail, or the marshmallows. "The challenge here is dealing with the sweetness of the marshmallows, or lack of time to cook the meat."

The judges are clear that they mete out punishment. Guarnaschelli says, "Our job is to decide which person committed the error that sends them home." At the end of each round, the chefs line up before the judges, hunched in self-conscious culpability, to await their fate. The question is not "whodunit?" but "who failed to do it?" that is, failed to deliver a palatable plate. Essentially, who murdered these food ingredients? The lineup is grueling, with the contestants glancing nervously at each other when the judge makes a scathing comment. If a competing chef bragged about the certainty of winning, the stern ruling of the judges might make them sorry for the initial confidence. While the competitors are experts, the judges are a supreme court, a culinary elite with unquestioned experience and taste that make the competitors cower.

The judges issue plenty of commentary during the contestants' mad dashes and spurts of flame on the stoves during the food preparation. They watch along with the viewers and contribute occasional commentaries designed to stir viewers' doubts about a successful outcome, like "Oh no, that pan is too hot" or "I can't believe he's cutting that piece of meat so soon," and even "I can't look." Their reactions are intense and dramatic, in the same tone as Poe's prisoner: "Unreal!— Even while I breathed there came to my nostrils the breath of the vapor of heated iron! A suffocating odor pervaded the prison!" (256).

Stoic silence is not the style in these judges' courtroom demeanor. Basically, they issue nonstop verdicts during the cooking, as if talking through the trial. "I don't think James is gonna finish," Alex says. During the food preparation phase, the judges speak in one voice, almost literally. "I think we're a little bit worried about —" Alex G. starts; "— everybody," says Aarón Sánchez, completing her comment.

Clearly the show does not have a strict real time "reality" although the food undergoes an actual time process. Comments from the judges appear to be spontaneous and unscripted. Likely, they are edited for the sake of time. The section that appears truncated is their process of making the deliberations. The judicial dissent or controversies seem too quickly dispatched. The judges appear to be in an ethereal zone between actual time and a space allowing all eternity for making up one's mind. The judges, essentially, could be in heaven.

The judges are like prosecutors trying a case, arriving at their judgments then voicing an opinion that results in rejecting one of the "suspects" in the lineup. Ted Allen asks, "Judges, do you know who will not make it to the next round?" They agree, too quickly. They are then ready to send one of the contestants the netherworld downstairs, condemning the outcast to an *oubliette*, a dungeon of oblivion.

After the grueling roast of each judging round, the crew of contenders marches away with hands behind them, like prisoners headed for yard exercise. They are regimented and rigid as the camera follows them offstage.

The chefs' breakroom is drab. No green room elegance here. The players perch on stools at a stainless steel table and commiserate about the judges' comments. They can also have a bottle of water, if they like. "Agitation of spirit kept me awake for many long hours, but at length I again slumbered. Upon arousing, I found by my side, as before, a loaf and a pitcher of water" (Poe 250). Like Poe's prisoner, they are now all on a subsistence diet.

Krishnendu Ray characterizes many of the Food Network shows as a type of "food porn." The shows play on a viewer's wish fulfillment, with the lemon chicken or seared scallops lovingly laid out before extreme closeup shots. Viewers then think, "That's so simple. I could do that." According to Ray (no relation to Rachael), as with filmed sex, the food objects are shiny, too good to be true. As with *Penthouse* centerfolds, the meal seems part of a lavish photo shoot, except the images are destined for the pages of *Gourmet*.

The suspense of *Chopped*, however, contradicts Ray's argument about food porn. Ray asserts that culinary shows make the food look so good and inviting that the viewer imagines himself carrying out those same actions. Watching the chefs on *Chopped* filet a rattlesnake or de-bone a rabbit emphasizes the reverse for most viewers, who are more likely to think, I could never do that nor would I want to. Education is not the major impetus of *Chopped*. Instead, the audience's primary motivation for watching may be to see experts fail in front of them. Through most of the contestants' preparation phase, the cameras do not ogle the food itself. This would be too much like watching the manufacture of sausage, as the harried chefs make mistakes, slopping on sauce for the plating presentation and arranging the tenderloin slices with shaking fingers. Instead, we gain a sense of the chefs stirring, swirling, bending, and rushing. Flames leap and smoke pours from the oven. The chefs are clearly harried. "And then there stole into my fancy, like a rich musical note, the thought of what sweet rest there must be in the grave" (Poe 246). On *Chopped*, the viewer's ability to follow actual food preparation is irrelevant. Humiliation is the program's central motif.

Activity reaches such a level during the cooking that camera shots of the chefs are interspersed with the action. The flustered contestant addresses the camera with thoughts and reactions about the difficulty of working with the basket ingredients. "I looked over at the mess on Jeffrey's plate and knew I did better than I thought." The brief respite matches that of Poe's prisoner, who thinks, "It seemed evident that mine was not, at least, the most hideous of fates" (248).

Then there were three. After the judges' verdict on one of the elimination rounds, the remaining contenders again flip open the baskets to start anew. "I saw clearly the doom which had been prepared for me, and congratulated myself upon the timely accident by which I had escaped. Another step before my fall, and the world had seen me no more" (250).

Along with other Food Network programming, this show's Nielsen ratings were very high in 2009. "The year 2009 was the best year ever for Food Network with record ratings, impressions and hit shows.... Food Network is aided by the bad economic times that spur people to gather around the television and learn new techniques for cooking at home and traveling vicariously through epicurious adventures" (McIntyre). However, numbers were down in 2011. Media commentator Raphael Brion notes that many new food programs had launched from other networks. "One would imagine that those channels cannibalized some FN viewers?" Another reason for viewer drop-off might be the sameness of the contests, and the judges' commentaries being too predictable. Even if the identity of the winner is typically a surprise, the decrease in viewership could be an audience reaction against the formula. The narrative arc is too familiar.

The chefs sweat under the studio lights, but again, the background of the work area is extremely dark. Chefs blame themselves for mistakes. "The tomatillo sauce is not thickening. I waited too long." The program's rivulet of guilt runs like spilled red wine. "Long suffering had nearly annihilated all my ordinary powers of mind. I was an imbecile — an idiot" (Poe 253).

Clearly tension mounts as chefs use dish towels to mop facial perspiration and avoid sweating into the food. Timekeeper Ted counts down. "Time's up!

Please step back." The chefs throw up their hands in surrender, like a running criminal caught by police at the end of a blind alley. "And now we'll find out what the chefs have to say about your entrees."

The judges issue their verdicts on the individual dishes. These are typically harsh critiques that inevitably find something wrong, too much salt or too little. "Too much," says Scott Conant. "Those flavors are in your face." Suspenseful music punctuates a judge's disparaging comment. Da-dum! A minor chord sounds a literal sour note among the feasting.

Since presentation counts, the dish must also look appealing. "The pork was cooked exactly right, but the dandelion greens are a casualty of war, tucked underneath," says from Alex. Even worse, what is most likely to send the competitor home is if all ingredients are not on the plate. "And then I suddenly fell calm, and lay smiling at the glittering death, as a child at some rare bauble" (Poe 253). The only way one contestant can emerge unscathed from that egregious oversight of one ingredient left off is if a rival has left off two.

The judges' panel seems Kafka-esque in its verdicts. Contenders are caught in a no-win situation. In addition to the rigid requirements of using disparate ingredients, the judges also ask that the chefs create dishes that reveal their personalities. The raters will downgrade a chef based on criteria outside the stated rules, such as failing to stay true to their heritages or their personalities or breaching kitchen etiquette, that is, leaving potato peels on the floor.

As the rank of competitors thins, suspense ratchets up. Who will remain alive on the chopping block? The question is never "who is innocent?" but "who has murdered the food the least?"

The narrative reaches its highest suspense as host Ted Allen holds his hand on the dish cover, prepared to reveal the creation of the unfortunate chef who will be "chopped." Then comes a commercial break. The show intensifies the competitive drama and stretches the narrative. "So, whose dish is on the chopping block?" A camera shot focuses on a disembodied hand that lifts the lid to reveal the dish. Poe's prisoner awaits his fate: "Down — certainly, relentlessly down! It vibrated within three inches of my bosom! I struggled violently — furiously" (254). Ted reads the verdict. "Chef, you have been chopped."

The losing chef, who has become a distinctive personality through revelatory offscreen dialogue, is now incriminated. "I struggled no more, but the agony of my soul found vent in one loud, long, and final scream of despair" (Poe 257). The camera follows the loser downstairs. What will he or she do? Show an actual emotion? Cry? Some of the players do, some are enraged, or proud, or disappointed in themselves. Depending on how the viewers feel about him, they can cheer or boo. The winner stands alone, almost in an anti-climactic haze: "there rushed to my mind a half-formed thought.... I felt that it was of joy — of hope" (Poe 253).

The tension in this prison kitchen with potential competitors being chopped or essentially executed out of this corner of the culinary world is not enough. Despite esoteric ingredients and a bizarre narrative bordering on sadomasochism, this show's suspense may not be enough raw meat to satisfy ravished viewers. The formula demands more intensity. In January 2011, news reports cited declining ratings for Food Network's cooking shows. This is undoubtedly due to competition from other networks like Bravo or Discovery TLC with programs offering exotic settings for cooking shows. Among these are Anthony Bourdain's *No Reservations, Man v. Food,* and *The Wild Within,* with adventurer Steven Rinella (Atkinson). Food trends on cooking shows are on the move toward ever "edgier culinary 'reality' competition shows." To meet this demand for exotic and bizarre food experiences, more programs are taking the action outside a restaurant kitchen and setting the cooking situation around a campfire in the Rockies or in a Philippines street bazaar. Declining ratings do not mean that the audience is turning off from the formula. Rather, viewers want the heat turned up. Viewers demand more tension and drama, more blood on the chopping block.

In this time of plenty, it is ironic that life-giving food is cast as a culprit. The story of *Chopped* is basically one of humiliation and failure. It carries the suspense of ambiguous guilt, a template that Poe designed. The audience follows the linearity of action. Along with the judges, we assess how the chefs process the food and how the judges stack up all the polenta. Their discerning sense of taste substitutes for Dupin's laser-sharp eye. As viewers we have no way of accessing this taste, except through language. The narrative suspends those moments of holding our attention and stretching the outcome. The withheld final verdict intensifies the vague guilt of all the chefs, even that of the bragging, unself-aware contestant whom we know will be the next to be chopped.

The popularity of this show's design testifies to how familiar this narrative template has become. It fits us. Folklorist Millie Rahn asserts that we are not what we eat, but rather "we eat what we are" (Rahn 30). This program — indeed, most of the shows on the Food Network — feeds into our culture's guilt about food. We objectify food as art, competition, and danger. Through the on-camera reality perspective of each character on *Chopped,* we experience a first-person narrative that situates us as judge and jury. What better way to externalize our collective guilt than with a crime drama, in which food is not a perfect result but the focus of another person's transgression?

CHAPTER 9

Poe at the Cineplex:
Of Dungeons and Dragon Tattoos

In Poe's "The Oval Portrait" (1842), a wounded traveler and his valet break into a deserted chateau to take shelter in the mountains. The narrator's chamber is furnished with luxurious, although shabby, furnishings. "Its walls were hung with tapestry and bedecked with manifold and multiform armorial trophies, tougher with an unusually great number of very spirited modern paintings in frames of rich golden arabesque" (Poe 290). The walls themselves are indented with crannies, shaped by the "bizarre architecture" of the building. The valet closes "the heavy shutters of the room," lights a "tall candelabrum," and draws back the curtains surrounding the bed.

The flickering candle casts light on a portrait in a shadowy corner of the chamber. The narrator catches a glimpse of a live-seeming image of a young woman. He squeezes his eyes shut. "It was an impulsive moment to gain time for thought — to make sure that my vision had not deceived me — to calm and subdue my fancy for a more sober and certain gaze" (290–291). A second glance verifies the palpable presence of the image. The flickering candle rivets his gaze to the portrait. In observing the framed image by the light of a flickering candle, the narrator examines the "spell of the picture in an absolute life-likeliness of expression" (291). The narrator then obtains a book to help explain the portraits, "a volume which discussed the paintings and their histories" (291). He slides into the experience narrated in the book, letting his imagination work. All is ready for the show. Light, color, action. With this construction of the tale-telling context, Poe sets up a narrative informed through verbal and graphic texts. He essentially envisions the modern cinematic experience.

The tale the narrator reads in the book explains how the woman sat for her portrait painter husband. As soon as he achieved the finishing touches on her portrait, she died. "Ah this is life, but now it's death."

Critics have often considered "The Oval Portrait" as an instance of the distant artist who does not care about actual life. In this respect, the artist figure is similar to Hawthorne's Owen Warland in "The Artist of the Beautiful," published four years later. The allegories of Hawthorne's art have not translated well to the screen, *The Scarlet Letter* (1995, dir. Roland Joffé) being a case in point. Demi Moore plays Hester Prynne and Gary Oldman is Dimmesdale in an overwrought drama that earned several Raspberry Awards. Whereas Hawthorne's story is a parable warning against too much artistic distance from life, Poe emphasizes the necessity of an artist staking everything on a vision, of taking in and shaping a fully realized experience. Poe understands that a medium with a visual component does not distance the reader/viewer, but immerses the audience deeper into truths of experience. In this respect, Poe creates stories with an eye toward full expression.

Add *Shutter Island* and *The Girl with the Dragon Tattoo* to the long list of films wielding powerful motifs from Poe's fiction. These films are so cutting edge, why should a writer from a hundred and eighty years ago matter?

Both movies, adapted from best-selling novels, use narrative conventions and generic twists original with Poe that appeal to 21st-century audiences. Motifs central to the Dupin short stories, "The Gold Bug," and "The Fall of the House of Usher" are made to order for contemporary visual media. Mismatched investigators reflect sporadic access to information, prompting viewers toward interactive deductions. Encoded text in the story gleams like a nugget of partially buried treasure enticing the audience to join the hunt for clues. Investigators on-screen bring the audience along on the chase as cameras creep along narrow hallways and down winding staircases. Contemporary projections of Poe onscreen testify to the sturdy conventions of his tell-tale art.

Martin Scorsese directed *Shutter Island* (2010), based on the same-titled 2003 novel by Dennis Lehane. *The Girl with the Dragon Tattoo* (2009), directed by Niels Arden Oplev, comes from the best-selling book *Män som hatar kvinnor* (*Men Who Hate Women*, 2008) by Stieg Larsson.

Poe's shadow falls across these films primarily in three ways: The "who" of the narrative is a "double" agent, double in the sense that two people work the case, following the standard set by Dupin and "I," the nameless narrator. The method of investigation is to gather, decipher, and "read" word puzzles, images or anagrams pointing to the toxic X, the narrative's villain. The place of investigation is a haunted house, but one that functions metaphorically as it props up a ramshackle mind.

Poe's original "double agent" convention occurs in his stories pairing C. Auguste Dupin with the unnamed, first-person narrator. These two are the prototypes for Holmes and Dr. Watson. Dupin takes the lead due to his sharp deductive powers. The unnamed narrator is "well-educated, a good writer, a keen observer, but slow to pick up on clues. Thus Dupin can explain to him — and through him to the reader — how he arrives at his conclusions" (Magistrale and Poger 24). This narrator expresses doubt at the start and ends up processing and admiring Dupin's achievement. In other words, the narrator's dullness serves to polish Dupin's brilliance. Richard Wilbur discusses these two figures as "warring principles of the poet's divided nature" (117). Critics regard the duality of this agent/narrator as two sides of the same personality. However, I contend that the two sides do not define a mind/body duality, nor do they form a traditional doppelgänger. Instead, Poe makes clear that these characters are two sides of the tale-telling principle. At times, Dupin tells or withholds information key to the narrative; at other times, the narrator retrieves information from newspapers or the marketplace to prompt Dupin toward another phase of the case. The convention works because for the most part, these two are asymmetrical. They have unequal access to information and display an unequal balance of power. Unified by the story process, these two are not separate characters, but shifting sides of the narrative construct.

In a film, the metaphoric quality to this double figure is more challenging to implement. Played by two actors, the unified personality appears to be two characters. Each walks around independent of the other. But as the narrative develops, viewers register that the two halves function as one, in service to the mystery to be solved. They form a psychological unit, each incomplete without the other. One of the pair is the agent, in the action sense, holding most of the cards, while the other watches or asks questions and listens. The power of insight then shifts over the course of the investigation. The two sides have no clear dividing line, and the audience accepts the two characters as a single story-shaping force similar to Poe's original convention.

In a film-viewing context, the audience also plays a role similar to the nameless narrator "I." The rows of rapt spectators form the presence watching, admiring, and responding to the investigators' accumulation of clues.

A more defined break in the narrative emerges when a film uses Poe's convention of codes and ciphers to develop the story. Like the unnamed narrator of "Murders in the Rue Morgue" and "The Purloined Letter," the teller of "The Gold Bug" is an early Watson. He responds to Legrand's explanations and theories with various naïve responses like "how is it possible to extort a meaning from all this jargon?" (Poe 206) or "how excessively odd. I was sure you were mad" (210). These have the effect of prompting Legrand to explain in more detail, to set up a dialectic that ultimately creates the meaning. Legrand describes the treasure map cipher during a discussion with his helpful narrator "I." The insertion of these mysterious symbols into the text creates a break in the line of words to compel a slower reading: dagger, asterisk, double closed parentheses? What do these marks mean? These encoded sections raise questions and trip up the reader, creating a series of suspenseful pauses.

Poe's two forces of character/narrator and questioning reader serve to break down the authority of the text in a way that challenges the role of fiction. Far from being a hunt for buried treasure, "The Gold Bug" frames a more profound search: how does a symbol relates to its meaning? Legrand's presentation of signifiers as clues moves narrator and reader along the horizon of words from states of knowing to not knowing and back again. With markings to be interpreted by gradual revelation, in "The Gold Bug," Poe attempts to replicate the structures and processes of how we understand language.

Poe's essay "Philosophy of Composition" articulates the requirement that a short story maintain "close circumscription of space." This narrows the lens on Aristotle's concept of the dramatic unity of time and space. In *Poe's Children*, Magistrale and Poger write, "Poe intensified the Gothic's configuration that linked personality and place, supplying examples of confined and subterraneous imagery with a psychodynamic correspondence to his male characters" (15).

"The Fall of the House of Usher" sets the metaphoric mode for structures in both *Girl* and *Shutter*. The narrator fixates on the mansion's "vacant eyelike windows" and grasps in one moment "an utter depression of the soul which I can compare to no earthly sensation more properly than to the afterdream of the reveler upon opium — the bitter lapse into everyday life — the hideous dropping off of the veil" (231). The narrator follows the window "eyes" toward a vision of the interior and altered states of mind. Writing half a century before Freud without a vocabulary to articulate psychological interiority, Poe's creative take on the dynamics of psycho-emotional states is cannily accurate.

Poe's three narrative conventions of the paired double protagonist, ciphers and anagrams as clues, and houses of the mind emerge almost intact in the recent films *Shutter Island* and *The Girl with the Dragon Tattoo*.

An unlikely double forms at the center of Scorsese's film with the partnership of Teddy Daniels and "Chuck Aule." Actually, the paired characters represent doubles of doubles. Neither character is who he appears to be, but only one knows that he is playing a role.

It is 1954. U. S. Marshal Teddy Daniels is assigned a mission to locate a missing patient from Ashecliff Hospital for the criminally insane on Shutter Island. His partner is Chuck Aule, proud to work with the famous Teddy Daniels. He calls Teddy "Boss" and defers to him as their investigation proceeds. Early in the film, audience members also become investigators, listening carefully for clues. "Teddy" is a nickname for Edward. As "teddy bear," it carries connotations of childhood. Teddy hardly fits the heroic image Chuck has painted. Our first view of Teddy is when he gets sick in the ferry bathroom. He sports a Band-Aid on his temple, and his face looks drawn and beat up. If we pay attention, we can catch the easy pun of "Chuck Aule," as in "Chuck it all," or "Take this job and shove it." Chuck's name is another way to express surrendering the psyche. Clearly, the two are not who they seem, but who are they?

Once Teddy and Chuck arrive on the island, they meet suspicious-acting administrators. Teddy becomes convinced that the hospital is working out a nefarious plot of mind control. After he drinks coffee, a blinding headache confuses him. He has trouble interviewing the inmates about the missing patient, Rachel Solando, he was called in to locate. He gets a tip that a person named Andrew Laeddis has valuable information about the case. When Teddy has hallucinations, the waking nightmares stall his search for Laeddis. To up the dramatic ante, a violent storm blows out the hospital's electrical system and releases the most dangerous patients from cellblock C.

A compliant Chuck agrees with Teddy most of the time. These two are *simpatico*, complementary in the same way as Dupin and his pair-of-eyes narrator. Eventually, Chuck falls off a cliff, and Teddy has to investigate alone. Or does he? Who really is the boss behind Teddy's actions? He fights his way toward the dangerous lighthouse. Its blinding ray could lead to mental obliteration, a revelation, or perhaps both.

Stieg Larsson takes Poe's basic "genius-narrator" formula and loosens it. We start with two investigators, Mikael Blomkvist and Lisbeth Salander, also an unlikely double, who trade roles as the film proceeds.

Blomkvist is a disgraced journalist asked to help elderly industrialist Henrik Vanger find out what happened to his niece Harriet, missing for thirty years. Through the security agency working with Vanger, Blomkvist learns about the extraordinary investigative skills of Lisbeth Salander, a diminutive, painfully shy girl-woman who kick-boxes, has a photographic memory, and is a computer hacker without peer.

Blomkvist starts in the driver's seat. Initially, Lisbeth had monitored Blomkvist's progress on the investigation from afar on her computer, and when he shows up expectedly at her apartment, her cover is blown. She is thrown off balance by his intrusion. As the aggressor barging into her apartment, Mikael could seize the power in the investigative relationship, if he were so inclined. But he is not. He needs her help and by responding to his plea, she emerges reluctantly from her self-imposed cyberworld isolation. Because Lisbeth has been damaged by men, when Blomkvist fails to give her his full attention, she withdraws yet again.

Soon the balance of power shifts in this detecting dyad. The film includes a scene in which she literally ends up driving the two of them, and ultimately she is the damsel who rescues the prince.

Onscreen, the faceted characters of *Shutter* and *Girl* appear in such a shimmery, incomplete way that the audience learns to piece together aspects of them. These people are like pointillist representations of human experience, with certain traits laid out. When their actions fail to match the build-up, the audience has to fill in the spaces.

The ciphers and anagrams in these two films become psychological mirrors of the characters trying to figure them out. Through anagrams, Teddy Daniels discovers the true missing persons of his mission. In the same way, Salander soon finds, to her horror, that in researching the cold cases of horrific crimes against women, she must relive her own traumas of abuse.

In working this case, Blomkvist also uncovers truths about himself. He exposes the quintessential men who hate women, Gottfried Vanger and his son Martin, Harriet's brother. He also comes to understand his own ways of treating women badly through his lackadaisical attitudes toward women. In the book, he has an ex-wife and a daughter whom he ignores. The film transforms him into a doting uncle. A few scenes show him in his sister's kitchen chatting it up with his niece. Still, his diffidence in dealing with Salander and Erika Berger ends up paining them both.

Blomkvist eventually uses Salander's information to locate the missing Harriet. When Salander saves Blomkvist's life, she releases him from literal and metaphoric restraints, but at what price to herself? Does her rage against Vanger re-open painful wounds from her past? Does Mikael repay the favor and release Salander from her prison? Blomkvist's debt of gratitude to Salander motivates him to rescue her in the trilogy's second installment, *The Girl Who Played with Fire*. Even though Blomkvist does not beat or mistreat women intentionally, his diffidence victimizes the women in his life.

Mikael grievously wounds Salander by going with Erika. The first film of the trilogy leaves open whether Blomkvist will ultimately be with Salander. He observes a video of her in a new identity and smiles in a patronizing way. The book clarifies that she has sincere feelings for him. She is too much of a realist to be carried away by romantic fantasy: "She had never in her life felt such a longing. She wanted Mikael Blomkvist to ring the doorbell and ... what then? Lift her off the ground? ... No, she really just wanted his company" (588). Then Salander sees Blomkvist with Erika, and the girl dumps into the trash the Elvis sign she had bought for him (588–589). On the page, his betrayal of her is much more straightforward.

Due to extreme trauma, Teddy loses his identity as a storyteller. After his breakdown due to alcoholism and his wife's death, his reputation as a law-enforcement officer is ruined. Thus, he has no real power to shape a narrative inside the justice system or out of it. In the closing scenes, Teddy pathetically reaffirms his status as teller of the case he will work on Shutter Island. He plays a role as an "agent" to gain a sense of redemption through the charade. In the film's final scene, Teddy asks Chuck, "Is it better to live as a monster or die as a good man?" He appears to have made his Parfittian choice. He goes to his fate with the split psyche he needs to survive each remaining moment.

When Blomkvist loses his position as an investigative journalist, he has to piece together the case on his own. This position places him outside his usual role with a city news organization. Working for Henrik Vanger, he has the old man's backing but no institutional support. Ultimately, he cedes power to Salander on the Wennerström case. We catch a brief glimpse of her as the film ends. Blomkvist knows what she is doing, and he smiles. She has grabbed power, but she still has not emerged into her own persona. She is in disguise, not herself.

Salander all but disappears in the second book, as she has gone into exile. Her re-emergence from her own mental prison takes longer than Mikael's. After her long exile in the second book, Blomkvist finds her only at the end, and she is so massively injured she is unaware that he is rescuing her. Her re-emergence from the prison of her psyche will take much longer. She crawls up from the earth in a birth ritual only to be locked back into the jail of her own debilitated body. Previously psychic traumas have imprisoned her; now actual physical trauma immobilizes her.

Ultimately, Teddy glimpses his actual identity as slayer of his wife. The lighthouse brings a blinding revelation of who he really is. He sees the "insoluble mystery" that the narrator of "Usher" mentions, the profound ineffable reality of the self. The clues all point to the truth that "Teddy Daniels" is an anagram for "Andrew Laeddis." Hunter and hunted are the same. But this epiphany lasts for only a quick moment. The blend of outside perspective with inner subjectivity, with seeing himself as he actually is, is so horrifically painful that he must lapse back into seeing Laeddis as "Other."

Santos' *The Dark Mirror* discusses the many shortcomings of psychotherapeutic culture in *film noir*. Movies made in the years immediately following World War II reflect the popular mind's lack of confidence in the psychiatric community's power to remedy war-induced traumas. Santos observes, "Psychotherapy, dream analysis, hypnosis, and drug therapy ... are usually shown to have less-than-desirable effect, and the treatment atmosphere or mental hospital becomes yet another *noir* locale for alienation and peril" (35). *Shutter Island* provides a contrasting view of therapy in the popular mind. Scorsese's update, or *nouveau film noir*, displays a public's confidence with psychiatric methods of healing. The methods of Teddy's Ashecliffe healers are sound and more than generous. The doctors construct a layer of role-playing narratives to lead Teddy gradually to the painful story at his core. His failure to retain that story has everything to do with his shattered self, not the healing culture. The perspective five extra decades later shifts onscreen attention to the de-stabilized self rather than the dysfunctional institution providing the ostensible care.

Onscreen, letters, maps, and symbols all but halt the action. The camera zooms in, as audience attention shifts from the flow of physical action to a character then to a smaller space of information. Television shows like *CSI* or *NCIS* or *Cold Case* spruce up these moments with special effects. High-def colors and closeup views of blood streams or splatters keep these images bright and sparkly as "zoom" sound effects play on the soundtrack. One would think that films would not trust this kind of action slow-down required of ciphers or codes. The immediacy of an image is usually the prime mover to propel an audience through the storyline. However, both *Shutter Island* and *Girl* incorporate a stream of coded text that needs deciphering.

In Lehane's work, images flash into Teddy's head about his past. His wife turns to ashes in his arms. What does the nightmare mean? Teddy's snippets of memories about his wife pose a meaning he must decipher. Prisoners scratch cryptic notes and slip these to him. He watches as crazed prisoners in the high-security cell block cover the cell walls with scribbles and obsessive phrases. The novel describes the scene: "Teddy backed away from the bars, turning to his left and noting that the entire left wall of the man's cell was covered in script, not an inch to spare, thousands of cramped, precise lines of it, the words so small they were unreadable unless you pressed your eyes to the wall" (235). These words are emblematic of the deranged narrative Teddy's damaged psyche tells to itself. He constructs a narrative, a false one, of what has happened, to give himself a quasi-memory, *q*-memory, as in Derek Parfit's philosophy of personality.

In a parallel narrative technique, the newspaper pictures of Harriet Vanger at the parade just before she disappeared pose question marks for Blomkvist. The key subtext to these clues is neither image or word, but time. Reading the cryptic texts correctly does not scroll out before the investigator a comprehensive view of what happened, but it does allow the perceiver to take in those moments, essentially to restore stopped time and move it forward again. Figuring out the meanings of his burning wife and his wife in her dripping wet dress allows Teddy to replay his personal history and comprehend what has happened. Reconstructing those last moments of Harriet's affords Blomkvist the opportunity to pick up her trail.

Poe's uses of codes break into the fabric of the text as a kind of proto-intertextuality, now a commonplace with postmodernist meta-fiction by authors like John Barth, Thomas Pynchon, or Mark Z. Danielewski. Poe's uninformed narrator suggests a "shadow" presence of the uninformed reader. This relationship mirrors that of the unnamed narrator in the Dupin stories.

Salander and Blomkvist each fail to receive a validation of experience from the ciphers. These written signs represent the uncanny reality that exists just beyond their abilities to comprehend them.

The intriguing point about the photographs of the missing Harriet Vanger at the parade is that these do not record merely her, but her point of view. Her objective image has one validity, to note her presence at the parade. It is a happy, festive time, and there is a poignant irony in her presence there, since the possibility hovers that her opportunity to enjoy any more of these moments has ended. The other intriguing element of these shots is that Blomkvist gathers more clues from the direction of Harriet's gaze. Her facial expression changes given what she sees. It remains for Blomkvist to figure out what she is looking at. As in Antonioni's film *Blow Up*, the image itself does not convey any final meaning. The key significance results from the interplay created when subjective gaze meets the object of that perception.

Another crucial clue to the case followed by Blomkvist involves biblical ciphers. Blomkvist fails to decipher the significance of these names and numbers. Interestingly, Salander is the one who first recognizes the context in which these symbols have to be read. By reinfusing language with a sacred element, she makes progress toward understanding that the case has a long history. She now frames Harriet's disappearance in that context.

Blomkvist is blind to this religious tie-in to the ciphers. He has lost an appreciation for the sacred quality of the word. As a cynical journalist, he has seen the degradation of language used for crass motives and commercial polemic. He has used it himself to expose the corrupt financial titan Wennerström and has suffered for it.

Another kind of clue that puzzles Salander and Blomkvist involves words from the internet. After Salander figures out the Biblical references, Blomkvist approves, but then he removes himself from the uses of language for charged meaning and enters a duplicitous realm of social small talk. He has dinner at the Vanger households. He leaves Salander to develop all the remaining coded leads. She gathers data from library archives, old newspapers, and old TV programs. Putting pictures and identities together, Salander looks for clues left as traces of crimes mirroring her own abuse.

As Teddy approaches Shutter Island, the outside of Ashecliffe Hospital looms before him as a Gothic castle with turrets constructed of gray blocks. Especially frightening is his view of the outside of cellblock C, which contains the most dangerous prisoners, the criminally insane. The inside of cellblock C is even more dangerous to Teddy, as it draws out painful memories, and he has a difficult time conducting the interviews and investigations he has been assigned.

In the cellblock, Teddy and Chuck agree to separate, Teddy to find Andrew Laeddis and Chuck to locate files. Once Teddy is alone, stairs and bars from cells whirl about him in a dizzying array of various planes without coherence. To recreate Teddy's imbalance, Director Scorsese uses 360-degree revolving and zoom-in/track-out shots, camera techniques from Hitchcock, whom Scorsese has long admired. Andrew Pulver of the *Guardian* reviewed the film when it first came out in March 2010 and notes a bit derisively that Scorsese "has taken the Hitchcockian atmosphere of murderous insanity and run with it." Still, despite the scene's derivative quality, the effect is an Escheresque collision of horizontal levels and walkways. The film transforms Poe's idea of a *mise en abîme* into knots of psychic disturbance. The disequilibrium overwhelms Teddy, moving him to question who and where he is. He is pulled deeper into the cell blocks and into his psyche.

Teddy's conversation with the prisoner George Noyes brings back a rush of memories:

> Teddy felt her in him, pressed at the base of his throat. He could see her sitting in the early July haze in that dark cottage light as city gets on summer nights just after sundown....
>
> Let her go, Noyce had said.
>
> "I can't," Teddy said and the words came out cracked and too high and he could feel screams welling in the center of his chest [242].

Houses of the mind represent an extreme psychological state expressed as a tortured environment. The dimensions of the cellblocks are deceptive, and the hope of escape turns out to be an illusion. Who are the guards and who are the inmates? Ironically, Teddy's confusion brings him closer to the truth that he is as caged as the rest of them.

The film version of Larsson's book reflects the motif of House of the Mind as the island. For Blomkvist, a cold, harsh present is juxtaposed against a glinting summer of memories. Possibilities of escape actually yield to no escape. As with the narrow causeway topography in Poe's "The Fall of the House of Usher," a shaky bridge separates everyday life from an island of disturbed, traumatized consciousness.

When Blomkvist is jailed as a result of the Wennerström libel suit, he comes out almost happier than he went in. Blomkvist is a charmed boy. He treats his stint in Rullåker Prison as a lark:

> His time at Rullåker had been unstressful and pleasant enough.... The daily routines reminded him of living in a youth hostel.... He asked for permission to keep his iBook in his cell so that he could continue to work on the book he was commissioned to write. His request was granted" [Larsson 275–276].

In a few months he is back at work, trapped in his real prison of failure, one of the mind.

Blomkvist has basically failed with his exposé of Wennerström. He was accused of falsifying data and of libel, a journalist's worst nightmare. He had to take the legal punishment, even though he knew the truth of his words. He had to settle for scraps, that he could work toward an eventual exposé in the future.

On Hedeby island in the cottage, Blomkvist and Salander are isolated from the rest of the world, but they are together in their captivity. He was in jail literal, and so has she been in captivity. He remains in a mental exile, and so is she still psychologically imprisoned by fear of her own brilliance and bitterness over her troubled past. Over the larger narrative arc of the trilogy, Larsson works out more developments between the two. Salander takes a longer time to emerge from her cage, and Blomkvist plays a consistent role in coaxing her out. Lisbeth's tattoo says as much. In 1995, Kathleen Gregory Klein wrote, "The Woman is the body in the library on whom the criminal writes his narrative of murder" (173). In a sense, the tattoo on Lisbeth documents her victimhood. A dragon is a symbol of the spirit. The dragon inked over her skin represents her paralyzed spirit, displayed on the outside because it cannot escape. However, Lisbeth takes consistent steps toward emerging from this prison, starting with the indicting tattoo she inks on the abdomen of her rapist, Advokat Bjurman: "I AM A SADISTIC PIG, A PERVERT, AND A RAPIST." She reverses Klein's dictate about the criminal's writing on the body, and as a victim, she writes her own narrative on the oppressor.

Salander's involvement in the cyberworld illustrates her extreme withdrawal from the tangible world. She is already diminutive, but she hunches in her hoodie to make herself smaller, nearly assuming a fetal position. Ironically, she travels with ease over the cyber-universe, but she has a minimal bodily presence in the world. Although her custom-designed hacker program gives her omnipotence, she has named it "Asphyxia," an inability to breathe, carrying a connotation of claustrophobia. Even her own mother calls her by her sister's name. Although Lisbeth's revenge against her attacker, Advokat Bjurman, is scathing and has film audiences cheering her on, even this revenge is cramped. She films her rape through a tunnel lens in her backpack.

Both Blomkvist and Salander move toward a gradual reconciliation with society, although Blomkvist achieves his resolution before she does. At the end of *Dragon Tattoo*, book and film, Salander is "at work" ripping off Wennerström by hacking into his bank accounts. She travels out in the world but wears another costume as "Irene." She does not yet achieve a spatial freedom as has Blomkvist, doing his work for Vanger outside the confines of a conventional office.

Haunted houses and structural details like stairs and doors appeal to film audiences because a film is itself a house of the mind. The wide-angle screen gleaming in the dark projects the patterns inside our heads across the wall in front of us. Cracked structures, too-low ceilings, dark hallways, and ominous staircases are outside images that reflect our often flawed thought processes and the anxieties that go with them. We experience a complete immersion in the film experience. When the film ends and the lights come on, like the narrator of "Usher," we retreat across the bridges and causeways to flee the surreal images of terror or pain or sorrow before the house collapses into the tarn.

Audiences love this formula. By all box office measures, these two films achieved popular success. *Shutter Island* earned $127,000 when it opened and shows a gross income of $41 million of June 2010. According to *Variety*, the Swedish-version of *Dragon* has grossed over $200 million worldwide so far. *Girl* opened with grosses of $335,000 in the U.S. and currently stands with over $10 million in profits.

More films about altered consciousness have followed. After *Shutter Island*, Christopher Nolan's *Inception* came out in July 2010. Trailers for *Inception* said that the movie would tap into a Poe-esque psychological blend of disturbed cognition: "Your mind is the scene of the crime." Audiences flocked to the film. *Inception* directed by Nolan and again featuring DiCaprio, grossed $62 million at its opening and continues to do a brisk business, with IMBD citing a gross of $289 million as of October 2010.

The main character of *Inception* has a number of parallels with Teddy Daniels/Laeddis. Like Teddy, the protagonist, Dom Cobb, grieves the death of his wife. Also like Teddy, the character's name presents itself as a kind of anagram: Dom Cobb, a slanted version of the high-tech "dot.com." As a result, we conclude that Cobb's consciousness lives in an altered state. Dreams are interchangeable with reality. From his point of view, his constructed half-lives emerge through odd perceptions and clusters of images that coalesce into characters. According to Parfit, the fusion coming from a character's psyche is born from his need to survive. The film plays between certainty and uncertainty about the physical and psychological survival of Dom Cobb.

Solid houses, cathedrals, and palaces unroll with excruciating slowness into spaces of Cobb's mind and those of the viewers. Locations at the shore or on an ice-frosted mountaintop make little everyday sense; as is the case with dreams, the impact is primarily metaphoric. Each scene is sketched in expressionistic outlines. The locale seems nearly alive, as conveyed in the "sentience of all vegetable things" in the world of the House of Usher. The backdrop is a reflection that breathes with the characters. "Your mind is the scene of the crime." *Inception* is as good as its word in following up on its promotional trailer: Objects melt into the subject's vision and mind as experience plays out as dreams. The concluding scenes pose questions that cast into doubt all that has gone on before.

Film audiences devoured *Inception*, as the puzzling narrative almost commands repeated viewings. The blogs lit up with viewers' interpretations, because nearly everyone seemed to have one. The images take on significance according to viewers' focalizations, and not all is channeled and shaped for audience consumption in the traditional way of films.

An American version of *Girl with the Dragon Tattoo* is on its way. Daniel Craig plays Mikael Blomkvist, and Rooney Mara was cast amid much fanfare as Lisbeth Salander. Set to be released in December 2011, it will be directed by David Fincher and produced by Scott Rudin, the same creative duo behind *The Social Network* (2010). The Fincher-Rudin connection to this project is no coincidence. These film-makers understand perceptions of the digital-savvy youth market. They know how cyber-culture has shaped young viewers' engagement with a story and can make this translation to the screen.

This comparison between a textual use of ciphers and message posted in cyberspace provides more evidence of Poe's familiarity with the self's inter-action with a story. When the camera zooms onto a message and the film audience has to readjust thinking about the story from images into a series of letters and words, that shift alters the shape of a narrative. It channels the stream of graphics into a symbolic landscape. The story is like a melody played in a different key with a shifted rhythm. What we think of as postmodernist literary technique finds full expression in these films using the building blocks of storytelling originated by Poe. Poe's fiction lays the groundwork for subtly shaded characters, for intertextuality, and for a blend of mind and space that now regularly takes place every time a person logs into cyberspace.

Audiences flocked to *Shutter Island* and *The Girl with the Dragon Tattoo* for several reasons. They are, foremost, well-written, compelling stories. Next, as commodities, the stories were already pre-sold, in a sense, through platforms established by the novels. As with most Poe-inflected narratives, the story essentially hinges on the mystery of words and a character's ability to "read" images that construct an interior story.

The people going through these events are full-bodied characters, familiar and recognizable as victims of conflict and trauma. These film characters have subtleties, but they are close to being the same as characters on television crime dramas or victims on the pseudo-documentaries that pass as true crime.

However, *Shutter* and *Girl* build on a fluidity or looseness of structure now familiar to most film-goers. This generation of cinema viewers regularly experiences the autonomy of information from the Web as it appears on lap-tops and podcasts, Droids, iPhones, and iPads. These messages are often framed out of a traditional context and decentralized, so the authority of the text is ceded even more to audience interpretation. The public's current thirst for disembodied investigators, fragmented narratives, and surreal haunted houses could also reflect the current popular equivocation over rapid shifts in delivery systems for entertainment media. The public is at once satisfied with the wealth of information, but uneasy over this relatively new autonomy of interpretation.

Contemporary audiences have a high tolerance for the disorientation of today's thriller films. The degree of disruption is similar to that of Poe's fiction with his undercurrents of ambiguity and indeterminate characters. In a sense, the ambiguous selves of William Wilson or the fused identity of the narrator in "The Tell-Tale Heart" find modern analogues in the digital world's social network.

Today's audiences have become accustomed to fluid identities, perhaps due to Facebook. They easily translate this familiarity of a personal shape-shifting to onscreen characters. They are used to personalities that do not cohere and may not develop organically as they might in conventional literary works. Like Dupin and his protean narrator, characters in many films today are like constructed identities from online social network. The onscreen characters grow out of a swirl of characteristics to be filled in by the audience. Characters that draw high interest from contemporary viewers are pixilated identities.

Multi-linearity of a story line is a second quality of Poe's fiction that translates smoothly to the screen. Today's film audiences are accustomed to hyperlinks leading to branchings of divergent perceptions. Through codes and ciphers, puzzles within puzzles, Poe's fiction presents a collision of worlds, language systems, and hierarchies of images. The *mise en abîme* of this work presents a rough texture to the text, creating multiple layers. These layers exist not merely in the sense of metaphors but in the juxtaposition of works inside works. Poe's fiction displays a texture of the same order as a hyperlink, a slippage into various sets of words and linguistic worlds, an option for new information, an explanation of the concept in the line of the sentence, a move into a new space.

Another facet of computer use affecting a viewer's story perception is the tunnel-like vision the user must adopt for the small screen. Poe's close circumscription of space presents a locked room, hermetically sealed environment that blocks external disturbances, but over which, paradoxically, the mind can roam. This paradox is woven into Poe's artistry. Even in an expansive environment, Poe creates claustrophobia. For instance, Pym is at sea on the *Grampus*, yet he is below decks in a stifling, suffocating box. The fusion quality of this perception is at work through images of envelopment. The psychodynamics linking personality and space that Magistrale and Poger pinpoint as the circumscription of space in Poe's work become literal and redefine themselves each time we log on and take residence in an online environment.

Using a computer and entering cyberreality emphasizes a paradox of intimacy and distance. We perceive an image or text through the tiny rectangle of the screen of an iPad or iPhone. We experience the image closeup, and it carries the illusion of appearing to us alone, yet we perceive an image with the potential of being shared worldwide. The internet is redefining public and private spaces. Privacy is fast disappearing. The line is fading between the inner sanctum of a home and the outside world. Yet when we use a computer, we have both the illusion of intimacy and that of openness. The appealing images of our screensavers lure us in with the illusion of openness. With the user's easy control over text and the process of writing, the computer fosters an atmosphere of intimacy. Two cases in point are recent instances of very public figures, a sports star and an elected representative, sending sexual images of themselves over cell phones or social websites. Private behavior slips all too easily into a public sphere.

With entertainment viewed on a personal electronic device, the viewer has no actual sense of receiving information along with a group, as in a movie theater. This is another reason for the illusion of privacy over the internet being both so persuasive and pervasive.

Poe himself as a directly named subject continues to come off the media assembly line. A film called *The Raven*, is coming out in 2011 from Relativity Media. Starring John Cusack and directed by James McTeigue, the story covers the last days of Poe's life. The writer spends these last few days chasing a murderer committing copycat crimes modeled on the ways of death from Poe's stories. The situation seems similar to the Poe "copycat" murderer who toys with Alex Cooper in Linda Fairstein's *Entombed*. Undoubtedly this onscreen version of *The Raven* will shuffle time, play with faulty memories, slipped intentions, or dreams from others. Audiences have always had a huge appetite for the spectacles that are visual overlays of houses of the mind. It could be argued that film's sacred quality comes from its full color replication of the inside of our heads. Throughout the history of film, viewers have worshipped this projected icon of ourselves. We are like the narrator of "The Fall of the House of Usher." We immerse ourselves in multiple narratives. Then as the film credits roll at story's end, we cross back over that "narrow causeway" into the light. We flee images of pain, terror, sorrow, or whatever else we discovered dwelling in the House of Film and return to our own constructed reality. At that point, whatever the house represents, a meaningless dream or an enduring truth, collapses into the tarn.

CHAPTER 10

Hurtling through Cyberspace

Over the past decade, the cyber-gaming world has exploded like a super-nova. In addition to a player's potent feeling of being in control, players become immersed in the small screen's stories. Video game developers have painted vast tracts of this universe with the blood-tinged imagery of Poe's fiction. Despite the upgrade to entertainment technology, the stories told through video-game platforms continue to pay homage to Poe's tell-tale art. Does a story's meaning change when a player wields a game controller from a Wii, PlayStation 3, or Xbox 360 instead of when a reader turns pages?

Poe's intense use of first-person narration is made to order for first-person, role-player video games. For stories on the page as well as on a computer monitor, a controlling perspective parcels out action, cementing the relationship between teller/tale, and reader/player. Poe's work of the 1830s and 1840s was so forward thinking that he continues to be relevant when reframed in a modern context. What is the position of Poe's narrative formula in the world of electronic narratives and how can we best view his place in the discourse about new media? Electronic means for delivering text may increase the speed of word messages. It may also offer control over fonts and color shades and applications at laser-fast speed. However, ultimately text shapes itself into a story, and Poe's narrative templates of fear and suspense and the search for truth continue to play a central role.

In the same way that Poe draws in the reader for intense interactivity, technology has advanced to the point where viewers of visual media can have that same involvement. Narrative interactivity has expanded to the point where objective viewers can affect screen motion through actual muscular movement, as in video games such as Wii and Kinect for Xbox 360.

Poe appeals to an audience reading about fear and gives them something to grasp as they try to take control over death in trying times. Detective programs on television are the equivalent of "comfort food." These programs make it safe for viewers to confront death, even if only in an onscreen incarnation. The narrative formula that Poe developed serves to structure most of these cyber-narratives as well. In addition, Poe focuses on death as a search for self-knowledge. He moves the reader/player's consciousness into horrific conflict and toward resolution, and provides an ultimate affirmation of life.

Narrative art evolves from written text to image to narrative interactivity, which means incorporating a literal idiom of communication through actions and gestures. What are the forces behind these shifts and developments in media? With everyday images morphing into nightmares and with underlying layers of anxiety and paranoia, Poe's fiction looks toward an image-oriented culture consistent with our contemporary world's preoccupation with personal and homeland security. Over the past decade, electronic communication devices have changed our lives enormously. Even if the general effect of this shift is to democratize the message and distribute control among many, the effect is destabilizing.

Cyberworlds on Film Screens

Connecting narrative text, image, and gesture, or at least a viewer's perceptual gestures, occurs in James Cameron's high-tech *Avatar* (2009), which received an Oscar nomination in 2010.

Although set over a century into the future, *Avatar 3D* sends characters we recognize on a psycho-fantastic voyage to the planet Pandora light-years from earth. Once there, modern characters transform from their earthly bodies into the giant, graceful forms of intelligent beings of the Na'vi tribe. This film is Poe-esque in its eco-action adventure theme and its use of Poe's tale-teller interaction with voice-over narration. In addition, Cameron's high-tech "performance capture" film technique builds an intimate connection between onscreen characters and film-viewers. Snakes or guns do not jump out at the viewers, but instead the audience is drawn in by a fully dimensioned landscape and character perceptions.

Even though actors usually create people to whom the audience can relate, in this film, viewers watch the process of how a character becomes an avatar. Through many tests, extensive training, and machine hookups, we see how paraplegic war veteran Jake Sully (Sam Worthington) becomes a human–Na'vi hybrid capable of living on Pandora among the Na'vi tribe. The basic construct of a crippled character finding freedom and a full range of movement and imagination in a fanciful realm is itself a metaphor for film. Movie characters have always been essentially onscreen avatars for the audience.

The most recent 3-D film release connected with James Cameron is *Sanctum* (2011), directed by Alister Grierson. While Cameron is not the director or writer, but the executive producer, his name is a major part of the film's marketing. In its basic plot of an expedition battling uncompromising forces of nature, *Sanctum* bears striking similarity to Poe's "A Descent into the Maelström." Not only does the film echo many motifs from the story, but its form, set with numerous *mise en abîme* shifts in story levels, displays a Poe-esque narrative structure. In addition, the storytelling context blends tale and teller through a circumscribed perspective enhanced through 3-D film-viewing technology.

Before the featured film *Sanctum* begins, the theater audience, now wearing 3-D glasses, receives samples of future high-def films to come. While this prelude is mostly a promotional come-on, these small *mise en abîme* structures form additional stories-within-stories for the viewer's immersion into the entire narrative of the 3-D film experience. Viewers are lured across Poe's narrow causeway adjacent to the tarn of imagination to enter the new realm of the tale.

Like Dupin, who dons dark glasses to see more clearly in "The Purloined Letter," audience viewers sport the vision-enhancing gear. The film trailers take advantage of this captive audience. Clearly, these viewers are part of the 3-D film target market. If they are in the theater, they want to enjoy 3-D. During a recent screening of *Sanctum*, I viewed several 3-D movie trailers before the actual film began. The film montage emphasizes a trend in viewer interactivity that requires a fuller engagement of the audience's perceptual identification with onscreen action.

The string of promotional trailers begins. Despite the different technology of film delivery, Poe's narrative structures continue to mark the stories. *Battle: Los Angeles* (dir. Jonathan Liebesman) is an apocalyptic film. Objects that at first appear to be comets or meteors streak across the heavens, landing with fiery crashes. Earth-bound observers soon realize that they are under attack, being "colonized" by machine-like aliens, the latest iteration of "Transformer" creatures. The crafts and missiles send shock waves and tsunami-sized waves of dirt onto the urban population. The 3-D effect intensifies flying shrapnel from falling buildings, exploding battleships, and giant weapons that fire shells directly at the audience. The vapor trails crisscross the sky, overwhelming a besieged Los Angeles. There is no hope for salvation. At trailer's end, the date of the film's opening, "3-11-2011," then morphs ominously into the words "*Battlefield: LA*." The numerical date, then, carries a kind of prediction for the end of the world.

Another 3-D preview trailer prior to *Sanctum* involves a bizarre cross-genre, *Cowboys and Aliens*. This film is a hybrid of standard popular conventions. Daniel Craig plays a lone cowboy waking in the desert with a start, wondering at the high-tech bracelet on his wrist. He wanders into a saloon of the Old West, but an electronic bracelet places him in the 21st century. Harrison Ford plays the grizzled cowboy. The two actors team up to face the strange, evil force from out of town. This time, the cowboys in black hats are aliens, highly machined life forms. UFOs the size of battleships hover over familiar urban scenes. These stealth aircraft descend without stealth. Shotgun shells flip out from the screen at the audience; the barrels of rifles point in the audience's collective face.

This continued film warning of impending apocalypse exploits the collective anxiety of a moviegoing public trying to deal with a shifting geopolitical landscape. Our films emphasize that we cannot rest easy in the power of the United States after 9-11, and the images on film betray our upset. In the wake of being attacked, we fear intrusion from other countries, and this paranoia translates onscreen into manageable attacks from outer space.

In addition, our culture now endures internal stresses from technology. The space aliens that descend in *Battle L.A.* and *Cowboys and Aliens* look like machines. These enemies represent not only an attack from outside, but they emphasize the very real stresses and tensions we endure daily from cell phones, emails, and texts. Cyber forces both run and challenge our everyday lives. The attention these devices demand, the reliance we have on them, and the betrayal we feel when they fail all collectively, come to the fore when techno-enemies attack through 3-D film technology.

Finally, like the narrator of "Usher," shaken to the core, but recovered and ready to proceed, the audience prepares to enter the inner *Sanctum* of the feature film.

In Papua New Guinea, a team of cave explorers fine-tunes its preparations to descend into the earth. The team's purpose is to chart one of the last unexplored cave systems in the world. The film is connected to Poe by its major emblem of a maelström-like, circular descent. Coming face to face with the environment promotes madness. The story also dips below the basic linear sequence of the narrative into several dimensions of a *mise en abîme*, embedded stories within the story.

To stamp a seal of authenticity, the introduction to *Sanctum* carries the label "inspired by a true story." A helicopter flies a young man, Josh, to see his father, a famed cave explorer named Frank, played by Richard Roxbergh. The 3-D visuals emphasize the immensity of an endless jungle, "the last primeval wilderness," as Carl emphasizes. Carl is a photographer hoping to capture photos worthy of being published in *National Geographic*. Carl's girl-friend Victoria and Josh are fresh from a Himalayan climb. Their presence on the expedition is tenuous. They are scalers of vertical ascents. This project requires them to descend and use scuba gear. While the three have some skills, their expertise is not exactly the right fit.

The helicopter carries this group of stock characters to the site, but 3-D adds many thrills to their entrance. The chopper affords viewers a bird's-eye view. An extreme long shot with a down-tilt follows a twisting river. The camera's perspective creates a disorienting stomach churn as it simulates the helicopter coming over a rise. The effect is startling as the audience catches its first glimpse of the circular, bottomless hole in the earth into which the group must drop. The geologic feature is Esa-Ala, "the mother of all caves."

The cave was created out of eons of rainwater cutting through limestone. In addition to this subjective long view, we soon see a map of the cave's interior on a laptop screen that proves this point. The contrast between close feeling and distant cogitation is a thematic motif continuing throughout the film. From a map on the tiny screen of a laptop, the audience sees that the immense cave descends through a series of horizontal steps, leading eventually to a tight place called "the Devil's Restriction." Then it follows a series of "unknown and unexplored" passages, heading eventually, by some mysterious way, to the sea. The structure of the cave basically lays out the form of the film's narrative. We know from the start that Josh and his father are on bad terms, as members of the expedition warn the son that his father is furious with him for some as yet unknown incident. The relationship between father and son has to work its way past unknown emotional encounters before the two can reach the freedom to feel, as represented by the cave's rivers flowing into the ocean.

On the surface, we view the normalcy of camp, people carrying supplies, natives walking along well-worn pathways flanked by tents. Once a heavy rain starts on the surface, trouble brews for the team in the cave system below. As the crew prepares to descend, an ancient man decked out in a tribal mask observes the group through the falling rain, an omen of bad things to come.

George is one of Frank's divers who tries to set Josh straight about his father. George's attitude is that Frank is a terrific guy, and Josh should drop the chip on his shoulder and take a lesson. George has been with Frank for a while and has suffered the blood-fizzing, nitrogen narcosis. George also at one point relates that he had picked up the clap when the team was diving into caves in Mexico. He wears a Ramones t-shirt with "Hey Ho Let's Go" scrawled across the back. The motto's energy relates to Frank's own driving force as he tries to rally the team later when the going gets tough through the caves. The motto also dispels the image of scientist George as a geek. Since *Twister* (1996), science-chasing characters in the movies are regular guys, slobs even, doing extraordinary things. This upending of the mad scientist stereotype has itself become another type.

The film plays out an Oedipal struggle. Frank's view is if you're going to explore, approach life with élan, and just do it. Frank has made exploring this cave his life's work, but the son disparages this goal and his father in general.

Josh wears a boar's tooth necklace that his father had given to him. Frank had killed the boar with his bare hands. Josh is disgusted that his father couldn't leave the tooth as it was, natural bone, but instead had it outfitted with a tiny torch. Josh shows the others, making a scatological comment about where one might shine this tiny light. At another point, Josh calls a tight squeeze in the tunnel "a sphincter passage." In fact, the camera's dolly shots moving through the network of tunnels seem to replicate images from a colonoscopy. Clearly, the film links human anatomy to the body of the earth. Human experience marks geographic landscape in a time-honored ritual of understanding. As with the hieroglyphic markings along the Cliffside in *Pym*, man attempts to overlay mysteries of the human body onto Mother Earth's greater mysteries.

Many of *Sanctum*'s 3-D camera angles catch viewers by surprise and even disturb. An especially alarming instance occurs as the divers first descend below water, and our point of view behind the 3-D glasses sinks with them. These immersive shots remind viewers of the weight of the 3-D glasses, and overwhelm us with the feeling of being underwater with the divers. The moment simulates the viewer's own drowning, as the waterline nears the viewer's faces and then rises above the nose, in a reenactment of water torture.

Robert Baird discusses the jolt that a visceral moment on screen makes on the consciousness of film viewers. He notes that "startles prove to us, in the very maw of virtual death, how very much alive we are" (22). The death moment of a film character at first alarms our nervous systems. Then we breathe a sigh of relief that we escaped, and within an instant, our neurophysiologies are back on track. We are ready to resume living in the film's realm.

The camera captures a wide spectrum of diving experiences, exhilaration as well as panic. The divers move in graceful ballets through the crystal water. Without bubbles or organisms in the water for a point of reference, the scuba-encased actors seem to be in free-fall. The camera follows seamlessly.

The camera is equally proficient in conveying reactions to danger. The most disturbing, stomach-churning scene occurs with Jude, a woman diver working alongside Frank. George warns Frank that Jude may not be prepared for the dive's challenges. Camera closeups show her tense face. Her every movement is hesitant. She checks her equipment three times. The others give her a chance to pull out, and she refuses. "I have not come this far to watch from the sidelines." From the outset, the narrative predicts that Jude will face a tough challenge. Every mention and shot of Jude primes us for her demise. She is uneasy swimming through the tight squeeze of the Devil's Restriction. She wedges herself between the sharp rocks, stirring up silt in the crystalline cave. Shifts between subjective and objective camera angles present a sense of viewer disequilibrium, adding to the suspense.

From the campsite above the abyss, three team members watch Jude over the remote feed. They are safe, in dry clothes, under a sky of atmosphere, not rock. By stark contrast, camera closeups show Jude encased in her wetsuit, cramped in her claustrophobic rock tunnel. Through the mask, her eyes flicker with fear. Viewers, behind their own 3-D glasses, lighter, but similar in feel and shape to a diving mask, squirm in discomfort.

Frank and Jude break through to an unexplored chamber, and its architecture is sublime. Stone edges appear as drips around a Gothic-shaped atrium. The stalactites glow, seemingly lit from behind. "It's like a cathedral," Jude says into the mask. They stare in awe at the stone buttresses. The next second, Jude's air hose explodes into a flurry of bubbles. The tiny air circles fly at us the viewers, putting us behind that face mask and overwhelming us with the situation. Frank tries to keep Jude alive by sharing air with her, encouraging her to watch him. He points at his own eyes, to keep her calm, but she panics and pulls away, partly in fear and in recognition that additional struggle is no use. She inhales water, and her eyes glaze over. She floats away, motionless, and her hair flies out in wavy Medusa strands. Later, we see from the computerized mapping that the new chamber has been named "St. Jude's Cathedral."

One of the divers is fatally injured and dying. As Josh protests that they cannot leave him, Frank assesses that the diver's body is broken, and he is too injured to continue. He's not completely dead, but we see the ruthlessness of Frank as he holds the diver underwater and performs a mercy drowning. The injured man struggles in the last paroxysm to hold onto life.

Two gigantic rushes of air, like the Usher whirlwind, cause the cave system to shudder. The cyclone aboveground floods the network underground caves, and the expedition has no choice but to descend. Frank's knife is a depth gauge to show how fast the water is rising. The crew wants to rest and wait for rescue, but the knife handle is quickly nearly submerged, making their protests useless. They have to move.

Frank starts to take the wetsuit off Jude's body so Victoria can wear it on the next leg of the trip. She adamantly refuses to wear the dead woman's suit. Victoria is a climber and inexperienced diver. Frank realizes the futility of arguing with her. Instead of wasting time, they start out. Of course, Victoria's bad decision comes back to haunt her.

Praying is futile. Frank tells them that there is no God down there. He lashes out at their weakness, saying that the young people today only want to play at being extreme adventurers. "You spend your lives wrapped in cotton wool." To Frank, the new generation knows nothing of the hard choices it takes to confront nature head on.

A torrential gush of water comes sluicing into the passage, and with difficulty, the explorers make their way through the honeycomb of passages. The cave starts to flood.

As Victoria tries to squeeze through the tight passage, the film's 3-D perspective captures her rising terror closeup. We hear her voice through the mask, sense her frustration with not getting through. She has to be the last one, so she will not block the passage for the others. The claustrophobic shots and orientation of being underwater combine for an intense visceral reaction. The audience holds it breath in the suspense. Will she make it? Or more accurately, will we make it? Will she make it on our behalf?

On the other side, the others wait and she does not appear through the tight passage. Frank prepares to go get her, but eventually, she does appear. As they make it into a cave with a space of air available, Victoria is of course hypothermic, because she has refused to wear Jude's wetsuit. Her climbing skills falter, and her ear gets caught in the climbing gear. She chooses to cut it off and falls from the line, dropping into the surging caldron of storm water.

Carl blames Frank for Victoria's death. Frank points out that she made her own choices, and the team must move ahead. Carl doesn't understand. "You stay, you die," Frank says. So Carl leaves with the only breathing equipment left. Josh assumes that Carl will return for them; Frank knows that he won't.

When Josh and Frank are alone in the depths of the cave, the fundamental Oedipal conflict of the story plays out more intensely. Frank says he needs to rest, but Josh urges him on. The two undergo a role reversal. The son begins to fuse identities with the father.

They make the ascent toward light together, and Frank continues reciting Coleridge's "Kubla Khan." Josh asks about the verse, eager for his father to teach him. "The sacred river ran/ In caverns measureless to man."

Father and son share their joy in climbing, as Frank feeds Josh the poem line by line. Together they make it to the top. Poetry and their newly fused relationship help them find the way. An overhead camera shot gives us a glimpse of the two from above, and the camera revolves to dizzying effect. Then Josh gives his father a hand up, yet another gesture reminiscent of the opening scene from *Vertigo*.

The two exhausted divers arrive on the floor of a circular pothole, but the surface of the hole is still several hundred feet in the air. A Japanese tank had fallen into the collapsed pothole. They get fuel from there and light torches. They announce their presence at the site by writing on the truck. They make their mark, together.

From this point, Josh's understanding of his father is clear. He sees that his father's friend George was correct, that his father is a man worth knowing. The enclosure of father by son is complete.

All would be well from here on, except that Frank and Josh encounter the photographer Carl. His face is smeared with dirt and blood, and he eats with his hands like an animal. Carl then attacks Frank, knocking him backwards onto a stalactite.

Carl the photographer has transformed into evil. He had wanted to photograph the natural features, eager for his shots to make the cover of *National Geographic*, but the cave defeats him with its reality. Josh, the newly converted poet, kills Carl, capturer of the image with a torch, setting him on fire with fuel from the ruined tank. The viewers see this immolation in slow-motion 3-D. The power of the word turns the prospect of a static image into an intense image of the burning form.

Frank lies on the ground writhing on the rock. He begs Josh to help him into the water. Eventually, father convinces his son to "help him" to this death. Josh basically administers the same act of death that Frank had done earlier for another team member. Josh drowns his father then lets him float away, arms extended in a Christ-like pose.

As Josh continues a frantic swim along the unknown passage, he uses a small air tank as long as he can, then sucks surface air bubbles for tiny whiffs of breath. His swimming form is backlit. He hears his father's voice in encouragement. "Time to go, Josh." He sees light and surfaces close to beach. As we see a few people on the beach rushing to his aid, we hear Josh's voice-over: "My father was a helluva guy, once you got to know him."

Sanctum takes the viewer into a preternatural world similar to a video game. It represents a growing film trend to create a hybrid narrative, blending conventions of film and gaming.

The concept of 3-D films has been around for several decades. However, it has been only recently that a full-bodied audience interaction with the narrative has expanded through actual muscular movement by way of gaming platforms like Wii and Xbox 360 Kinect.

As a writer, critic, and reviewer of books on science and exploration, Poe had a keen interest in how moving parts fit together. He was a technology buff. Antebellum development of technology during Poe's time was still at a primitive state. In *On Photography*, Susan Sontag notes, "The first cameras, made in France and England in the early 1840s, had only inventors and buffs to operate them. Since there were no professional photographers, there could not be amateurs either" (7). Still, Poe recognized very early the powers and dangers of the daguerreotype image.

The concept of reading a written text is analogous to appraising information in the cyberworld. Poe's writing casts a skeptical eye on technology's contribution to actual knowledge. It may be that Poe's thinking about technology and its impact on the image was so forward that our narrative culture has only now caught up to him.

In adapting to electronic media, we currently experience many of the issues Poe grappled with in his fiction. His writings connect presciently with the same questions posed by cyberspace, defining the public areas and retaining privacy, the role of mind in technology, the implications and limits of physical sensations through media and artifice. Poe's thorough scrutiny about how we read and tell a tale applies equally to how we read messages sent via electronic means. Reading and puzzling over reading has an analogue as well to the messages we receive from cyberspace. Does having so many facts available at our fingertips make us smarter and increase our capacity to know the world? How does accumulation of knowledge add up to truth?

Poe demonstrates an accurate take on the mechanics of gamesmanship as well as the psychology of games and challenges as shown in his article "Maelzel's Chess Player" (1836). This sketch presents his fascination with the workings, both mechanical and human, behind this machine. In the late 1820s, the show, for that is what it was, had played in Boston, Philadelphia and Baltimore. Eventually, the Automaton came to Richmond, which is where Poe probably viewed it sometime in late 1893 (Wimsatt 144–145). In this sketch, Poe takes the position of a skeptical observer of a machine that seems to play chess. The Automaton offers any challenger to step forward to the chessboard to play the machine, which inevitably wins. Poe has an interest in pulling back the curtain on this exhibit.

As Poe describes it, the Automaton presents the top half of a human-like figure perched on the base of a trunk-sized cabinet on castors. The show's impresario, Maelzel, wheels the machine out and introduces the Automaton, with its player figure, called the Turk, to the crowd.

As part of Maelzel's demonstration of the chess machine, the impresario pulls aside the panels to reveal to spectators that there is not enough space in the bottom trunk that could conceal a human figure. The trunk's inside appears as a complex, Rube Goldberg–type contraption, with the inner workings of gears and belts, "wheels, pinions, levers, and other machinery" (435). This flourish in the demonstration assures the spectators that no chicanery is involved behind the Automaton's capabilities. "The Chess-Player is a pure machine and performs its operations without any immediate human agency" (423).

Atop the chest is a life-sized human figure viewed from the waist up. The figure is called the Turk, due to his turban. "The eyes roll unnaturally in the head, without any corresponding motions of the lids or brows. The arm particularly performs its operations in an exceedingly stiff, awkward, jerking, and rectangular manner" (434). Poe assesses quickly that Maelzel's flashy attempt to lay out the machine's innards is all smoke and mirrors. The purpose of the Turk's herky-jerky motion is to distract. "Were the Automaton life-like in its motions, the spectator would be more apt to attributes it operations to their true cause (that is, to human agency within)" (434).

Overall, the grotesque head of the Turk seems related to the figure in the coin-operated arcade fantasy machine at the fairground in the film *Big* (1988). When the young Josh Baskin (David Moscow) inserts a coin into the slot and makes a wish to be, the turbaned head grants his wish, turning him overnight into an adult Josh (Tom Hanks).

The Turk head in *Big* clearly works through a supernatural agency. In fact, the machine works only when the electric plug is pulled out of the electrical outlet. In our time, we prefer the romance of not knowing how a twelve-year-old can physically age twenty years overnight. We need this mystery since the technology for most of our modern devices manifest a pervasive complexity that we would find overwhelming.

To contrast, Poe's sketch takes apart Maelzel's trick machine, piece by piece, to debunk any possible claims of a ghost in the machine. In this process, he uses the inductive method for which Dupin later becomes famous. As W. K. Wimsatt notes, Poe's early biographer Hervey Allen identifies this incident as being the first in Poe's writing of using the method of the ratiocinative detection (139). Other observers over the years had forwarded explanations, such as a dwarf being hidden inside, a premise earning Poe's derision: "The whole hypothesis was too obviously absurd to require comment or refutation" (428). However, he clearly cannot help devoting space to comment on the absurdity.

Poe points out that Maelzel's apparent show of the Automaton's inner workings distracts the spectators through its apparent disclosure. But at this time, the transparency obscures the man's presence in the box. A person shifts inside when the doors to the cabinet at the base are opened and then inhabits the body of the Turk, so he can play chess and operate the arms. "He sees the chessboard through the bosom of the Turk, which is of gauze" (431). For Poe, the machine poses a threat to human intelligence. A secondary purpose to the report, Poe being Poe, is that he needs to make sure that Maelzel does not get the better of him as spectator with the deception. The writer has the sensibility of a man who does not take kindly to being lumped with the gawking masses willing to be tricked. However, above all, Poe emphasizes that the agency of the human mind is still in control.

After going through a painstaking analysis of arm positions, dimensions of the doors, timing of the ritual, and lighting of the scene, the sketch determines conclusively that a man is in fact inside. And who is this man? None other than Maelzel's assistant, a man named Schlumberger. Poe connects the dots between dates when Schlumberger had been ill, and days on which the Automaton had been shut down with no explanation offered. Poe writes, "The inferences from all this we leave, without farther [sic] comment, to the reader" (438).

In our time, viewers want to emphasize a machine's supernatural qualities, as in the grant-a-wish machine in *Big*. In Poe's time, he wants to be clear of how the machine's empirical workings to define its limits. For us, the technological processes running the hardware, chips, with microcircuitry are too amazing to contemplate. Our entertainment prefers the supernatural explanations.

Poe's conclusion about this machine is that regardless of the workings, it requires a human mind to anticipate the chess moves and challenge the spectators who might take it on: "its movements are regulated by *mind*— by some person who sees the board of the antagonist" (432–422). And it is not Maelzel's mind that controls the machine's chess movements, but that of the unobtrusive assistant who helps him assemble the apparatus and wheels it out before the audience on castors. In a sense, the sketch's exposé sets up a scenario in which the butler did it. The secret to the Automaton rests with the humble helper, hiding in plain sight. Even after all the dissection of the parts of this puzzle, the final identification of the human agent inside the machine, the ultimate mystery of the mind remains.

Poe's Need for Speed

In several works, Poe captures the physical sensations of media-triggering physicality and imbalance. His narrative mirrors the visceral jolt of video games, by overwhelming the reader with all the images and people from a watcher's point of view.

Poe's interest in the potential of technology was partly a response to his time. David Bell uses early-19th-century novels to show "the way speed and communication were being woven into the fabric of social perception" (Bell 1). Even prior to the railroad, people were adjusting to a more rapid pace in their daily lives. Writers like Dickens and Stendhal had captured this pace with "an endoscopic warping of space — in short, true cinematic vocation" (Bell 135).

In this context, Poe uses words to simulate physical imbalance and instability, whirling, falling. There's a visceral quality to the narrator's horror, to feeling ill, sick with fear, and terrified. Previous chapters discuss dizzying descents powering the narrative. Another sketch takes the reader far into a video-game-like realm of thrills.

"The Unparalleled Adventure of One Hans Pfaal" follows a narrator who goes up on a balloon trip to the moon. The town fathers of Rotterdam watch over him, and with the names Supurbus von Underduk and Rubadub, who are fellows from the Rotterdam College of Astronomers, Poe makes clear that this story is a put-on. But despite the tale's comic tone, the compelling description of a high-wire adventure draws us in.

By chance, the once again unnamed narrator finds a pamphlet in a bookseller's stall. He begins reading and cannot help but want to build a balloon. He studies pneumatics and puts together his inflatable. Due to the terrible treatment he feels he had suffered from the College of Astronomers, he decides to attempt a balloon trip to the moon. He busies himself with preparations. "My balloon was soon completed. It would contain more than forty thousand cubic feet of gas; would take me up easily, I calculated, with all my implements" (9). But all does not proceed smoothly with the trip, as an explosion rips under him, blood throbbing in his head.

> The balloon at first collapsed, then furiously expanded, then whirled round and round with sickening velocity, and finally, reeling and staggering like a drunken man, hurled me over the rim of the car, and left me dangling, at terrific height, with my head downward, and my face outward.... I gasped convulsively for breath — a shudder resembling a fit of the ague agitated every nerve and muscle in my frame — I felt my eyes starting from their sockets — a horrible nausea overwhelmed me — and at length I lost all consciousness in a swoon [11].

When he awakes, the balloon is high over the ocean, with no land in sight. Once he regains his composure, he prepares for the long voyage in a crippled state. He is like the astronauts as depicted in the film *Apollo 13* (1995, dir. Ron Howard). He is firm of purpose and convinced in the value of control over technology in rescuing himself.

He snatches a momentary happiness over the process of figuring out what to do. He explains with great detail the operation, which passes for high-tech in the nineteenth century. He figures out the atmosphere according to gravity and density. He makes arrangements for breathing in a vacuum. Combining romantic sensibility with science-fiction mechanics, his operations show an element of early "steam punk."

Hans Pfaal then mentions his thoughts about committing suicide, but he decides instead to escape from his horrible life, not through death but by trying to be successful in reaching someplace else: "I began to find difficulty in drawing my breath. My head, too, was excessively painful; And having felt for some time a moisture about my cheeks, I at length discovered it to be blood, which was oozing quite fast from the drums of my ears" (19). The altitude gives him muscle spasms, and he begins bleeding from his nose, ears, and eyes. After he gains control of those conditions, however, he acclimates to the altitude enough so he can keep a journal.

Over the course of nine days, he records his encounters with a comet, anticipates seeing the North Pole, going higher and higher and seeing ice, treated to a grand view of the continents splayed over the earth's surface, such as what only NASA astronauts are privy to.

Then he does indeed reach the moon. "It lay beneath me like a chart." He notes the "indentures of its surface" (33). He sees the conical volcanoes and notes the absence of any oceans. When the balloon begins dropping like a stone toward the moon's surface, "with horrible rapidity," he cuts off the basket, "and thus clinging to the net-work," he plunges "headlong into the very heart of a fantastical-looking city" and the ugly small people living there stand around looking at him, "like a parcel of idiots" (36).

The last entry in the journal says that he will tell the astronomers about the secrets of his journey and his life on the dark side of the moon in painstaking detail, "but I must have my reward" (37). He asks for a pardon, since he had killed his creditors before he left town. As the town fathers agree between them that the pardon must indeed happen, the reader is then treated to a view of Hans Pfaal and his creditors drinking in a tavern with plenty of money in their pockets. Clearly, the learned society of astronomers had no more wit or discernment than the gawping idiots allegedly populating the plains of the moon.

While this satire is a transparent jab at pomposity in learning and elite professors, Poe interlaces enough extreme motion to provide a verisimilitude of terror. Hans Pfaal's adventure unfolds with one visceral thrill after another. Like a *Mission to Mars* ride in Disney World, Poe paces his account as action-packed hurtling through space.

This connection between Poe and the motion-filled but controlled rocketry of video gaming promises that for the future Poe will only continue to have more relevance. The power of his imaginary world matches the virtual worlds that come to life on the screens of cell phones, laptops, and wall-sized plasma TVs.

During the balloon voyage of Hans Pfaal, a vertical drop is the focus. In "A Descent into the Maelström" (1841), a swirling, nausea-inducing experience replicates the phobia of centrifugal force causing a person to fly into the void. The story is prefaced by an epigram from Joseph Granville about the "unsearchableness of His works." The phrase highlights the story's emphasis on the ineffability of the natural world and man's place in it.

The story's unnamed narrator and an old man ascend the headlands off the Norwegian coast, as the older climber prepares to tell a tale. The purpose of their ascent is to set the context for the elder man's experience. The tale promises to be wild and incredible. Once the pair reaches the summit of the steep cliff, they look over the ocean, and the narrator essentially collapses.

The old man narrator of this story begins his account of a previous terrifying experience that had turned his black hair white in a single day: "Do you know I can scarcely look over this little cliff without getting giddy?" (Poe 127). The narrator is so fearful that he lies prone and hugs the ground: "Nothing would have tempted me to within a half dozen yards of its brink.... I looked dizzily and beheld a wise expanse of ocean" (127–128). The narrator's perceived lack of borders and the possibility of flying off into the Great Unknowable Beyond is a form of vertigo.

Derek Parfit's concept of personality fusion is again relevant here. Surrendering the self via a funnel-like shape suggests falling into another story. An encircled place for fusion in the middle of a story comes up a number of times, as swirls in the ocean or drops off cliffs.

This story combines geographic wonder with psychological upset. Poe captures in amazing detail what can occur to a person suffering from many dimensions of vertigo. "In truth so deeply was I excited by the perilous position of my companion, that I fell at full length upon the ground, clung to the shrubs around me, and dared not even glance upward at the sky" (127). The narrator suffers from more than acrophobia. His sensation goes beyond a well-reasoned fear of falling. The narrator experiences emotional vertigo, the self's sense of a loss of equilibrium between inner and outer space. The psychic gyroscope is disrupted by the centrifugal force of an integrated center flying apart into a void.

Danielle Quinodoz elaborates on this theory based on her clinical experiences. She describes the phenomenon in *Emotional Vertigo: Between Anxiety and Pleasure* (1997). Quinodox emphasizes that even though the more well-known form of vertigo is fear of falling, an equally disturbing experience is a person's fear of flying apart. It is connected to a misperception of the self. With so much internal space coming forward and threatening to press outward, the self's form of destruction comes by being attracted to the void (Quinodox 59–60). With "A Descent into the Maelström," Poe develops all dimensions to this fear in great detail.

Vertigo is also connected to the self's experience with time. The fear of the void dramatizes the conflict between being and nothingness. The person may also vacillate between stability and disequilibrium through a "fusion-related vertigo" (21). The lack of control is so severe that the person carries the irrational fear of being destroyed along with another contingent personality. The narrator exhibits this same fear in the early pages of the story.

Finally, the narrator can look out into the expanse: "I looked dizzily, and beheld a wide expanse of ocean" (128). Finally, he can appreciate the old man's story. The narrator first detects the whirlpool's approach from its disturbing rumble, gradually getting louder, "like the moaning of a vast herd of buffaloes"

(128). Then the sea begins to swirl, switching directions in its chop, until the ocean "lashed into ungovernable fury" (129). After a short time, the entire whirlpool is at full force:

> The vast bed of the waters seamed and scarred into a thousand conflicting channels, burst suddenly into phrensied [sic] convulsion — heaving, boiling, hissing — gyrating in gigantic and innumerable vortices, and all whirling and plunging [129].

This disequilibrium sets the stage for the man's tale, softens up the narrator as recipient of the man's story. "You have had a good look at the whirl now," the old storyteller says (131). Now he is ready.

The silver-haired man's narrative relates how he and his two brothers had their usual routine of fishing when a storm disrupted their usual route and drove their fishing schooner into the dangerous part of the channel. Seeing the maelström from a distance is terrifying enough for the narrator, so the old man's recreation of actually being sucked into the gigantic whirlpool stirs up a paralyzing fear.

Fortunately, as readers of this story we do not have to imagine the horror. Poe's narrator registers the terror for us. The action lurches in paroxysms of disaster, with the storm tossing the small brig from one gigantic ocean swell to another. The sky turns copper. Wind and driving spray turn daytime visibility to night (133). The mainmast blows off and takes one brother with it, "who had lashed himself to it for safety" (133), as in Longfellow's poem "The Wreck of the Hesperus" (1839).

A break in the clouds reveals the moon as it "blazed forth with a luster" (134). "The whirl of the Ström was in full fury." The wind shrieks and howls as from "a thousand steam vessels" (135), so the old man cannot hear his own thoughts. "And then down we came with a sweep, a slide, and a plunge that made me feel sick and dizzy, as if I was falling down some lofty mountain-top in a dream" (134–135). After the account takes the reader to the brink of the abyss, the old man pauses for a moment of philosophical reflection: "how magnificent a thing it was to die in such a manner." Poe adds a moment of the sublime, taking the long view as the old man feels privileged to have a "view of so wonderful a manifestation of God's power" (135). Poe creates a moment of perfectly poised suspense, with action halted above, below, and in the surroundings. He conceives a full-dimensioned scene with simultaneous vertical and horizontal views. The moon gleams through a narrow break in the cloud cover, and below is the depth of the abyss.

In this moment of garish light, the boat hangs in midair, suspended in the middle of the funnel as the action recoils and gears up to take one more swipe at the ship. In a particularly brilliant depiction, Poe provides a glimpse of the funnel's "perfectly smooth sides [which] might have been mistaken for ebony" (136). Then the storm resumes in earnest, whipping the small craft in circles.

For this section, Poe uses language the way a thrill-ride builder relies on gravity. The next onslaught from the whirlpool sweeps away rational thought and the human ability to take in the world. Wind and spray "blind, deafen, and strangle" (136). We feel the "sickening sweep" (136) of the old man's descent into the boiling water. "Round and round we swept — not with any uniform movement — but in dizzying swings and jerks" (137). The old man describes the miasma of fog that arcs upward in a sweeping rainbow "like that narrow and tottering bridge ... the only pathway between Time and Eternity" (137). Again, Poe takes a moment to define that subtle switch between one mode of thought and another, the silk-fine line between illusion and reality. This monumental swirl draws everything in, boxes, and crates, house furniture, trees, and other boats. At this juncture, the old man pulls back from the frenzy to debate using these floating items in his suspended state. His thinking is similar, perhaps, to Dorothy's, as she senses the wicked witch flying next to her in the tornado leveling farmhouses across the plains of Kansas as it whisks her to Oz. As a result of the old man's experience, losing his brothers and experiencing terror, his hair turns from black to white virtually in minutes. He steps out of the gradual progression of time.

Because the tale never returns to the frame of the narrator, we have no explicit information on whether this listener believes the old man's story. Poe fails to give us the listener's reaction. The story lacks explicit closure. However, Poe drops a large breadcrumb of meaning to clarify that the narrator has been a completely credulous auditor. At the tale's beginning, he is so prostrate with fear on the land overlooking the maelström that we can assume his willing pair of ears. He is eager to believe in the horror of the old man's experience. He is convinced of how the intensity of fear and horror can enact a physical change to age a person. He has felt it.

While the physical motion associated with this tale presents readers with many overwhelming jolts, a more central suggestion is the whirlpool itself. As an emblem of the story within the story, the whirlpool is not only *the* story but *any* story. It represents the reader's or viewer's abdication of control in the face of a powerful narrative.

The narrator senses the majesty of the story's allure. The plane of ocean descends, and white trails of ocean foam extend every which way. "Suddenly, very suddenly — this assumed a distinct and definite existence" (129). The narrator suspends a part of his consciousness and imaginatively fuses himself meanings created from the old man's words. He descends into the *mise en abîme*, the story within the story, represented by the swirling pool. The descent represents a loss of psychic control but it carries the payoff of expanding experience.

Similarly, a video-game player participates willingly in the disturbing instability of the game. The controller rumbles in hand. The screen of his POV turns blood red as a signal that enemies are shooting and draining the life of his avatar. The player may not ask to be led to destruction, but he welcomes the opportunity to try to beat the odds. If the game means the player's loss by way of a horrible, sometimes graphic "death," there is always a "reset" button. The game is once again afoot.

Poe's meditations on soaring journeys through space are not the only writings containing parallels to today's new media. In "The Man of the Crowd" (1840), Poe dramatizes a charged situation resonating with tensions from today's cyberculture. This tale explores issues of maintaining privacy in a public sphere. Through the interiority of the narrator's consciousness, the deceptively straightforward sketch carries profound epistemological ramifications of gathering information and locating knowledge. This tale presents a strikingly similar parallel between a nineteenth-century observer and a modern user of the internet. It is almost as if Poe had zapped forward through time into 2011 then returned to 1840 to compose his sketch.

Poe prefaces the tale with a quotation in German about a particular book: "*er lasst sich nicht kesen.*" He translates the phrase: "it does not permit itself to be read." He also observes, "There are some secrets which do not permit themselves to be told" (475).

Like many a frantic seeker of free wi-fi today, the narrator sits in the coffee shop of a London hotel. Remaining purposely vague, he refers to the location only by the letter D —. At first he peruses advertisements and newspapers, puffing on a cigar, taking his leisure. He had recently been ill, but now he has a lucid gaze, blinking in a clear world. "I felt a calm but inquisitive in every thing" (475). The panorama meeting his cleared vision is the parade of people passing outside. He watches the world through rectangles of glass described as "a bow-window" and "the smoky panes into the street" (475). He is essentially surfing the web.

Outside, a stream of people command his interest, and he scrutinizes the panoply of humanity, reveling in the many categories of people labeled by class, occupation, or mood. He watches the "tides of population rushing past the door." His observation only intensifies when the street lamps illuminate the crowd, swelling him with feeling: "the tumultuous sea of human heads filled me, therefore, with a delicious novelty of emotion" (475). The energy this narrator takes from the spectrum of people is similar to a vision of Whitman's America. Whereas Whitman finds joy and solace of being among others, this narrator remains shielded by the glass. He does not join them. He is like a lurker on Facebook, a voyeur fixated on the stream of humanity.

Not only does he sit and watch, but he sits in judgment. He makes distinctions about the people based on surface appearance, such as clothing, facial characteristics, and manners of walking. This tale's narrator draws conclusions about the parade of people as they pass. He uses the method of inductive reasoning that Poe would develop later with Dupin in "The Murders in the Rue Morgue," published in *Graham's* the following year.

When this storyteller fixates on an old man whose face and demeanor are unreadable, the narrator chases him, fascinated. He follows him into the marketplace, an emblem of the American republic. The story's motifs also work according to Parfit's concepts of fission and fusion, with this teller's personality hovering between isolation and belonging. The narrator's classification of each passerby appears to stem from the vantage point that he perceives as superior. The story gains momentum through its interplay between the individual and the group, an ongoing American tension.

Certainly the era had its concerns over changing dynamics of private and public marketplace. An issue of heated discussion concerned uses of photography for recreating a person's image. "The visual media of Poe's time helped inaugurate the illusion of access by 'almost anyone' to people at an inaccessible distance, including those 'long dead'" (Renza 62). The cynical Poe refused to jump onto the bandwagon hauling many of his contemporaries who were applauding picture-taking technology. Poe worried that through visual reproductions with the daguerreotype, for instance, "it becomes less and less possible to observe not only other persons and events but also one's personal, spatio-temporal experience of them *sans* their technological reproducibility" (62–63). This comment has at least as much to do with today's issues of privacy through cyber-use as it does for Poe's time.

Louis Renza suggests that the narrator's observed "prey" is an old man, because he "represents an older mode of social privacy that still haunts the American scene" (Renza 65). Certainly the narrator's "recent illness" connects him to the old man. The narrator has had a bout with mortality and the old man's condition may be a harbinger of the narrator's future. By following the unknowable fellow with a dogged tread, the narrator traces a horizontal line of a yet another *mise en abîme*.

The narrator chases the old man only to find time and again that he has just missed him. John T. Irwin says, "There will always be one more step needed in order to make the act of thinking and the content of thought coincide" (Irwin 12). The narrator spends all night and most of the next day following the man through all kinds of environments. Tailing the old man takes him around a square and then in circle. He crosses and re-crosses. He heads down wide boulevards and narrow, obscure alleyways, tracing a discernible, yet still incomprehensible pattern. He loses sight of his quarry around one corner and catches up with him the next. Eventually, the pursuer knows, or thinks he knows, a pattern to the man's movements.

The narrator approaches for a confrontation: "And as the shades of the second evening came on, I grew wearied unto death, and stopping fully in front of the wanderer, gazed at him steadfastly in the face. He noticed me not, but resumed his solemn walk" (Poe 481). What does he learn? The old man's lined face presents a "type and genius of deep crime." What is this crime? He refuses to be alone.

Commentators consider that this sketch's teller is a kind of proto-detective. "Luckily I wore a pair of caoutchouc overshoes, and could move about in perfect silence" (Poe 480). As Patricia Merivale notes, this is the first instance in American detective literature of a protagonist "tailing" a mark while wearing "gumshoes" (106). He also wears a disguise, a kerchief over his face. He is "undercover." The text does not say that the quarry of the narrator's chase is, in fact, a criminal, but that in this culture, to be a man of the crowd who maintains a separate identity while connecting with the group is a crime. For all the stakeouts and tailing in the best detective traditions, this narrator is not an actual detective, nor is the old man actually a criminal. He is only a seeker of himself, and sadly, his chase remains unrewarded.

The narrator's observations have the goal of trying to know, trying to satisfy his curiosity, but this is a futile quest. The narrator can never know his quarry's motivations, or the "wild history" that drives the old man to be with people. Patricia Merivale notes the impossibility of discerning between the chase and the object of the chase, since the object of the chase is ultimately unknowable (108). John Irwin also characterizes this quality of the search: "The commitment to an increasingly self-conscious analytic posture that animates this cumulative series of interpretations produces at last a kind of intellectual vertigo, a not uncharacteristic side effect of thought about thought — the rational animal turning in circles trying to catch itself by a tale [sic] it doesn't have" (11).

Ultimately, the theme of the unknowable void at the heart of experience leads to this self-reflexivity. After extracting this trope of the futile chase for the old man, Poe redirects our attention to the narrative by ending the story as it began, with the German phrase that there are some books that cannot be read. Our awareness of this element of the ineffable is ultimately a creative act, as it impels more efforts to reach that zone beyond. Poe sets up his narrative in such a way as to elude resolution.

The purpose of the narrator "reading" the old man's drives and motivations is for him to see that the meaning of a heart is impossible to attain by viewing a group. Where the two meanings of self and group meet is in the concept of the computer. As in the situation constructed in "The Man of the

Crowd," a computer screen gives the user an illusion of focus where no actual focus exists. As in the tension between the self and the group, a particularly American conflict, the computer user maintains his isolation and exits as a conundrum to others and himself. Poe's teeming marketplace where way leads onto way is the nineteenth-century equivalent to cyberspace.

Identity and Movement in Narrative

A recent study conducted in Great Britain notes that young people prefer their virtual lives to their own reality. Psychotherapist Peter Bradley studied young teenagers living lives filled to the brim with internet use. This report about virtual lives draws disturbing conclusions. "Around 47 per cent of children said they behaved differently online than they did in their normal lives with many claiming it made them feel more powerful and confident" (Thomas). When children change their appearances, breaking from their actual identities, and maintain a consistent contact with strangers, they obviously court disaster. They fail to see the consequences of this high-risk behavior as they sit at their laptop screens or use cell phones in familiar surroundings.

On the BBC survey, this response from young people was typical: "You can say anything online. You can talk to people that you don't normally speak to and you can edit your pictures so you look better. It is as if you are a completely different person" (Thomas). The construct of an expanding, changing, or contracting personality that Poe develops in "William Wilson," for instance, has a strong parallel to the online presence that more young people cultivate. Identity becomes fluid. Parfit's concepts of fission and fusion forces pulling apart our sense of a single self have come to fruition.

The love affair of young people with the internet and their changing identities sets up a dangerous paradox in terms of security. In *Born Digital*, Palfrey and Gasser emphasize the amorphous nature of online relationships: "They are often fleeting; they are easy to enter into with a few mouse clicks; and they are easy to leave, without so much as a goodbye" (33). Palfrey and Gasser also note the sad reality that easy online ties can leave long-lasting problems due to identity theft. To continue the metaphor, the quick online romance may have lingering effects, the cyber-equivalent of an STD. "The identity of a sixteen-year-old is characterized by instability; it can change frequently. But when it is expressed online, it is also characterized by insecurity.... This kind of insecurity isn't inherent in the concept of identity, digital or otherwise" (33). In other words, with love the old-fashioned way, the worst damage that could happen is a broken heart; with online romances, the damage could be a stolen identity and ruined future.

Poe's narrative vocabulary speaks to our culture with tremendous resonance. His stories fall naturally into the channels of video gaming, because his narrative structures are so familiar to contemporary audiences. Poe's blood-drenched ethos has infused our popular culture for at least the last thirty years. How many video-game designers, for better or worse, have been raised on the Poe idiom of horror and suspense that colors our culture?

Video gaming may be the entertainment system of the future, but it utilizes narrative constructs from the past. PlayStation, Wii, and Xbox integrate viewer interactivity via physical motion into the light, color, and sounds on the screen's projections.

Wii training games promote a video narrative of physical fitness. Each game offers the onscreen version of the player, the Mii (pronounced "me"), the tremendous possibility of self-improvement. It encourages the person behind the Mii to be successful at weight reduction or cardio fitness by completing a course of persistence and working through the pain. The Wii system costs less than an actual gym membership for a year, but given the space needed, use of a Wii realistically means that people will probably not work out together. Despite TV ads or website demos showing an entire family playing games or cheering each other on before the oversized flat-screen TV, working out on the Wii is more likely an individual pursuit, similar to reading or phone texting.

The game features no two-way communication in words with the onscreen avatar, only gestures. The onscreen avatar trainer speaks a canned instruction to correct the home user if the remote is not held correctly, or if the control device attached to a leg is not moving in a way consistent with a successful workout.

It is no coincidence that the avatar in this platform of games is called the Mii/Me. Just as the "I" in "private eye" refers back to the source of a gaze, so the Mii defines a ready-made character identity that the player alters for his own personality. It bounces the viewer's gaze onto the self in an ultimate fusion of identity.

What features of video games are similar to Poe's narrative elements? Action plays out in a context of a distinctive physical landscape, although the environment can bend according to the user's whim. The screen offers the player options of selecting his own weather condition or time of day. The player's mind and imagination work with technological design to create the story's landscape, an independent Storyville.

Conflict is embedded in nearly every video game at many levels. For Wii fitness games, the Mii establishes goals to compete with itself (Mii-self?). With combat games such as *Call of Duty*, *SOCOM: US Navy Seals*, or *SplinterCell*, conflict takes on an edge between a single player and the elimination of figures representing adversaries. Multi-player modes set up online games, in which competition is fierce. Other kinds of conflicts involve a player's avatar racing against the clock, gathering money or prizes, or reaching a defined checkpoint before being killed. The investigator gathers clues toward reaching a solution to the crime, and frequently has to travel a labyrinth of city alleyways, a road, corridor through a mall, ramps in a parking garage, or other routes to reach the bomb or hostage in time. Actual life rarely sets such intense life-or-death deadlines. Essentially, these basic stories combine elements from thriller or detective narratives first established by Poe.

A virtual game contains suspense in whether a player's avatar can move to the next world or level, or die by the gradual death by a thousand cuts (although there usually are fewer than a thousand). Monsters spring from the side passage of a cave or a World War II German sniper shoots from the upper window of a bombed-out church. Is it possible to drink the potion, find the food, or apply the first aid in time?

Many of Poe's stories and sketches feature a first-person narrator, an anonymous but focalized center of consciousness. In video gaming, first-person role-player games replicate this tale-teller situation. From the initial time of playing, the player can set up a profile or identity, but this is not essential. Basically, the avatar on the screen is as significant or meaningless as the player makes it.

A video-game controller has a dimension of tactility that a literary text cannot have. Whereas story content may include a tactile image describing a rough or cold surface, the video-game controller has a rumble feature that transmits a vibration to the hands. Through actual appeal to three physical senses, the video game edges out the sensate capability of fiction, although Poe comes closer than most writers, with his sound-infused sentences.

In literature, shifts in perspective are not as obvious as an onscreen game. A reader has to stay alert to transitions in the text, subtle shifts in levels of reality. Similarly, Poe's shifts occur through a *mise en abîme*, if the work is about a play within a play, for instance, or sets up a narrative frame.

Literacy of a verbal text requires focalization of imagination. We engage our memories or create images of experiences we have never had. By contrast, a television remote is easier to engage than the imagination. Switching television channels and lowering or increasing the volume with an electronic device is commonplace. A video-game remote expands on the powers of the TV remote. To direct games, players wield focalized action by way of remote controllers. The controller switch causes a figure to run, walk, jump, paddle, shift left or right, drive, punch, shoot, or even fly.

Technological design of the remote has advanced to the point where two different remotes can work the two sides of the body. Kinect from Xbox represents the latest phase in user interface evolution. It does away with the awkwardness of wires, since a person does not need even to hold the remote. The figure on the screen moves in accordance with the player's own movements. "Kinect's camera is powered by both hardware and software. And it does two things: generate a three-dimensional (moving) image of the objects in its field of view, and recognize (moving) human beings among those objects" (Carmody).

The sophisticated electronic device incorporates a camera into the home hardware. "The camera transmits invisible near-infrared light and measures its 'time of flight' after it reflects off the objects" (Carmody). This sweep of the camera's eye recognizes people in the room. If a chair in the player's den interferes with the camera's view, the camera tells the player move the chair. "When you step in front of it, the camera 'knows' who you are." In this constructed narrative, is the unblinking camera lens like the Evil Eye of the old man in "The Tell-Tale Heart"? Or the casually roving, searching eye of the narrator in "The Man in the Crowd"?

The user can talk to onscreen players through a headset. Games with militaristic names feature weaponry, but strategy and planning are involved as well. In the game SOCOM's *Medal of Honor* or *Call of Duty*, the player gives vocal commands in a military jargon to onscreen figures: "Go to Romeo," "Sweep Alpha," or "Set Flashbang." Although the screen has a limited vocabulary, the concept of a full game user interface, or GUI in the trade, is expanding.

What is the ramification of this gamer surveillance? Is Kinect a kind of Foucaultian panopticon watching us? Is this relentless gaze even more surreptitious and uncanny because we control it ourselves? We can turn it off, but do we? It's not a two-way communication.

How does this way toward electronic narrative relate to literature? If the reader trades in a book or Kindle for a game controller, is the interaction between tale and teller the same? If the people with these controllers and therefore the illusion of control are playing games, do they risk having fewer adventures in an exterior world? Are players destined to stay immersed in their cyberworlds? Poe asked this question when the mechanical reproduction of images was new. How many do?

Certainly literature can be escapist, as games now seem to be largely an escape. But the games also hold benefits. They can model decision-making situations to simulate demonstrations of ethics or show patterns to propel people into new situations. Other beneficial effects of video games are helping people to set priorities and understand proportions. Still, in stacking the games' educational results next to entertainment value, we have to wonder if these media are promoting more solitude in the home, fostering isolation, even alienation.

As in a literary narrative, a game offers perspective. In first-person role-player games, pressing a button shifts between first- and third-person points of view. The avatar brings this point of view to the video game's plot. Individual actions come from buttons on the remote, which prompt the avatar to perform certain tasks. For instance, in PlayStation, pressing a triangle or circle on the joystick controller causes the avatar to jump or use a weapon. As in a story, a string of events created by the pressed buttons builds falling or rising actions which follow a narrative arc or storyline.

The avatar proceeds along the road or journey. It has free will to roam among the rooms in the haunted house, to descend to the basement or explore the attic. The bomber pilot has a map to follow tracing the route for a bombing raid, picking up supplies along the way to replenish weaponry, amass wealth, or extend life. A video-game remote is new, but the stories it helps the avatar to navigate are time-worn, developed by Poe.

The Future of Tale-Telling Art

In many ways, Poe was prescient about how the American tale could develop through a blend of different art forms. As a poet, he worked sound into the story; he conceptualized the significance of a story told with a combination of image and text. He worked an element of physical movement into the narrative, and connected this momentum thematically to explorations, both in the environment and the self.

Poe's fiction also looks ahead to how words intersect with images. Technology has now turned that same struggle into film. The next phase of technological development in narrative is to infuse story with an action-oriented medium, moving art closer to physicality. Such a combination of action-oriented story currently exists in nascent form through video games.

Two controversies currently divide theories about video games, and Poe plays a role in each. The first considers whether video games are art. Mark Wolf notes that all genres go through phases of development. When new visions come onto the scene, acceptance by traditional thinkers or practitioners may be slow, as was the case in the art world with works by Duchamp, Dali, or Warhol. Art history provides a precedent for what is going on in the gaming world as it struggles for aesthetic acceptance.

A few years ago, film critic Roger Ebert declared that video games could not be considered "art." Immediately following his assertion, readers and bloggers presented a flurry of dissenting opinions, but Ebert could only reassert his objection: "the nature of the medium prevents it from moving beyond craftsmanship to the stature of art." Ebert's critical qualm stops short of identifying what aspect of the medium serves as a major limitation. In form, is the video game a film? Television program? Literary text? A video-game carries some qualities of all these types of artistic entertainments. The hybrid nature of these games may pose questions about categories and judgment criteria, but those questions should not be stumbling blocks. Poe's "Eureka" sets a similar model as a work difficult to categorize. Is it a philosophical tract? A critical essay? A poem, as he himself wanted it to be labeled? That a video-game might achieve longevity as an interdisciplinary artistic genre is not impossible to consider.

In blog formats, the issue provokes serious consideration. Leigh Edwards answers Ebert: "The problem is that games can be more than a text, and the author may choose to focus on any element of a game's composition over any other. A game can be successful because its environment is particularly immersive, or if its narrative is well constructed or open-ended, but it doesn't have to be both.... From that perspective, video games can indeed be art, and as such, they represent an artistic medium with its own values that are constructed outside of similar mediums" (Edwards).

A second controversy in the gaming world concerns a rift between ludologists, that is, theorists tracing the logic and design of video games and narratologists, concentrating on story structure. In a 2005 keynote address to DiGRA (Digital Games Research Association), Janet H. Murray lays out a central argument dividing the gaming community. The battle lines are drawn between objectivists and subjective-emotive models of gaming. The two camps are also called ludologists and narratologists.

According to Murray, ludologists are formalists about games and game theory. They press for examining games "in their own right, rather than as 'colonized' examples of film or narrative.... They think of games as 'configurational' structures, which require us to actively manipulate their components. Through the study of form they have raised questions about games in themselves, boundaries between video games and other cultural forms."

On the other side of the controversy are narratologists, who take a more subjective view of games and gamers. Murray appears to come down on the side of the narratologists, because she finds that the game theorists "are willing to dismiss many salient aspects of the game experience, such as the feeling of immersion, the enactment of violent or sexual events, the performative dimension of game play, and even the personal experience of winning or losing." Despite her address giving a perceptual edge to those narrative proponents, in the end, Murray makes a plea for calm and compromise in the divisive controversy rocking the intellectual gaming community. She calls for a more complementary approach to studies of gaming, leading to a "multi-dimensional, open-ended puzzle that we all are engaged in cooperatively solving."

Considering any other writer in connection with video games would tend to emphasize the story quality to games, but Poe himself did have an interest in game theory. It could be argued that "The Purloined Letter" has elements to please both game formalists and narrative modelists. After Dupin has produced the incriminating letter and astounds the prefect, he launches into a discussion of a schoolboy's success in playing the marble game of "even and odd" (Poe 215). The game segment has tangential thematic relationships with Dupin's one-upsmanship over both the police prefect and Minister D —, thief of the letter. Each plays to win and lord it over the other. A recent article in *Science News* takes a games analysis point of view about the story to illustrate how Poe has revealed an error in game theory (Rehmeyer).

This concept of odd-even and gamesmanship coupled with the chase of "The Purloined Letter" contains parallel to the "ludology versus narratology" controversy rumbling through the gaming world today.

Poe expresses the abstract formality favored by ludologists in Dupin's discussion of the odd/even game. The diegetic story begins to flow after that, when Dupin takes action to retrieve the letter and present it with a flourish to Inspector G —. Time resumes.

To be sure, video-game culture has many areas for study that Poe never influenced. Still it makes sense to examine Poe's narratives with an eye toward gaming. Incorporating physical sensations into his stories, his tales embed a visceral quality that gaming platforms seek to replicate. He has also affected the structure of games themselves, with his tunneled, anonymous first-person narration surfacing in gaming as first-person role player modes.

Poe's narratives show a linear structure filled with swoops and swirls into alternative realities. Through their fearful, terror-inducing moments, the tales recreate what Murray calls the "immersive" quality of gaming. In addition, the drama of winning and losing essential to every game is part of Poe's design. Competition is built into the detective story as a form. By recreating the crime, locating the missing letter, or identifying a killer, the detective wins, controlling morality, language, and even death.

Poe's implausible narratives hardly present a mimetic mirror of experience. Still, comparing the tales to video games can help game theorists and players to see gaming as a metaphor of life's struggles. The interactivity of video games engages the player/viewer/reader through problematic experiences. In turn, literary critics seeing Poe through a video-game metaphor can gain insight into how Poe's fiction captures a storytelling vision that we continue to discover.

Conclusion

Why do we continue to read Poe? Based on this evidence striating popular entertainment, we want to believe in our own powers to solve the big mysteries of our existence. The detective narrative centers on the power of controlling time and ultimately understanding death. The story of detection that solves intricate puzzles asserts that we can overcome the limitations of language. Tales of psychological imbalance assert that we can know the depths of our own minds. Reading stories of morbid horror help to objectify the mysterious workings of our bodies. Adventure narratives place us in an unforgiving environment, and advance the fanciful illusion that we can read our way out of the danger. Or is it an illusion? Poe's characters change or languish due to the very real agency of words. Ultimately, writing and reading about death is life-affirming.

Two hundred years after his birth, Poe's insights about the human heart continue to fascinate and provoke us into learning about ourselves. Because 2009 marked Poe's 200th birthday, the author drew much attention. A recent anthology giving tribute to Poe is titled *In The Shadow of the Master*. Mystery novelist Michael Connelly introduces the volume. In his essay "What Poe Hath Wrought," Connelly writes of Poe:

> He walked across a field of pristine grass, not a single blade broken. Today that path has been worn down to a deep trench that crosses the imagination of the whole world. If you look at best-seller lists, movie charts, and television ratings, they are simply dominated by the mystery genre and its many odd shoots. The tendrils of imagination behind these contemporary works can be traced all the way back to Poe [xix].

Connelly is one of many writers firmly in Poe's literary debt, but he refuses to elaborate: "I'm not going to get analytical about Poe's life or work here. I leave that to his disciples" (xx). This volume of essays takes a few steps toward the gauntlet that Connelly has left on the luxuriant grass. Still, the challenge continues to echo.

Works Cited

Ackroyd, Peter. *Poe: A Life Cut Short*. New York: Nan A. Talese, 2009.

Allen, Hervey. *Israfel: The Life and Times of Edgar Allan Poe*. New York: Farrar & Rinehart, 1934.

Almén, Byron. *A Theory of Musical Narrative*. Bloomington: Indiana University Press, 2008.

Anderson, Karen G. "*January* Interview: Dennis Lehane." *January* (Aug 1999). http://jan uarymagazine.com/profiles/lehane1999.html.

Andrejevic, Mark. *iSpy: Surveillance and Power in the Interactive Era*. Lawrence: University Press of Kansas, 2007.

Arehart-Treichel, Joan. "Study Cautions Against Assumptions About Serial Killers' Behavior." *Psychiatric News* 45, no. 16 (20 Aug 2010).

Atkinson, Claire. "Chefs Losing Heat, Viewers Fleeing Scripps Food Network, HGTV." *New York Post* 20 Jan 2011.

Baird, Robert. "The Startle Effect: Implications for Spectator Cognition and Media Theory." *Film Quarterly* 53, no. 3 (Spring 2000): 12–24.

Bal, Mieke. *Narratology: Introduction to the Theory of Narrative*. 2d ed. Toronto: University of Toronto Press, 1997.

Barber, Paul. *Vampires, Burial, and Death: Folklore and Reality*. New Haven: Yale University Press, 1988.

Baudrillard, Jean. "Simulacra and Simulations." *Jean Baudrillard, Selected Writings*, edited by Mark Poster, 166–184. Palo Alto, CA: Stanford University Press, 1988. http://www.standford.edu/dept/HPS/Baudrillard/Baudrillard_Simulacra.html.

Beecher, Donald. "Suspense." *Philosophy and Literature* 31, no. 2 (Oct 2007): 255–279.

Bell, David F. *Real Time: Accelerating Narrative from Balzac to Zola*. Urbana: University of Illinois Press, 2004.

Berry, Steve. *The Templar Legacy*. New York: Ballantine Books, 2006.

Bertens, Hans, and Theo D'haen. *Contemporary American Crime Fiction*. Houndmills: Palgrave, 2001.

Big. Dir. Penny Marshall, Perf. Tom Hanks, Elizabeth Perkins. Twentieth-Century–Fox Film Corporation, 1988. Film.

Biressi, Anita. *Crime, Fear, and the Law in True Crime Stories*. New York: Palgrave, 2001.

Body Heat. Dir. Lawrence Kasdan. Perf. William Hurt, Kathleen Turner. Film.

Bones. Perf. Emily Deschanel. Fox Network, 2005–2011. Television program.

Bongiovi, Jon, and Richard Sambora. "Wanted: Dead or Alive." Perf. Jon Bon Jovi. *Slippery When Wet*. Sony ATV Tunes, LLC, Bon Jovi Publishing, 1986. Album.

Boyd, David, and R. Barton Palmer, eds. *After Hitchcock: Influence, Imitation, and Intertextuality*. Austin: University of Texas Press, 2006.

Bowman, David. "Detective Melodrama on TV." *Journal of University Film Association* 27, no. 2 (1975): 40–42, 46.

Brion, Raphael. "The Food Network's Ratings Decline." *Eater National.* 20 Jan 2010. http://eater.com/archives/2011/01/20/the-food-networks-ratingsdrop.

Brown, Dan. *The DaVinci Code.* New York: Doubleday, 2003.

_____. *The Lost Symbol.* New York: Doubleday, 2009.

Brownlee, Shannon, and Jeanne Lenzer. "Shots in the Dark." *The Atlantic* 304, no. 4 (Nov 2009): 44–54.

Bruner, Rob. "The Books that Hooked the World." *Entertainment Weekly* 1108 (25 Jun 2010): 37–45.

Burns, Gus. "DNA Case Load Backs up as Michigan State Police Crime Lab Turn-around Stretches Six Months or Longer." *Saginaw News* [Michigan]. Apr 18, 2010. http://www.mlive.com/news/saginaw/index.ssf/2010/04/dna_caseload_backs_up_as_michi.html.

Burroughs, Edgar Rice. *Tarzan of the Apes.* New York: Ballantine, 1973.

Canada, Mark. "Flight into Fancy: Poe's Discovery of the Right Brain." *Southern Literary Journal* 33, no. 2 (Spring 2001): 62–79.

Carey-Webb, Allen. *"Heart of Darkness, Tarzan,* and the 'Third World': Canons and Encounters in World Literature, English 109." *College Literature* 19–20 (Oct 1992–Feb 1993): 121–141.

Carmody, Tim. "How Motion Detection Works in Xbox Kinect." *Wired.* 2 Nov 2010. http://www.wired.com/gadgetlab/2010/11/tonights-release-xbox-kinect-how-does-it-work/.

Carroll, Noel. *The Philosophy of Horror.* New York: Routledge, 1990.

"The Case of the Curious Bride." *Perry Mason.* Perf. Raymond Burr, William Hopper, Barbara Hale, CBS. 1958. Television program.

Cates, Irina. "Montana State Crime Lab Seeing Increase in Case Load." *KTVQ News* [Billings, MT]. 3 Dec. 2010. http://www.ktvq.com/news/mt-state-crime-lab-seeing-increase-in-case-load/.

Cawelti, John G. *Adventure, Mystery, and Romance: Formula Stories as Art and Popular Culture.* Chicago: University of Chicago Press, 1977.

Cawelti, John G., and Bruce A. Rosenberg. *The Spy Story.* Chicago: Chicago University Press, 1987.

Central Intelligence Agency. *FAQs.* 20 Nov 2010. https://www.cia.gov/about–cia/faqs/index.html.

Connelly, Michael. *Bloodwork.* New York: Warner Books, 1998.

_____. *The Scarecrow.* New York: Grand Central Publishing, 2010.

_____, ed. *In the Shadow of the Master: Classic Poe Tales and Essays by Jeffery Deaver et al.* New York: William Morrow, 2009.

Coppel, Alec, and Samuel A. Taylor. *Vertigo.* Based on the novel *D'Entre les Morts* by Pierre Boileau and Thomas Narcejac. 12 Sep 1957. Screenplay. http://www.dailyscript.com/scripts/vertigo.html.

Dateline NBC. "Kate Snow Interview with Sharron Chasson." Feb 13, 2011.

DeLisi, Matt, Michael G. Vaughn, Kevin M. Beaver, John Paul Wright. "The Hannibal Lecter Myth: Psychopathy and Verbal Intelligence in the MacArthur Violence Risk Assessment Study." *Journal of Psychopathology and Behavioral Assessment* 32, no. 2 (Jun 2010): 169.

Dowler, Ken, and Thomas Fleming. "Constructing Crime, Media, Crime, and Popular Culture." *Canadian Journal of Criminology and Criminal Justice* 48, no. 6 (Oct 2006): 837–844.

Dussere, Erik. "Out of the Past, into the Supermarket: Consuming Film Noir." *Film Quarterly* 60, no. 1 (Autumn 2006): 16–27.

Ebert, Roger. "Answer Man." *Chicago Sun–Times.* 27 Nov 2005. http://rogerebert.sun times.com/apps/pbcs.dll/section?category=ANSWERMAN&date=20051127.

Edgar Allan Poe Society of Baltimore. *The Letters of Edgar Allan Poe.* EAP to George W. Eveleth. 4 Jan 1848 (LTR-259). 24 Dec 2009. http://www.eapoe.org/letters/p4801040.htm.

Edwards, Leigh. "Are Video Games Art?" *Pop Culture Universe: Icons, Idols, Ideas.* Santa Barbara, CA: ABC-CLIO, 14 Feb 2011.

Englehardt, Tom. Interview with Jonathan Schell. "The Fate of the Earth, the Bush Years." *Salon.* 5 Dec 2007. http://www.salon.com/news/feature/2007/12/05/nuclear_weapons/.

Federal Bureau of Investigation. "Crime in the United States: Preliminary Annual Uniform Crime Report: January to December 2009." Washington, DC: Department of Justice. 24 May 2010. http://www.fbi.gov/ucr/prelimsem2009/index.html.

Fairstein, Linda. "Alex Cooper Crime Novels: FAQs." *Alex Cooper.* http://www.linda fairstein.com/.

_____. *Entombed.* New York: Pocket Star, 2005.

Fisher, Benjamin. *The Cambridge Introduction to Edgar Allan Poe.* Cambridge: Cambridge University Press, 2008.

Forbes, Ron. "How You Become the Controller," *Xbox Engineering Blog.* 29 Dec 2010. http://www.xbox.com/en-US/Live/EngineeringBlog/122910-HowYouBecomethe Controller.

48 Hours. "A Case For Murder." Nov 15, 2009. CBS.

_____. "The Lady in the Harbor." Jan 23, 2009. CBS.

Frank, Lawrence. "Edgar Allan Poe's Evolutionary Reverie." *Nineteenth-Century Literature* 50, no. 2 (Sep 1995): 168–188.

Franklin, Nancy. "Brooklyn Dodger: HBO's New Comedy about a Writer Turned Private Eye." *New Yorker.* 28 Sep 2009. http://www.newyorker.com/arts/critics/television/2009/09/28/090928crte_television_franklin#ixzz19LZl1iZ0.

Frye, Northrop. *Anatomy of Criticism: Four Essays.* Princeton: Princeton University Press, 1971.

Fukuchi, Curtis. "Poe's Providential *Narrative of Arthur Gordon Pym,*" *ESQ: A Journal of the American Renaissance* 27, no. 3 (1981): 147–156.

Gargano, James W. "The Question of Poe's Narrators." *Poe: A Collection of Critical Essays.* Ed. Robert Regan. Englewood Cliffs, NJ: Prentice-Hall, 1967. 164–171.

Geherin, David. *Scene of the Crime: The Importance of Place in Crime and Mystery Fiction.* Jefferson, NC: McFarland, 2008.

"The Getaway." *Dexter.* Perf. Michael C. Hall. Showtime. 13 Dec 2009.

The Girl with the Dragon Tattoo (Män som hatar kvinnor). Dir. Niels Arden Oplev, Perf. Michael Nyqvist, Noomi Rapace. 2009.

Grella, George. "The Hard-Boiled Detective Novel." *Detective Fiction: A Collection of Critical Essays,* edited by Robin W. Winks, 108–120. Englewood Cliffs, NJ: Prentice-Hall, 1980.

Grimes, Martha. *The Black Cat: A Richard Jury Mystery.* New York: Viking, 2010.

Haley, Kevin. "Visual Culture and 'The Man of the Crowd.'" *Nineteenth-Century Literature* 56, no. 4 (Mar 2002): 445–465.

Hall, Adam. [Jonquil Trevor.] *The Quiller Memorandum.* New York: Simon & Schuster, 1965.

Hartmann, Jonathan. *The Marketing of Edgar Allan Poe.* New York: Routledge, 2008.

Heffernan, Virginia. "Honk? No, Pray if You Hear a Loud Crack." *New York Times* 22 Jun 2007.

Hoffman, Daniel. *Poe Poe Poe Poe Poe Poe Poe.* New York: Doubleday, 1972.

Hollinger, Karen. "'The Look,' Narrativity, and the Female Spectator in *Vertigo.*" *Journal of Film and Video* 39, no. 4 (Fall 1987): 18–27.

Holmslund, Christine. "'Sexuality and Power in Male Doppelgänger Cinema: The Case of Clint Eastwood's 'Tightrope.'" *Cinema Journal* 26, no. 1 (Autumn 1986): 31–42.

Horsley, Lee. *The Noir Thriller*. New York: Palgrave, 2001.

Hühn, Peter. "The Detective as Reader: Narrativity and Reading Concepts in Detective Fiction." *Modern Fiction Studies* 33 (1987): 451–466.

Irwin, John T. *American Hieroglyphics: The Symbol of the Egyptian Hieroglyphics in the American Renaissance*. New Haven: Yale University Press, 1980.

Jacoby, Henry, ed. *House and Philosophy: Everybody Lies*. Hoboken, NJ: John Wiley and Sons, 2009.

Jung, C. G. *Four Archetypes*. Bollingen Series. Trans. R. F. C. Hull. Princeton: Princeton University Press, 1969.

Kafalenos, Emma. "Not (Yet) Knowing: Epistemological Effects of Deferred and Suppressed Information in Narrative." *Narratologies: New Perspectives on Narrative Analysis*, edited by David Herman, 33–65. Columbus: Ohio State University Press, 1999.

Kane, Margaret. "Edgar Allan Poe and Architecture." *The Sewanee Review* 40, no. 2 (Apr–Jun 1932): 149–160.

Kaufman, Frederick. "Debbie Does Salad: The Food Network at the Frontiers of Pornography." *Harper's* (Oct 2005). http://frederickkaufman.typepad.com/harpersmag/harper_kaufman.html.

Kelleher, Michael D., and C. L. Kelleher. *Murder Most Rare: The Female Serial Killer*. New York: Random House, 1998.

Kelly, R. Gordon. *Mystery Fiction and Modern Life*. Jackson: University Press of Mississippi, 1998.

Kerbel, Matthew R. *If It Bleeds, It Leads: An Anatomy of Television News*. Boulder, CO: Westview Press, 2001.

Klein, Kathleen Gregory. "Habeas Corpus: Feminism and Detective Fiction." *Women's Detective Fiction*, edited by Glenwood Irons, 171–189. Toronto: University of Toronto Press, 1995.

Kopley, Richard. *Edgar Allan Poe and the Dupin Mysteries*. New York: Palgrave Macmillan, 2008.

_____, ed. *Poe's Pym: Critical Explorations*. Durham: Duke University Press, 1992.

Kurz, Jeffery. "The Tell-Tale Cipher." *Salon*. 8 Mar 2000.

Lacan, Jacques. "Seminar on 'The Purloined Letter.'" Trans. Jeffrey Mehlman. *The Purloined Poe: Lacan, Derrida, and Psychoanalytic Reading*, edited by John P. Muller and William J. Richardson, 28–54. Baltimore: Johns Hopkins University Press, 1988.

Larsson, Stieg. *The Girl with the Dragon Tattoo*. Trans. Reg Keeland. New York: Vintage, 2009.

Laura. Dir. Otto Preminger. Perf. Gene Tierney, Dana Andrews. Twentieth-Century–Fox, 1944. Film.

Laverty, Carroll. "The Death's-Head on the Gold Bug." *American Literature* 12 (Mar 1940): 88–91.

Lawrence, D. H. *Studies in Classic American Literature*. New York: Penguin Classics, 1990.

Lehane, Dennis. Author Website. http://www.dennislehanebooks.com/.

_____. Interview. Karen G. Anderson. "*January* Interview: Dennis Lehane." *January* (Aug 1999). http://januarymagazine.com/profiles/lehane1999.html.

_____. *Shutter Island*. New York: Harper Perennial, 2003.

"LJ Talks to Robert Skinner." *Library Journal*. 31 Jan 2006.

Linderman, Deborah. "The *Mise-en-Abîme* in Hitchcock's *Vertigo*." *Cinema Journal* 30, no. 4 (Summer 1991): 51–74.

Lippman, Laura. *What the Dead Know*. New York: HarperCollins, 2007.

"Living Proof, Part One." 2010. TNT Network. Perf. Kyra Sedgwick. Television program.

Long, Carolyn Morrow. *A New Orleans Voudou Priestess: The Legend and Reality of Marie Laveau*. Gainesville: University Press of Florida, 2006.

Lovink, Geert. *Uncanny Networks: Dialogues with the Virtual Intelligentsia.* Cambridge: MIT Press, 2002.

Magistrale, Tony, and Sidney Poger. *Poe's Children: Connections between Tales of Terror and Detection.* New York: Peter Lang, 1999.

Manovich, Lev. *The Language of New Media.* Cambridge: MIT Press, 2001.

Maslin, Janet. Review of *Tightrope.* Dir. Richard Tuggle. *New York Times Online.* 17 Aug 1984. http://www.nytimes.com/1984/08/17/movies/film-tightrope-new-clint-east wood-thriller.html?scp=2&sq=Aug+17+1984&st=nyt.

May, Charles E. *EAP: A Study of the Short Fiction.* Boston: Twayne, 1991.

McIntyre, April. "Food Network Scores Historic Ratings High, Sign of the Times?" *Monsters and Critics.* 16 Dec 2009. http://www.monstersandcritics.com/smallscreen/news/article_1519564.php/Food-Network-scores-historic-ratings-high-sign-of-the-times.

McKeithan, D. M. "Two Sources of Poe's *Narrative of Arthur Gordon Pym.*" *University of Texas Bulletin,* 13 (1933): 127–137.

Mellow, James R. *Nathaniel Hawthorne in His Times.* Boston: Houghton Mifflin, 1980.

Meltzer, Brad. *The Book of Lies.* New York: Grand Central Publishing, 2008.

_____. *The Inner Circle.* New York: Grand Central Publishing, 2010.

Merivale, Patricia, and Susan Elizabeth Sweeney, eds. *Detecting Texts. The Metaphysical Detective Story from Poe to Postmodernism.* Philadelphia: University of Pennsylvania Press, 1999.

Meyers, Jeffrey. *Edgar Allan Poe: His Life and Legacy.* New York: Cooper Square Press, 2000.

Mills, Bruce. *Poe, Fuller, and the Mesmeric Arts: Transition States in the American Renaissance.* Columbia: University of Missouri Press, 2006.

"Mr. Monk and the Red Herring." *Monk.* Perf. Tony Shaloub. USA Network. 21 Jan 2005. Television program.

Moore, Joe, and Lynn Scholes. *The Grail Conspiracy.* Woodbury, MN: Midnight Ink, 2006.

Morris, Christopher D. *The Hanging Figure: On Suspense and the Films of Alfred Hitchcock.* Westport, CT: Praeger 2002.

Moynihan, Sinéad. "Marginal Man and Hard-Boiled Detective: Racial Passing in Robert Skinner's Wesley Farrell Series." *Clues* 26, no. 3 (Spring 2008): 56–69.

Murder by Numbers. Dir. Barbet Schroeder. Warner Bros. Pictures, Perf. Sandra Bullock, Ryan Gosling. 2002.

Muller, John P., and William J. Richardson, eds. *The Purloined Poe: Lacan, Derrida, and Psychoanalytic Reading.* Baltimore: Johns Hopkins University Press, 1988.

Mulvey, Laura. "Visual Pleasure and Narrative Cinema." *Screen* 16, no. 3 (Autumn 1975): 6–18.

Murray, Janet H. "The Last Word on Ludology v. Narratology in Game Studies." *Keynote.* DiGRA [Digital Games Research Association] 2005, 17 Jun 2005. http://lcc.gatech.edu/~murray/digra05/lastword.pdf.

"Next of Kin, Part One." *The Closer.* 2002. TNT Network. Perf. Kyra Sedgwick. Television program.

Numb3rs. Perf. Rob Morrow. CBS Network. 2005–2010. Television program.

Palfrey, John, and Urs Gasser. *Born Digital: Understanding the First Generation of Digital Natives.* New York: Perseus Book Groups, 2008.

Parfit, Derek. "The Indeterminacy of Identity: A Reply to Brueckner." *Philosophical Studies: An International Journal for Philosophy in the Analytic Tradition* 70, no. 1 (Apr 1993): 23–33.

Parfit, Derek. "Personal Identity." *The Philosophical Review* 80, no. 1 (Jan 1971): 3–27.

Perry, Dennis R. *Hitchcock and Poe: The Legacy of Delight and Terror.* Lanham, MD: Scarecrow, 2003.

_____. "Imps of the Perverse: Discovering the Poe/Hitchcock Connection." *Literature Film Quarterly* 24, no. 4 (1996): 9.

Philbin, Tom, and Michael Philbin. *The Killer Book of True Crime*. Naperville, IL: Sourcebooks, 2007.

Poe, Edgar Allan. *The Complete Tales and Poems of Edgar Allan Poe*. New York: Vintage Books, 1975.

Priest, Dana, and William Arkin. "Top Secret America." *Washington Post*. 19 Jul 2010. https://www.cia.gov/about–cia/faqs/index.html#employeenumbers.

Prosser, Simon. "The Two-Dimensional Content of Consciousness." *Philosophical Studies: An International Journal for Philosophy in the Analytic Tradition* 136, no. 3 (Dec 2007): 319–349.

Pulver, Andrew. "Martin Scorsese Master of the Hitchcock Tribute." *Guardian UK* 20 Mar 2010. http://www.guardian.co.uk/film/2010/mar/10/martin-scorsese-shutter-islandhitchcock.

Quinodoz, Danielle. *Emotional Vertigo: Between Anxiety and Pleasure*. Trans. Arnold Pomeranz. New York: Routledge, 1997.

Rahn, Millie. "Laying a Place at the Table: Creating Public Foodways from Scratch." *Journal of American Folklore* 119, no. 471 (Winter 2006): 30–46.

Rank, Otto. *Beyond Psychology*. New York: Dover Publications, 1941.

"Rattle and Roll." *Chopped*. The Food Network. 2010. Television program.

The Raven. Dir. James McTeigue. Perf. John Cusack. Relativity Media, 2011.

Ray, Krishnendu. "Domesticating Cuisine Food and Aesthetics on American Television." *Gastronomics: The Journal of Food and Culture* 7, no. 1 (Winter 2007): 50–63.

Reddy, Maureen T. *Traces, Codes, and Clues: Reading Race in Crime Fiction*. New Brunswick, NJ: Rutgers University Press, 2003.

Rehmeyer, Julie. "The Tell-Tale Anecdote: An Edgar Allan Poe Story Reveals a Flaw in Game Theory." *Science News* 20 Jun 2008. http://www.sciencenews.org/view/.

Reiss, Benjamin. *Theaters of Madness: Insane Asylums and 19th-Century American Culture*. Chicago: Chicago University Press, 2008.

Renza, Louis A. *Edgar Allan Poe, Wallace Stevens, and the Poetics of American Privacy*. Baton Rouge: Louisiana State University Press, 2002.

Ricoeur, Paul. *Time and Narrative*, vol. 2. Trans. Kathleen McLaughlin and David Pellauer. Chicago: University of Chicago Press, 1985. Originally *Temps et Récit*, by Editions du Seuil, 1984.

Rivkin, Julie, and Michael Ryan, eds. *Literary Theory: An Anthology*, 2d ed. Malden, MA: Blackwell, 2004.

Rizzoli and Isles. Perf. Angie Harmon, Sasha Alexander. TNT Network. 2010.

Ron, Moshe. "The Restricted Abyss: Nine Problems in the Theory of *Mise en Abyme*." *Poetics Today* 8, no. 2 (1987): 411–438.

Rosenheim, Shawn James. *The Cryptographic Imagination: Secret Writing from Edgar Poe to the Internet*. Baltimore: Johns Hopkins University Press, 1997.

Roth, Martin. "Inside 'The Masque of the Red Death.'" *SubStance* 13, no. 43 (1984): 50–53.

_____. *Strictly Murder! A Writer's Guide to Criminal Homicide*. Los Angeles: Siles Press, 1998.

Rozan, S. J. *S. J. Rozan*. 2008. http://www.sjrozan.com/.

Santos, Marlisa. *The Dark Mirror: Psychiatry and Film Noir*. Lanham, MD: Lexington Books, 2010.

Saussure, F. *Course in General Linguistics*. Ed. C. Bally and A. Sechehaye. Trans. W. Baskin. New York: McGraw Hill, 1966.

Schell, Jonathan. *The Fate of the Earth*. Palo Alto: Stanford University Press, 1982.

_____. *The Seventh Decade: The New Shape of Nuclear Danger*. New York: Holt Paperbacks, 2008.

Schenkel, Elmar. "Unwritten Texts: H. G. Wells's Exploration of Narrative in his Early Essays." *Investigations into Narrative Structures*, edited by Christian Todenhagen and Wolfgang Thiele, 243–255. New York: Lang, 2002.

Shaffer, Lawrence. "Obsessed with *Vertigo*." *The Massachusetts Review* 25, no. 3 (Autumn 1984): 383–397.

Shields, David. "Men and Games and Guns." *The Yale Review* 91, no. 3 (28 Jun 2008): 39–46.

Shutter Island. Dir. Martin Scorsese. Perf. Leonardo DiCaprio, Mark Ruffalo, Ben Kingsley. 2003.

Silverman, Kenneth. *Edgar A. Poe: Mournful and Never-Ending Remembrance*. New York: HarperCollins, 1991.

Skinner, Robert. *Skin Deep, Blood Red*. New York: Kensington, 1997.

Sontag, Susan. *On Photography*. New York: Farrar, Straus, and Giroux, 1973.

Spoto, Donald. *The Art of Alfred Hitchcock: Fifty Years of His Motion Pictures*, 2d ed. New York: Anchor Books, 1992.

Standish, David. *Hollow Earth: The Long and Curious History of Imagining Strange Lands*. Cambridge, MA: De Capo Press, 2006.

Stark, S. D. "Perry Mason Meets Sonny Crockett: The History of Lawyers and Police as Heroes." *University of Miami Law Review* 42, no.1 (Sep 1987): 229–283.

"Step Right Up." *Chopped*. The Food Network. 2010. Television program.

"Strike Three." 2009. TNT Network. Perf. Kyra Sedgwick. Television program.

Sullivan, Ruth. "William Wilson's Double." *Studies in Romanticism* 15, no. 2 (Spring 1976): 253–263.

Swift, Harriet. "Looking for Mystery Street: New Orleans and the Detective Novel — Why So Few?" *Mystery Readers Journal: New Orleans Mysteries* 12, no. 2 (Summer 1996). http://www.mysteryreaders.org/Issues/Orleans.html#Swift.

Tenney, Tabitha. *Female Quixotism. Exhibited in the Romantic Opinions and Extravagant Adventures of Dorcasina Sheldon*. Boston: J. P. Peaslee, 1825. Google Books Online.

Thomas, Liz. "Generation Net: The Youngsters Who Prefer Their Virtual Lives to the Real World." *Mail Online*. 8 Feb 2011. http://www.dailymail.co.uk/sciencetech/arti cle-1354702/Children-happier-virtual-lives-real-world.html#ixzz1E3ZjiIba.

Tightrope. Dir. Richard Tuggle. Perf. Clint Eastwood, Genevieve Bujold. Screenplay by Richard Tuggle. Warner Bros. Pictures, 1984. Film. Warner Home Video, 2003. DVD.

Travers, Peter. "*Tightrope*: Review." *Rolling Stone* 2 Oct. 2001, 128.

Tresch, John. "Extra! Extra! Poe Invents Science Fiction!" *The Cambridge Companion to Edgar Allan Poe*. Edited by Kevin J. Hayes. 117. New York: Cambridge University Press, 2002.

Truffaut, François. *Hitchcock*. New York: Simon & Schuster, 1967.

Tucker, Ken. "The 'Chicago Code' Premier Review: Did the Super Bowl Promos Inspire You to Watch It?" *Entertainment Weekly*. 7 Feb 2011. http://watching-tv.ew.com/2011/ 02/07/chicago-code-jennifer-bealssuper–bowl/.

Twain, Mark (Samuel Clemens). "Fenimore Cooper's Literary Offences." Project Guten- berg. 22 Feb 2010.

Tynan, Daniel J. "J. N. Reynolds' *Voyage of the Potomac*: Another Source for *The Narrative of Arthur Gordon Pym*." *Poe Studies* 4, no. 2 (Dec 1971): 35–37.

Vallas, Léon. *Claude Debussy: His Life and Works*. Trans. Maire and Grace O'Brien. New York: Dover Publications, 1973.

Van der Kolk, Bessel A., and Alexander C. McFarlane. "The Black Hole of Trauma." *Literary Theory: An Anthology*, 2d ed., edited by Julie Rivkin and Michael Ryan, 487– 502. Malden, MA: Blackwell, 2004.

Vertigo. Dir. Alfred Hitchcock. Perf. James Stewart, Kim Novak. Paramount Pictures, 1958. Film. Collector's Edition. Universal Studios, 1998. DVD.

Vyhnanek, Louis. *Unorganized Crime: New Orleans in the 1920s*. Lafayette: University of Southwestern Louisiana, 1998.

Walsh, John Evangelist. *Midnight Dreary: The Mysterious Death of Edgar Allan Poe*. New York: Palgrave Macmillan, 2000.

Wenk, Arthur B. *Claude Debussy and the Poets*. Berkeley: University of California Press, 1976.

Whalen, Terence. *E. A. Poe and the Masses*. Princeton: Princeton University Press, 1999.

Wickliffe, Andrew. "Tightrope." *The Stop Button: An Appreciation of Amusements*. 4 Dec 2006. http://www.thestopbutton.com/2006/12/04/tightrope-1984/.

Wilbur, Richard. "The House of Poe." *Poe: A Collection of Critical Essays*, edited by Richard Regan. 117. Englewood Cliffs, NJ: Prentice-Hall, 1963.

Wimsatt, W. K., Jr. "Poe and the Chess Automaton." *American Literature* 11, no. 2 (May 1939): 138–151.

Wolf, Mark J. P. "Considering Video Games as Art." *Pop Culture Universe: Icons, Idols, Ideas*. Santa Barbara, CA: ABC-CLIO. 6 Jan 2011.

Wood, Robin. *Hitchcock's Films Revisited*. New York: Columbia University Press, 1989.

Woolf, Paul. "The Movies in the Rue Morgue: Adapting Edgar Allan Poe for the Screen." *Nineteenth-Century American Fiction on Screen*, edited by Ed. R. Barton Palmer, 43–61. Cambridge, MA: Cambridge University Press, 2007.

Yanal, Robert J. "The Paradox of Suspense." *The British Journal of Aesthetics* 36 (1996): 146–158.

Index